CAMALDOLESE SPIRITUALITY

Camaldolese Spirituality

Essential Sources

Translations, Notes, and Introduction

by Peter-Damian Belisle

Ercam Editions
Bloomingdale, Ohio

Nihil Obstat and Imprimatur:
P. Lanfranco Longhi, Er. Cam.
Superior Major

Copyright © 2007 by Holy Family Hermitage
Corrected impression
All rights reserved

ISBN 978-0-9728132-5-9

Library of Congress Control Number: 2006924018

Printed in the United States of America

Acknowledgments

Brunone Querfurtensi. *Vita Quinque Fratrum Eremitarum (Vita Vel Passio Benedicti et Iohannis Sociorumque Suorum)*. Monumenta Poloniae Historica, Series nova, Tomus IV, Fasc. 3, Recensuit, praefatione notisque instruxit Hedvigis Karwaskinska. Warszawa: panstwowe Wydawnictwo Naukowe, 1973.

Petri Damiani. *Vita Beati Romualdi*. A.c. Giovanni Tabacco. Roma: Istituto Storico Italiano per il Medeo Evo, 1957.

Petri Damiani. "Epistula XXVIII." *Die Briefe des Petrus Damiani*. A.c. K. Reindel, vol. 1, München: Monumenta Germaniae Historica, 1983.

Consuetudo Camaldulensis. "Rodulphi constitutiones." "Liber eremitice regule." Edizione critica e traduzione. A.c. Pierluigi Licciardello. Firenze: SISMEL—Edizioni del Galluzzo, 2004, pp. CXLV-131 con 2 tavv. f.t. "Edizione Nazionale dei testi mediolatini, 8."

*   *   *

First of all, St. Peter Damian was a hermit, even the ultimate theorist of the eremitic life in the Latin Church, at the very moment when the schism between East and West was consummated. In his interesting work entitled *The Life of Blessed Romuald*, he has left us one of the most significant fruits of the monastic experience of the undivided Church. For him, the eremitic life constitutes a strong recall for all Christians to the primacy of Christ and to His Lordship. It is an invitation to discover the love that Christ, from His relationship with His Father, has for the Church; a love that the hermit, in turn, ought to foster *with*, *through*, and *in* Christ towards all the people of God. So keenly did he sense the presence of the universal Church in the eremitic life that he wrote, in the ecclesiological tract entitled *Dominus vobiscum*, that the Church is, at the same time, one in all and all in each of its members....Peter Damian, conscious of his own limitations—he loved to define himself as *peccator monachus* [sinner monk]—handed on to his contemporaries the awareness that effective Christian witness can develop only through a constant, harmonious tension between the two fundamental poles of life—solitude and communion. Is this teaching not also valid for our times?

Pope Benedict XVI, 20 February 2007
for the Damian millennium

TABLE OF CONTENTS

I   General Introduction

II   The Life of the Five Hermit Brothers
by Bruno-Boniface of Querfurt

III   The Life of Blessed Romuald
by Peter Damian of Fonte Avellana

IV Letter 28 *Dominus Vobiscum* (The Lord Be With You)
by Peter Damian of Fonte Avellana

V   Constitutions
by Rudolf of Camaldoli

VI   Book of the Eremitical Rule
by Rudolf of Camaldoli

I

GENERAL INTRODUCTION

1. Romualdian/Camaldolese Context

At the turn of the first millennium AD, an amazing set of factors came together to form within the Christian monastic ambit a reform movement known as Romualdian. Centered on the life and ministry of a quasi-itinerant hermit named Romuald of Ravenna (c. 952-1027), this reform was a precursor to the great Gregorian Reform enacted during the latter part of the eleventh century by the strong-willed and powerful monk Hildebrand, who took the name Gregory VII as pope (r. 1073-1085). The Romualdian movement helped the monastic world and the Church as a whole prepare for the important work of this ecclesiastical reform.

The imperial power stood in the process of strengthening its strategic bonds of support and centralizing its power. Questions about succession to the crown were ironing themselves out, not without the inevitable turmoil and bloodshed running through history's corridors of power. Alliances and secessions, revolts and rebellions were all part of the relatively final struggles in a feudalistic world, to clutch power and stave off aggression. It was a time of ongoing struggle in a seemingly endless stream of little wars. These wars needed funding and, often as not, monasteries and abbeys with their endowments and holdings became prized plums in the frantic search for reserves to fill the war chests.

Just as money could purchase power, at times brutally so, it could also, unfortunately, buy influence and position in a Church trying to establish its place in such a society. The heretical pockets of simony were deep, and many were the bishoprics, abbacies, and parishes acquired merely through the crass exchange of money. Reform-minded ecclesiastics fought an uphill struggle throughout the late tenth and eleventh centuries. The acquisition of papal power was, unfortunately, as tempting as temporal power. Various powerful noble families vied with one another to control the elections of popes. And in a Church where money could purchase ecclesiastical standing and power, we should not be surprised to discover that sexual mores had grown lax among a clergy put in place through the exchange of coins. Rich fathers would buy Church positions for their sons who felt little or no inclination to follow the Church's ascetical disciplines of clerical celibacy or continence. Some of these situations became for all practical purposes quasi-dynastic, as fathers passed on parochial benefices to their sons. And all sorts of sexual misconduct began to surface, referred to by history's scribes as Nicolaitism: priests with wives and children, priests with mistresses or concubines, clergy cohabiting in same-sex unions, and other references to various forms of incontinence.

At times when history's pendulum swings so far in one direction, the pendulum's return often presages dramatic events in the opposite direction. The tenth to twelfth centuries formed a period of increasing monastic reform. Certainly the Cluniac reform encompassed the most territory and wielded considerable power for a group of

Benedictine monks. With its centralized power and strict uniformity, Cluny planted its roots throughout France, and spread its tendrils in Italy, Spain, and Germany, as well as into England and Scotland. Deriving its strength from the grace-filled stewardship of five strong and holy abbots during a two-hundred-year period, the Cluniac reform affected the entire Church of its day. Other similar monastic reforms took their cue from Cluny and changed the face of continental monasticism: Gorze Abbey, Brogue Abbey, the Abbey of Fleury, and Our Lady of Einsiedeln Abbey. Anglo-Saxon monasticism drew inspiration from Fleury and enacted significant reforms at the Council of Winchester. To this picture we add the Romualdian reform—including the Congregation of the Holy Cross at Fonte Avellana—and the Vallombrosan reform of St. John Gualbert (995-1073). And of course, just around the corner, history will find the Carthusian reform, the Cistercian phenomenon, and all the "New Orders" following the Rule of St. Augustine.

Within the Church politic, reform-minded clergy concerned themselves not only with the widespread abuses of simony and Nicolaitism, but also with the increasingly urgent need to stabilize and empower the papacy, while maintaining its integrity separate from the political Empire. Hildebrand's Gregorian Reform became the late eleventh-century vehicle to accomplish these tasks, but several popes prior to Gregory VII significantly prepared the way for his reform through a number of decrees and local Church synods. The Lateran Synod of 1059 established precise procedures for papal elections. Various popes utilized reform-minded legates to solve disputes and extirpate heresy. Slowly the papacy came into its own as a temporal power within the Empire, while it struggled to wrest itself from temporal powers' meddling, particularly by lay investiture. St. Peter Damian of Fonte Avellana (1007-1072) became one of two monk-cardinals (Humbert of Silva Candida being the other) who helped the Church articulate its theology against simony. Pope Leo IX (r. 1049-1054) eventually chose Peter Damian's work for this theological expression.

This is the world in which Romualdian hermits enacted their monastic reform work and conducted Church reforms both on the local church level and on the institutional plane. This is the arena in which two reform-minded hermit monks, Romuald of Ravenna and Peter Damian of Fonte Avellana, became intimately involved with the political forces of the Empire: Romuald with his young admirer Emperor Otto III, and later with Henry II; Peter Damian with various ecclesiastical and temporal powers connected with imperial politics and interests.

The two principal sources for our knowledge of Romuald of Ravenna are *The Life of the Five Hermit Brothers*[1] by Bruno-Boniface of Querfurt and *The Life of Blessed Romuald*[2] by Peter Damian. Romuald was born c. 952 in Ravenna to noble parents, Count Serge and his Byzantine wife whose name we do not know. Subsequent to a personal crisis occasioned by witnessing his father kill a relative over a land dispute,

---

[1] The critical editions of this work: (a) Bruno-Boniface di Querfurt, *Passio Sanctorum Benedicti et Johannis ac Sociorum Eorundem*, ed., Wojciech Ketrzynski, Monumenta Poloniae Historica 6: 388-428 (Cracow, 1893); (b) S. Bruno di Querfurt, *Vita dei Cinque Fratelli*, trans. B. Ignesti (Camaldoli: Edizioni Camaldoli, 1951).

[2] The critical editions of this work: (a) St. Petrus Damianus, *Opera Omnia*, PL 144-145 (1853); (b) St. Petrus Damianus, *Vita Beati Romualdi*, ed., Giovanni Tabacco (Roma, Istituto Italiano, 1957).

Romuald became a monk at the nearby Benedictine Abbey of St. Apollinaris in Classe, an abbey recently introduced to the Cluniac reform. However, seemingly immune to reform sensibilities at the time, Classe's monks struck the fervent young monk as hopelessly stuck in their ways and unreformable. After three or four years of life with Romuald, the abbot and monks of Classe were evidently only too willing to allow him to live outside the abbey in an Eastern model of abba/disciple relationship of solitary life with a rustic hermit named Marino. The two of them later became involved with the Doge of Venice, Peter Orséolo I, through whom they met Abbot Guarinus of St. Michel of Cuixá Abbey in the south of France, near the Pyrenees. Abbot Guarinus was returning from a pilgrimage to the Holy Land. At his invitation, all of them (including Doge Peter Orséolo and two other companions, John Gradenigo and John Morosini) left Venice by night and hurried to Cuixá where the Doge became a monk of the Abbey, while Romuald and companions began to live an eremitical life together in the nearby woods. There they read scripture and monastic literature. Romuald found himself becoming a spiritual mentor whose wisdom derived from an intense life of prayer and solitude.

Romuald left Cuixá to return home and help his father Serge remain in the monastery where he had become a monk a few years previously. From that time onwards, Romuald began his work of founding hermitages and reforming extant monasteries and hermitages. It can be somewhat confusing to try to follow Romuald's itinerary of monastic reform work, but we can discern several important periods. When Romuald initiated a monastic life with a group of Germans who had been part of the Ottonian court and entourage,

5

Romuald began a close spiritual mentorship of the young Emperor Otto III, who became not only Romuald's patron but also, we are told, his devoted follower and would-be monk. Forced to become abbot of his former community at Classe by Otto, Romuald dramatically resigned this abbacy after only a little more than one year's worth of trying to tolerate the Classe monks' continued obstinacy against reform. It was at the Peréo foundation in swamplands outside Ravenna that Otto's cousin and former court chaplain, Bruno-Boniface of Querfurt (with Otto's inspiration and help), promoted the "mission to the East" in the Romualdian movement. Through this missionary response to Boleslas of Poland's request for monk-missionaries, there could be a "triple good": a monastery for beginners, a hermitage for the mature life in "golden solitude", and the possibility for preaching the Gospel to unbelievers and even experiencing martyrdom in the process.

Due to historical circumstances, the life at Peréo fell apart at the seams, and this "mission to the East" that Romuald reluctantly permitted met with disaster, at least from an initial foundational point of view. Romuald never again saw Bruno-Boniface who, after moving to another remote hermitage, later became a missionary archbishop and suffered martyrdom. Nor did Romuald again see Otto III, who traveled to Rome to squelch a local rebellion and died tragically at the age of twenty-three. Then Romuald moved to Istria (Dalmatia), where his family may have owned land, and formed a monastic foundation there where he lived as a spiritual mentor and recluse for three years. During that time, Romuald reportedly developed mystical, contemplative gifts, whereby he enjoyed a profound comprehension of Sacred

Scripture, the gift of tears, and prophetic awareness.

This was followed by another period of foundation that included a long stay at the Abbey of St. Mary of Sitria and then another period of foundation travels. Camaldoli in Tuscany proved to be one of his last, if not the last, foundation of Romuald, in 1023.[3] He died in 1027 in a small hermitage near the monastery of Valdicastro. He had lived his life in the ministry of monastic reform. Personally drawn to greater solitude throughout his life, Romuald devoted himself to providing the possibility for solitaries to come into a communal setting under the *Rule of St. Benedict* (RB) and a superior, where they could live a life formed by the *Rule*, accountable to a superior, and juridically approved. Romuald founded many monasteries and hermitages; he also reformed many other already extant houses and absorbed them in his Romualdian reform. All the while, he was an outspoken opponent of simony and monastic laxity. His reform spread when Peter Damian of Fonte Avellana, Romuald's biographer, embraced and continued the work of the Romualdian reform at Fonte Avellana and among all its foundations and reformed houses.

Romuald was a humble and charismatic monk whose freedom of spirit and purity of heart allowed him to live as a prophetic flame of monastic reform in a world passing through a dark period. As a Benedictine monk, he centered his life on the Word of God and urged his fellow monks

---

[3] The actual document deeding the church there to the monks of Camaldoli by the Bishop of Arezzo, after they had lived there some years, is dated August 10, 1027. Cf. Giuseppe Vedovato, *Camaldoli e la sua Congregazione dalle Origini al 1184; Storia e Documentazione*, Italia Benedettina 13 (Cesena, Centro Storico Benedettino Italiano, 1994) 126.

always to do likewise. He was a solitary of solitaries, to the point of occasional eccentricity. Above all, he was a mystic and a saint whose life Peter Damian made a paradigm for posterity.

The Romualdian reform movement consisted not only in those houses founded, refounded, or reformed by Romuald and his associates, but also those houses that Fonte Avellana founded or reformed under Peter Damian, during the time before the canonical establishment of either the Avellanita Congregation[4] or the Camaldolese Congregation.[5] This reform sought, in effect, to join the former ascetical rigor of the desert monastic tradition to the contemporary Benedictine way of life. Its spirituality combined the regulations of the *Rule of St. Benedict* with the charismatic and prophetic asceticism contained in the *Life of Antony* and desert monastic literature—the *Apophthegmata*, *The Lives of the Fathers*, and John Cassian's *Conferences*. The Romualdian vision wanted to organize the eremitical life by emphasizing greater silence, solitude, and fasting for its hermits and cenobites living under Benedict's *Rule*.[6]

Most of the Romualdian foundations were rather small,

---

[4] Pope Gregory VII established the Avellanita Congregation (Avellaniti, Congregation of the Holy Cross of Fonte Avellana, Congregation of the Doves) on April 10, 1076. Pope Pius V (r. 1566-1572) later suppressed this congregation and joined it to the Camaldolese Congregation.

[5] Pope Paschal II (r. 1099-1118) established the Camaldolese Congregation as an autonomous union of hermitages and monasteries under Camaldoli in 1105 (*Ad hoc nos*) and 1113 (*Gratias Deo*).

[6] Cf. Mansueto Della Santa, *Ricerche Sull'Idea Monastica di San Pier Damiano* (Camaldoli, Edizioni Camaldoli, 1961). Also see Peter-Damian Belisle, "Primitive Romualdian/Camaldolese Spirituality" *Cistercian Studies Quarterly* 31:4 (1996) 413-429.

though later Camaldolese centuries would reverse this tendency. Some of them did not endure beyond their first or second generation. With the Romualdian accent on greater solitude as its fervent guiding impulse, this tendency did not present the hardship we might presume from our twenty-first-century standpoint. Surely, faith and spirituality, as well as strong bonds of fraternal support and love, had to be sound for such a movement to thrive. Giovanni Tabacco[7] has studied this aspect of the Romualdian world and shown how intrinsic to the success of Romuald's reform were the interpersonal bonds of deep friendship among his followers. These bonds are illustrated by Romuald's own personal friendships with several of his disciples, as well as relationships among followers at Ravenna, Cuixá, Montecassino, Peréo, Poland, and Fonte Avellana. Not only did these friendships exist, but also they developed a great desire to share their experience of God as a fruit of their shared solitude. The followers of Romuald became known for the great love they manifested among themselves and toward others.

Solitude was certainly the mainstay at the heart of the Romualdian reform movement. Intrinsically important as solitude was to Romuald's own personal spirituality and monastic journey, he was determined to devote his life to helping provide an atmosphere where Christian solitaries might live safely, as well as accountably vis-à-vis Church authorities. Developing a recognized environment

---

[7] Cf. Giovanni Tabacco, "*Privilegium amoris*: aspetti della spiritualità romualdina," *Il Saggiatore* IV (1954) 1-20. Also see a French rendition of Tabacco's work in Louis-Albert M.-A. Lassus, "L'Amour et l'amitié chez les premiers ermites camaldules," *Revue d'Ascetique e de Mystique* 39 (1963) 302-318.

where hermits could live together under a superior and the guidance of the *Rule of St. Benedict*, Romuald of Ravenna was concerned with ensuring autonomy and respectability for the eremitical life. Under Romuald's leadership, cenobites and hermits could live together, but under a hermit superior, once again stressing the importance of solitude within the ambit of the Romualdian world. The core of that world is essentially always the same: "a small group of solitaries bonded *pro privilegio amoris*."[8] This "privilege of love" is founded on loving God intensely and sharing that love through the interpersonal relationships of monastic community. But why solitude, more specifically?

Romualdians followed the fervent example of their charismatic leader and sought deeper solitude in order to speak with God and to challenge evil head-on, much like the ascetics of ancient desert monasticism. This desire to hold conversations with God regularly, to center one's whole life on the Word of God, and to commune with that Word with tears of compunction and contemplative joy is the Word-centered dialogue of Romualdian spirituality, enjoying a world of solitude that filled a spectrum colored by light moments of captured union, and by deeper hues of temporary periods of gifted contemplation, resting on a profound base of permanent reclusion and communion. The desire to challenge evil openly is clearly illustrated by Peter Damian's *Life of Blessed Romuald*,[9] as well as many of his later monastic works for the Romualdian movement. It is a return

---

[8]   Giovanni Tabacco, "Romualdo di Ravenna e gli inizi dell'eremitismo camaldolese," *L'Eremitismo in Occidente Nei Secoli XI e XII* (Milan: SEVEP, 1965) 100.

[9]   Cf. Peter Damian, *VR* 7, 16-18, 32-33, 49, 58, 60-63, 70.

to the voluntary "white" martyrdom of desert monasticism. Solitude became the Romualdian voluntary martyrdom.

One does not miss, however, the constant interplay of action and contemplation in the life of the enigmatic Romuald. His life seems to comprise a series of long itinerant journeys of founding, refounding, and reforming monastic houses, followed by intense periods (sometimes lasting for years) of reclusive solitude. He felt constantly restless to bear fruit. Apostolic concern would also express itself in evangelization (for example, the "mission to the East") and later Camaldolese concerns for guest ministry and care for the sick, expressed in various sets of early Camaldolese constitutions.[10] The later Camaldolese centuries would add to the experience of the Romualdian decades a distinctly apostolic thrust to Romualdian-Camaldolese spirituality. This would lead to scholarship, education, the arts, hospitals, active Church ministry on the hierarchical level, and missionary work, but the spirituality would continue to remain Benedictine monastic contemplative spirituality.

The Romualdian world centered around two power bases during those decades immediately following Romuald's death: Fonte Avellana and Camaldoli. This situation lasted several centuries before power and influence began to shift. Four years after Peter Damian's death (1072), his former friend

---

[10] Cf. *Consuetudo Camaldulenses. Rodulphi Constitutiones. Liber Eremitice Regule.* A.c. Pierluigi Licciardello (Firenze: SISMEL—Edizioni del Galluzzo, 2004); Martino III, *Constitutiones Camaldulenses a 1253*, in *Annales Camaldulenses Ordinis Sancti Benedicti*, Venetiae, 1755-1773, VI, App., col. 1-65; Gerardo I., *Constitutiones Camaldulenses a 1279*, in *Annales Camaldulenses...* VI, App., col. 240-255; Bonaventura da Fano, *Constitutiones* (1328), in *Annales Camaldulenses...* VI, App., col. 272-287.

and correspondent Pope Gregory VII officially constituted Fonte Avellana and all its dependencies as a congregation— the Congregation of the Holy Cross of Fonte Avellana, variously known as Avellaniti, the Avellanita Congregation, and Congregation of the Doves. Camaldoli became the head of what was soon to develop into the powerful and influential Camaldolese Congregation under Pope Paschal II, who established it as an autonomous union of hermitages and monasteries under Camaldoli. Already by 1113, when the second stage of its juridical establishment was confirmed by the papal bull *Gratias Deo*, Camaldoli had gathered around itself an impressive group of hermitages, monasteries, churches, and dependencies. The twelfth century became a period of constant growth, as popes and bishops bestowed further dependencies on Camaldoli's stewardship. This also proved a time of conflict for Camaldoli, as it struggled to ward off pressure from the Arezzo bishops and assert its protection under papal exemption. Success in this venture was a key element in Camaldoli's further expansion.

The thirteenth century proved another period of growth for the Camaldolese, particularly once Pope Innocent IV (r. 1243-1254) permitted the congregation to receive entire monastic congregations into its own union. Through a series of constitutions, the congregation developed its interior life as it experienced greater exterior complexity, including new legislation allowing new candidates to the eremitical life only after at least three years of cenobitical experience within the congregation. The fourteenth century became a time for urban development and, although Camaldoli would remain a revered hermitage within the congregation, its power passed to other Camaldolese hermitages and monasteries whose superiors would be elected Priors General. Among these were St. Matthias of Murano (Venice), Holy Mary of the Angels (Florence), St. Michael of Murano (Venice), and St. Hippolytus (Faenza). The urbanization of Camaldoli mirrored a parallel development in the secular sphere.

In 1338, the congregation reorganized itself into nine groups, each with its own center for studies. The fifteenth and sixteenth centuries were years of Renaissance studies and artistic achievements. Both Holy Mary of the Angels and Fonte Buono (Camaldoli) became centers for humanist endeavors. The former became known both for its college conducted for the youth of Florence and for its flourishing output in the arts (painting, miniature painting, transcription and illumination of manuscripts, drawing, tapestries, embroidery, and metalwork). Some of its more famous artists included Lorenzo Monaco, Silvestro Dei Gherarducci, Jacopo Dei Francesche, and Simone Camaldolese. Camaldoli, which also ran a school at Fonte Buono, became a center for ongoing humanist dialogue. St. Michael of Murano also staffed a respected school and developed a famous library.

But this time of exterior development also proved to be a time of general interior decadence that Priors General Ambrogio Traversari, Mariotto Allegri, and Pietro Delfino tried to combat within the congregation by means of various reforms. It lacked unity in its organization and customs, but attempts at consolidation during this period only seemed to favor further fragmentation. In 1446, St. Michael of Murano became the head of a new autonomous Camaldolese congregation, balancing power and influence in the Camaldolese world with the Hermits of Tuscany and a weakened Camaldoli. Paul Giustiniani had joined

Camaldoli in 1510, and, when his good friend became Pope Leo X (r. 1513-1521), he found help in legislating reform at the 1514 General Chapter. Elected superior of Camaldoli in 1516, Giustiniani continued to try to effect unpopular reforms at the hermitage of Camaldoli. While still superior, he departed Camaldoli with Leo's blessing and gathered around himself a group of like-minded hermits that later became the Camaldolese Hermits of Monte Corona.

Pope Leo X had approved a reunion of all Camaldolese houses in 1513, but this weak union seemed doomed. An attempt to bring Camaldoli and Monte Corona back together in 1540 failed, as did another attempt ordered by Pope Urban VIII (r. 1623-1644) in 1634. This union was dissolved thirty-three years later by Pope Clement IX (r. 1667-1669). Pope Pius V (r. 1566-1572) had dissolved the Avellanita Congregation in 1569 and bestowed Fonte Avellana and its dependencies upon the Camaldolese Congregation. Another separate, exclusively eremitical Camaldolese congregation began in Piedmont in 1601, modeling itself on the customs of Monte Corona. Yet another eremitical Camaldolese congregation began in seventeenth-century France, also adopting the customs and constitutions of Monte Corona, but remaining an autonomous entity. In 1616, the union between Camaldoli and Murano dissolved into two officially separate branches: eremitical (Hermits of Tuscany) and cenobitical (Murano). Once the French group became established, there were five autonomous congregations, all calling themselves Camaldolese, four of them eremitical: the Hermits of Tuscany (Camaldoli), the Cenobites of St. Michael of Murano, Monte Corona, the Piedmontese, and the French congregations. The family of Romuald had broken apart into various factions, but disunity did not preclude growth.

During the seventeenth century, Murano, Monte Corona, and the Hermits of Tuscany (Camaldoli) all experienced remarkable growth.[11] The eighteenth century proved equally prosperous until revolutionary forces began to sweep the continent, suppressing the French Camaldolese (1770), the Piedmontese Camaldolese (1801), and all Italian religious orders (1810) during the Napoleonic occupation. Though some groups of Camaldolese resumed the regular life during the nineteenth century, all the Camaldolese houses were once again suppressed by the Italian Republic between 1855 and 1873. Most never recovered during the twentieth-century period of recuperation and reacquisition.

The congregations of Camaldoli, Monte Corona, and Murano slowly revived, but Pope Pius XI (r. 1922-1939) suppressed the latter cenobites in 1935, closing half their remaining houses and bestowing five others on Camaldoli. Camaldoli slowly regained its strength, particularly due to the reforming efforts of two of its Priors General—Anselm Giabbani and Benedict Calati. Camaldoli once again became a spiritual center, showing further expansion in the United States, Brazil, and India, while the Monte Corona congregation expanded to the United States, Colombia, and Venezuela. In 1966, Camaldoli juridically joined the greater Benedictine Confederation, published new Camaldolese constitutions in 1985, and focused energy on ecumenical and interreligious dialogue. Through Romualdian inspiration and Camaldolese development, both remaining congregations

---

[11] Cf. Giuseppe M. Croce, "I Camaldolesi nel Settecento: tra la 'rusticitas' degli eremiti e l'erudizione dei cenobiti," *Settecento Monastico Italiano* (Cesena: Badia S. Maria del Monte, 1990).

of Camaldolese—the Camaldolese Benedictines and the Camaldolese Hermits of Monte Corona—stand witness to an enduring, unique charism within the history of monastic spirituality.

2. *Bruno-Boniface of Querfurt*

Bruno was born in 974 to Ida and Bruno, countess and count of Querfurt in Saxony, and thereby related to the Ottonian dynasty then in power within the Empire. Enjoying the benefit of a good education in the city of Magdeburg's cathedral school, Bruno studied grammar, rhetoric, theology, Scripture studies, and the liberal arts. His classmate was the chronicler Thietmar, whose later work provides us with valuable references to Bruno's ecclesiastical career. Ordained priest in 997, Bruno served his cousin Otto III as his court chaplain, until he became a professed monk of SS. Alexis and Boniface monastery near Rome. Bruno's two religious heroes were the then recently canonized martyr St. Adalbert, who had been murdered as a missionary to the Slavic peoples, and St. Boniface (+754), who earlier had also become a missionary archbishop to pagan tribes and martyr. Bruno added the latter saint's name to his own, in deference to the great fame and work of Boniface. Drawn to Romuald of Ravenna while he was in and about Rome at this time, Bruno-Boniface received permission to follow the wandering hermit to a monastic settlement near Tivoli, where, accompanied by one Tammo and other German soldiers of Otto's military guard, they began to live the monastic life together. Later pressured to leave Tivoli by jealous interests in the city of Rome who did not appreciate the growing influence and reputation accruing to this Romualdian band formed around Romuald himself, they moved to the countryside near Ravenna with the blessing and patronage of Emperor Otto III. Otto himself, and Pope Sylvester II also, left a rebellious Rome at this time and moved to Ravenna.

Both Bruno-Boniface of Querfurt and his cousin Emperor Otto III came forcefully into Romuald's life at this time and helped to form the spirituality of the Romualdian world. Whether Bruno-Boniface or Otto had the more original stake in proposing what became known in the Romualdian movement as the "triple good"—the monastery/cenobitic life for beginners; the hermitage/golden solitude for the more advanced monks; and evangelization/martyrdom for those desiring it—its conception probably was a collaborative effort. Otto's "mission to the East" proposal, and his ineffective structure for monastic life which he proposed at Peréo, could very well have been Brunonian in inspiration. Bruno-Boniface himself had become a monk in Rome, living cenobitically at SS. Alexis and Boniface prior to becoming Romuald's disciple.

The idea of a Romualdian monk first living in a cenobium as a first stage to monastic life—a model found in the works of John Cassian, for example—is likely the work of Bruno-Boniface. His own personal experience of impressive imperial monasteries and Saxon piety would have allowed him to view the cenobium as preparation for the eremitical experience in Romualdian reform. Otto himself harbored aspirations for both monasticism and missionary work, so his proposal to respond to Duke Boleslas' request for monk-missionaries by sending a Romualdian group to the Slavic regions drew strength from his own personal hopes in this regard. Feeling debilitated by the climate of the swamps near Peréo, as well as by his own inaction in contrast to the glorious example set by St. Adalbert vis-à-vis the expressed need for missionaries, Bruno-Boniface wanted to leave Peréo. He convinced Benedict, Romuald's close disciple, whom he had met at Montecassino with John Gradenigo and whom Romuald personally wanted to assume authority at Peréo, to volunteer for this Ottonian "mission to the East". Benedict came to prefer the idea of becoming a monk-martyr to the possibility of being an abbot. Persuading Bruno-Boniface to use his influence to convince Otto to veto Romuald's proposal to name him abbot of Peréo, Benedict was able to volunteer for the Slavic mission that Romuald reluctantly allowed to proceed.

Discouraged by this turn of events, Romuald decided to leave Peréo and begin once again in Istria. The disciples Benedict and John departed for Poland. Otto decided to leave for Rome to squelch that city's rebellion against the Empire. Bruno-Boniface had already received permission to move away to another hermitage where he might escape his disappointment with the doomed Peréo foundation. He deeply loved Romuald and felt drawn to the Romualdian world, but he was also tied to the Empire by blood, history, and personal experience. Motivated by the examples of SS. Boniface and Adalbert, he felt called to missionary life and martyrdom,[12] and therefore he planned to join Benedict and John in Poland once he had received permission from the

---

[12] Cf. Jean Leclercq, "San Romualdo e il Monachesimo Missionario," *Momenti e Figure di Storia Monastica Italiana*, ed. Valerio Cattana, Italia Benedettina 16 (Cesena: Centro Storico Benedettina Italiano, 1993) and Jerzy Kloczowski, "L'Eremitisme dans les territoires slaves occidentaux," *L'Eremitismo in Occidente Nei Secoli XI e XII* (Milan: SEVEP, 1965).

pope to evangelize the Slavs. Bruno-Boniface was ordained archbishop *Ad Gentes* by Pope Sylvester II (r. 999-1003) and given the pallium to accomplish his proposed missionary work in 1002.

Bruno-Boniface spent much time in Germany, caught up in a war of the Emperor's, as well as, quite probably, in some monastic foundation work. He gathered information on the life and martyrdom of St. Adalbert while on a journey to the East, but he was not in contact with his former confreres in Poland who, until their deaths, had been awaiting his arrival with the papal permission to evangelize. Bruno-Boniface had already begun to write the *Life of Saint Adalbert* and was now able to correct and revise his work. Later, with further research accomplished in Poland, Bruno-Boniface wrote *The Life of the Five Hermit Brothers* during two periods: 1006 and 1008. He accomplished missionary work in Hungary, Russia, Prussia, and possibly Scandinavia, before being martyred with eighteen other German monks in 1009 along the Prussian/Lithuanian border.

Otto III died tragically at the age of twenty-three in early 1002 while on that journey to put down the rebellion in Rome. He was never again to see Romuald, his spiritual mentor. He was not able to realize his missionary aspirations nor his monastic inclinations. Benedict and John, however, were able to make their monastic foundation with the generous help of a grateful Duke Boleslas in Poland. They began to draw disciples to their Romualdian manner of life. Two of these, Isaac and Matthew, were martyred with the Italian founders, along with their cook Cristin, in 1003. When he received word of their violent deaths, how remorseful Bruno-Boniface must have felt at his own tardiness in communicating with his former confreres, who depended upon his promised tasks. He had convinced his good friend Benedict to go on an envisioned quest, inspired by missionary evangelization and the possible prospect of martyrdom. He himself went on to accomplish admirable ecclesiastical work, however unknown that work remained to the unsuspecting Benedict and John in Duke Boleslas' territory.

Bruno-Boniface of Querfurt's reason for writing *The Life of the Five Hermit Brothers* seems twofold, or even threefold. From the original Latin title assigned to this work (*Passio Sanctorum Benedicti et Johannis ac Sociorum Eorundem—The Passion of SS. Benedict and John and Their Companions*), we can see that his original intention was to set forth their cause of canonization as martyred saints. Through the interior evidence of the document's illustrations of Benedict's and John's connections to their holy Master Romuald, climaxing in the final chapter accenting Romuald as a spiritual master, we can also assume that a second important motivation of the author was to underline the spiritual import of Romuald, and to illustrate the unique influence the Romualdian world held in early eleventh-century Italy as well as in the Church's missionary efforts in the East. We can conjecture yet a third reason for Bruno-Boniface's writing this work, that is, the remorse he feels for preferring to spend his time on pursuits other than those originally planned with Benedict without communicating any change of plan. And so, he pursues his own agenda, as his confreres suffer death while waiting for word from him.

Combining his own memories of the years 998-1004 with the oral research he conducted at the site of the Polish hermitage and with knowledgeable members of Boleslas' court, Bruno-Boniface wrote the story of the life, death, and subsequent miracles of the five martyred brethren. The first eight chapters set forth the background, chapters nine through fourteen describe their actual murder, and chapters fifteen through thirty-one depict various miraculous events following upon the martyrdom. A final concluding chapter depicts Romuald of Ravenna as the spiritual master whose influence underpins their monastic world. Bruno-Boniface's Latin has an educated, difficult style, somewhat turgid at times. Biblical in expression, with added classical allusions, some of which are vague or lost to us, his work is sophisticated and follows the basic structure for hagiographical writings of his day. Beneath its surface one feels the presence of Bruno-Boniface's earlier work, *The Life of Saint Adalbert*. Bruno-Boniface's *The Life of the Five Hermit Brothers* became lost to history until R. Kade discovered a manuscript dating to 1204 and published the text in *Monumenta Germaniae Historica* in 1888. This was followed by a revised and corrected version by W. Ketrzynski in *Monumenta Poloniae Historica* five years later.

Through this text we come to know the history of some of Romuald's first generation of disciples, and we also catch glimpses of a Romualdian world in which loving friendship, love of solitude and the monastic cell, and the so-called "triple good" stand out as guiding principles. In the concluding chapter highlighting Romuald's influence, we read what has come to be known as the *"Little (or Brief) Rule of Romuald"*—a collection of succinct reflections. It is an extraordinary little text uniting the Romualdian hermit with the teachings of the monastic desert tradition, the ancient hesychastic spirituality of the East, and the emerging currents of monastic reform in the eleventh century. All this is expressed in an apophatic style characterized by an extreme simplicity. It is a very brief compendium of monastic wisdom, as we might expect to find among the favorite sayings of an ancient Egyptian monk, Syriac ascetic, Palestinian hermit, or solitary on Mount Sinai.

3. *Peter Damian of Fonte Avellana*

Thanks to biographical references within Peter Damian's many works, the biography written by his secretary and successor, St. John of Lodi,[13] and extensive historical ecclesiastical documentation, we can piece together a substantial life-sketch of Peter Damian. Even if John of Lodi's biography of Peter Damian is not very historically oriented in deference to hagiographical exigencies, at least we derive from it a good sense of Peter Damian's personality.

Peter Damian was born in 1007 in Ravenna, the youngest of at least six children. He was orphaned during childhood. His older brother Damian, a priest of Ravenna, became Peter's patron and had him educated at Faenza (1022-1025), where he studied grammar and rhetoric, and at Parma (c. 1030), where he studied the liberal arts, Scripture, theology, and law. Peter added his brother's name to his own as a sign of gratitude and devotion. Before becoming a monk, Peter Damian taught rhetoric in Ravenna, gathering disciples around him as his reputation grew. He joined the hermitage of Fonte Avellana (c. 1035), already under the influence of the Romualdian monastic reform. At some point, Peter Damian

---

[13] Cf. Ioannes Lodensis, St. *Vita B. Petri Damiani*. PL 144, cl. 113-180.

was ordained priest. In 1040, the prior of Fonte Avellana sent him to the Abbey of Pomposa where he taught Scripture to the monks for almost two years. Around 1042, Peter Damian reformed the monastery of St. Vincent al Furlo in the Romualdian mould. While there, he began writing *The Life of Blessed Romuald.*

In 1043, Peter Damian became prior of Fonte Avellana and began an impressive phase of construction that improved the extant hermitage and added to the monastic complex. He introduced lay *conversi*[14] into the Avellanita lifestyle, thereby increasing the possibilities for development. He also began a lifelong project of gathering books and manuscripts for the hermitage's library, all the while writing his own impressive body of spiritual and theological works. Like his hero, St. Romuald, Peter Damian made numerous foundations and reformed other hermitages and monasteries—all in the Romualdian manner of monastic reform.

Created cardinal archbishop of Ostia by Pope Stephen IX in 1057, Peter Damian began a life of active Church reform, serving as a powerful and effective troubleshooter for a number of popes who sent him to trouble spots and Church synods throughout the Empire. His more important assignments as papal legate were: to Milan (1059) with Anselm of Lucca (later Pope Alexander II), to address a simoniacal controversy; to the Abbey of Cluny (1063), to mediate between the monks and the local bishop regarding power and wealth; to Florence (1066-1067), to mediate another similar dispute between the Vallombrosan monks

---

[14] *Conversi* were lay brothers attached to the community for purposes of work, who prayed more simply and less liturgically, and who often dwelled in the nearby fields and forests where they worked for the community.

and their local bishop; and to Frankfurt (1069), to represent the pope at an important Church reform synod. In 1071, Peter Damian traveled to the Abbey of Montecassino with Pope Alexander II to dedicate the abbey church, renovated by Abbot Desiderius (later Pope Victor III). His final ecclesiastical mission journey was to his native city of Ravenna, where he had the great joy of officially lifting Church sanctions on that city. While on his return trip from Ravenna, Peter Damian became ill and died in Faenza in 1072. There his body is entombed in the cathedral. Four years later, his good friend Hildebrand (now Pope Gregory VII) elevated Fonte Avellana and its dependencies to the status of a congregation.

Peter Damian was a very intelligent and talented individual. Difficult at times, he could be severe and uncompromising when he thought a given situation called for unswerving principles. Feared by many Church leaders of his day—particularly by simoniacal bishops against whom he waged incessant battle—he became a target for focused hatred by still others, who were probably the source of his title, the "monitor of the popes". He was a staunch promoter of Church and monastic reform. He was certainly a precursor to what later became known as the Gregorian reform movement in the Church. One can easily describe Peter Damian using extremes: absolutely fearless, demanding, zealous, intense, a tireless crusader. Many popes used him as their articulate spokesman and intransigent weapon of effective reform. From his works we can discern an ongoing struggle within him to balance his personal need for monastic silence and solitude with his ecclesiastical vocation to active Church reform work. Peter Damian was a complex individual whose many theological, spiritual, and poetical works reflect that articulated complexity.

Peter Damian wrote many works and was later named a Doctor of the Church by Pope Leo XII in 1828. He wrote in an epistolary literary form, directing his "letters" to various monks, ecclesiastical individuals, and nobles. Thankfully, his rhetorical style was also a bit autobiographical, giving us precious glimpses into the lives, events, and movements of his time. His more important works vis-à-vis Church reform are the *Liber Gratissimus*, a work against simony that was ultimately adopted by the pope as doctrine for the universal Church, and the *Liber Gomorrhianus*, a work notorious for its explicit depiction of contemporary sexual mores among the clergy of Peter Damian's day. From the perspective of the Romualdian monastic reform movement, the most important works of Peter Damian's literary output were writings such as: *The Life of Blessed Romuald*, the *Dominus Vobiscum*, the so-called *Avellanita Constitutions*, and the *Rule of the Eremitical Life*, as well as other works of monastic theology and spirituality. In addition to his general ascetical corpus, Peter Damian also wrote biographies of a number of saints, various hymns, prayers, and poetry.

Among recurrent themes in his literary endeavors, certainly central are those proposed by the Romualdian monastic reform: greater silence, solitude, fasting, prayer centered particularly on psalmody, and the penitential life. This last theme appears often in Peter Damian's writings, unsurprisingly so because the monks of Fonte Avellana referred to themselves in Peter Damian's time as "*penitentes*". During his priorship, the Avellanita monk was a spiritual athlete of the ascetical life, much in the spirit of primitive desert monasticism. Four days a week, for example, the monks maintained a very strict fast, and they did so perpetually during the Advent and Lenten seasons. Compunction of heart and the gift of tears are recurrent themes throughout his more distinctly ascetical works. The passion of Christ centered on the cross is never far from Peter Damian's mind and heart. (His future congregation would be called the Congregation of the Holy Cross of Fonte Avellana.) The pendulum swinging between the ministerial care for souls in the Church and the need for monks to "flee" the world to save their own souls underlines the ongoing struggle Peter Damian personally felt in his own life as hermit-monk and cardinal archbishop. The active/ contemplative struggle becomes a major theme flowing through his works. But his balanced ecclesiology remains sound, beautifully articulated in his *Dominus Vobiscum*, as well as in several other works. One final, recurring theme that should be mentioned is demonology. For Peter Damian, monastic solitude is constantly challenged by demons.[15] This theme recurs throughout his *Life of Blessed Romuald*. The psychological struggles and dangers inherent in the solitary lifestyle, expressed in contemporary hagiographical imagery and ascetical terminology, are not matters left untouched by Peter Damian's work of monastic reform.

The Life of Blessed Romuald was Peter Damian's first major piece of writing. His sources were Scripture, Augustine, Jerome, Palladius, John Cassian, Basil, Benedict, Gregory the Great, and, of course, the figure of Romuald himself. It is important to remember that one is not reading history

---

[15] Cf. Petrus Damianus, *De Fuga Dignitatem Ecclesiasticarum*, PL 145.

in Romuald's *Life* as one might expect to read rigorous, documented, scientific history. Romuald of Ravenna, for Peter Damian, was an heroic figure of almost mythic proportions, a person of saintly virtue, and an important model to imitate in the significant work of eleventh-century monastic reform. Peter Damian's question is: "How does one live an authentic eremitical life?" His response is to look at the witness and message of Romuald, who lived as though he were a combination of St. Antony the Great and St. Benedict of Nursia. For Peter Damian, Romuald brought hermits together to live juridically accountable lives under a religious superior guided by the *Rule of St. Benedict*, and so wed the desert monastic tradition to Benedictine communal life and prayer. This first work of Peter Damian's became an important vehicle for eleventh-century monastic reform, laying the foundation for the Romualdian world and, subsequently, Camaldolese spirituality.

Peter Damian sets forth Romuald of Ravenna as a meta-historical figure. Beginning with an account of his traumatic conversion experience and entrance into the Benedictine cenobitical life, and passing through a description of a transitional phase of development in an Eastern model of master/disciple relationship in solitude, Romuald is portrayed as becoming an accomplished spiritual mentor and ascetical hermit. Gathering many followers around him, Romuald spent his life in alternating periods of active foundation and reformation work and long periods of eremitical reclusion. Peter Damian describes the struggle between Romuald's spiritual need for a nurturing solitude and his call to keep saving souls and providing more monastic opportunities for others. Romuald is shown as a sapiential figure and mystic whose gift of tears pours out in contemplative joy, compunction of heart, eager expectation, and fervent beseeching. He is a prophet of monastic reform, bringing scattered hermits into community. He is a master of monastic discretion. He is an enigmatic wanderer who seems to travel from one solitary place to another— founding, reforming, and teaching a way of monastic peace. He is an abbot, a hermit, a loner, a father to so many, a joker, a recluse, a Master, and love's martyr. For Peter Damian, he is all of these things and more.

Peter Damian's *Life of Blessed Romuald* became a vehicle for important monastic reform. It gave new flesh to desert bones that thrilled to speak with God in the heart of solitude, to move from Word-centered reading, meditation, and prayer into contemplative union, and to challenge the presence of evil boldly in a spirit of voluntary "martyrdom" that mirrored the earlier "white" martyrdom of the desert. And in the midst of this solitary struggle, we discover Romuald's amazing openness to a world that needed saving, evangelizing, and love. Later, Camaldolese life would build upon this Romualdian foundation in an articulation of the interplay between contemplation's gift and action's historical necessity.

The so-called *Dominus Vobiscum* (The Lord Be With You), Peter Damian's Letter 28, is, after the *Life of Blessed Romuald*, probably the most popular of his works, showing an eloquent, mystical side of the author in its discussion of the meaning of Church as the Mystical Body of Christ. Peter Damian establishes a place for the hermit in Church life, both in its sacramental expression and in its more basic, ecclesiological membership. Obviously, this was a centrally important question for Romualdian monastic spirituality's emphasis on solitude and the eremitical vocation in the Church.

The first part of the work answers the question of how the solitary is a member of the Church, indeed *is* the Church itself, as the Church is in the solitary. A second section elaborates Peter Damian's ecclesial vision of the Mystical Body of Christ, in which each and every member is substantially the very Church itself. And so, solitude takes on a plurality while community is expressed in singularity! What holds it all together is an "adhesive"[16] of love from which emanates presence. The third and final section of Letter 28 is a beautifully poetic and evocative praise of the eremitical life. The hermit's cell is, naturally enough from a hermit's perspective, the *locus* for spiritual evolution. The cell is a desert paradise, which is surely a Romualdian tenet, given the opening lines of Romuald's *Little Rule* contained in Bruno-Boniface of Querfurt's testament. The cell is a school where one learns the heavenly arts and a garden of delights filled with colors and scents. It is a mirror for souls in whose reflection self-knowledge can be understood. The cell is a bridal chamber of contemplative union, a fountain of life, refuge, haven, and healing nurse. It is a meeting-place between heaven and earth, a crossroads of communion. But it is also a purgatory for cleansing and purification, a furnace, a kiln, a bath, and workshop. And at times, it can be a hell where battles are fought with demonic forces. But above all, Peter Damian reminds his readers that monastic solitude is meant for love.

---

[16] Cf. André Louf, "Solitudo Pluralis." *Solitude And Communion; Papers on the Hermit Life given at St. David's, Wales in the Autumn of 1975* (Oxford, SLG Press, 1977) 130.

4. Rudolf of Camaldoli

Tradition holds that Camaldoli was one of the last foundations, if not the final one, of Romuald of Ravenna before he died at Valdicastro in 1027. The fourth prior of Camaldoli was named Rudolf and, even though we know little about him, we know even less about the other Priors General of the Camaldolese Congregation who were also named Rudolf in the following century. Rudolf I of Camaldoli served as prior from 1074 to c. 1088. Still under the force of the "old" monasticism, Rudolf I was prior for life. During his tenure the slowly increasing aggregate of Camaldoli and its dependencies moved closer to its official erection as congregation (1105, 1113). The *Constitutions* attributed to Blessed Rudolf of Camaldoli are dated c. 1080.

A former hypothesis held that Rudolf I penned his *Constitutions* c. 1080 and followed them with a second version in 1085. However, recent historical research and textual studies regarding style and particular notes of interior evidence point to a much later date[17] of composition for the second work given here, *The Book of Eremitical Rule.* Rudolf II of Camaldoli was Prior General of the Camaldolese Congregation from 1152 to 1158. By then, Camaldoli was representative of the "new" monasticism mirroring the development of the Cistercians

---

[17] Cf. *Consuetudo Camaldulensis. Rodulphi Constitutiones. Liber Eremitice Regule.* A.c. Pierluigi Licciardello (Firenze; SISMEL-Galluzzo, 2004); Pierluigi Licciardello, "Ricerche sui Rodolfo priori de Camaldoli (1080-1180)" *Vita Monastica* 220 (2002) 48-67; Giuseppe Vedovato. *Camaldoli e la Sua Congregazione Dalle origini al 1184; Storia e Documentazione* (Cesena: Badia di S. Maria del Monte, 1994); Cécile Caby. *De L'Érémitisme Rural au Monachisme Urbain: Les Camaldules en Italie à la Fin du Moyen Âge* (Rome: École Française, 1999).

and Carthusians, complete with its self-monitoring general chapters, visitations, etc. The Congregation's increase in size and power engendered a proportional amount of problems between Camaldoli and its dependencies. When given the benefice of the nearby abbey of Prataglia by a friend, Rudolf II was forced to resign as Prior General in 1158, though historical references to his continued presence at Camaldoli continue to appear during subsequent years. This was a period of monastic change and turmoil at Camaldoli. There appear to have been a number of superiors at both the Hermitage of Camaldoli and the (Camaldoli) Monastery of Fonte Buono further down the mountain. Rudolf, for example, is mentioned as prior of the Monastery in 1177. The name Rudolf of Camaldoli once again appears as Prior General for a few months only in 1180, until he was named Bishop of Ancona. It would seem likely that this third Rudolf and Rudolf II of Camaldoli are the same person, as well as the author of the second work attributed to Rudolf of Camaldoli, *The Book of Eremitical Rule*. Even though this latter work seems to have appeared before 1176, its final redaction can be dated through historical testimonies to post-1158.

The *Constitutions* of Rudolf I form the earliest legislation we have from Camaldoli. It is a description of life in the Hermitage of Camaldoli within a few decades of its original foundation. In particular, it focuses on practices of monastic food and fasting, various aspects of ascetical practices at Camaldoli, and the relationship between the hermits of Camaldoli and the monks of Fonte Buono. Rudolf's sources include: Scripture; the *Rule of St. Benedict*; the stories about St. Romuald and the Romualdian world; and Peter Damian's monastic works, particularly the *Life of Blessed Romuald* and the so-called Avellanita *Constitutions*. Rudolf depends upon this latter work that served as a guide to the customs of life at the monastery of Fonte Avellana. The fasting practices for both Fonte Avellana and Camaldoli, for example, are almost identical, though Camaldoli evidently maintained a bit more rigor and austerity. Rudolf I, in fact, sets forth the full ascetical rigor of the "old" monasticism. He discusses the original foundation of Camaldoli, filling in a lacuna within Peter Damian's work that does not mention Camaldoli, Camaldoli's founding community (Peter Dagnino, Peter, Benedict, Giso, and Teuzo), Fonte Buono, or the role of Bishop Teodald of Arezzo.

Crucial for Rudolf I is his careful clarification of the status of both the *hospitium* of Fonte Buono and the Hermitage of Camaldoli. Fonte Buono's monks are there to take care of guests and pilgrims, as well as functioning as a community of cenobitical formation, unlike Fonte Avellana where postulants entered directly into the hermitage community. Fonte Buono functioned as a place for obedience and service. The Hermitage, however, is designed exclusively in Rudolf's work as a place for contemplation, distanced from all the noise, wealth, and prestige of the world. Yet Camaldoli maintained a quasi-feudal supremacy over the monks of Fonte Buono, who cared for the hermits' needs. Rudolf assumes that the greater the distance from the world and its confusion, the greater the possibility for contemplative perfection. He sounds absolute in his pronouncements, although he continually stresses the need for the Hermitage to remain a hermitage and never become a cenobitical house. He does not think its prior should ever become an abbot. For Rudolf, the hermit's cell becomes the *locus* for physical mortification and spiritual battle. Through various ascetical practices (e.g. fasting, prolonged prayer, tears, silence, genuflections, penances), the hermit of Camaldoli yearns for a mystical vision of God. There is, of course, incipient individualism here, just as there was in desert monastic spirituality and in the works of Peter Damian. Fonte Avellana and Camaldoli were surely more individualistic in spirituality than Cluny or Gorze, but that is probably so among all the more eremitical movements of monastic reform.

When we turn to the *Book of Eremitical Rule*, we find a work qualitatively different from Rudolf's *Constitutions*. It is a longer work, more rhetorical and stylistically complex. This Rudolf (Rudolf II-III) of Camaldoli's emphasis is not simply juridical in nature, but also more spiritual, exegetical, and certainly theological. Called the "*doctor eximius*" (gifted doctor), Rudolf II-III was an educated and cultured literary exegete and theologian. His documented sources are multiple: the Scriptures, Augustine, Peter Damian, *Rule of St. Benedict*, Bernard of Clairvaux, Bruno of Segni, Eusebius, Jerome, Gregory the Great, Prosper of Aquitaine, Prudentius, Rhaban Maurus, the *Lives of the Fathers*, and even Seneca.

The first ten chapters of the work of Rudolf II-III are devoted to giving eremitical examples from history and describing the actual foundation of Camaldoli. This latter description sets forth a tale about a landowner named Maldulus in the territory of Arezzo who gives a field in the mountains to Romuald, after a dream featuring Jacob's ladder and white-clad figures ascending the ladder into the heavens. This anecdote would later become a focus of sworn testimony to legally protect Camaldoli's concerns from the bishops of Arezzo when Prior Raniero of St. Michael's Abbey in Arezzo swore before a papal legate that he had personally been present in 1182 at the reading of a document dated 1012 regarding the gift to Romuald. This was one of history's legends that would safeguard Camaldoli's autonomy for centuries to come. Chapters 11-37 of the *Book of Eremitical Rule* discuss the legislated practices and customs in a more detailed fashion than is found in the *Constitutions*. Chapter 38 discusses the active and contemplative dimensions of the eremitical life, with action entering directly into contemplation as a necessary ascetical preparation.[18] Chapters 39-47 form a virtual ladder of perfection in eremitical spirituality, discussing humility, obedience, moderation, piety, patience, silence, meditation, and the perfection of love. These virtues of Rudolf II-III somewhat soften the brunt of Rudolf I's "old" monastic rigor. The final seven chapters concern the prior of Camaldoli—how he should live and govern the community.

5. *Critical Texts Used*

Brunone Querfurtensi. *Vita Quinque Fratrum Eremitarum (Vita Vel Passio Benedicti et Iohannis Sociorumque Suorum)*. Series nova, Tomus IV, Fasc. 3, Recensuit, praefatione notisque instruxit Hedvigis Karwasinska. Warszawa: Panstwowe Wydawnictwo Naukowe, 1973.

Petri Damiani. *Vita Beati Romualdi*. A.c. Giovanni Tabacco. Roma: Istituto Storico Italiano per il Medeo Evo, 1957.

---

[18] Cf. Benedetto Calati. *Sapienza Monastica. Saggi di Storia, Spiritualità e Problemi Monastici*. A.c. A Cislaghi e G. Remondi (Roma: Studia Anselmiana, 1994) 550-557.

Petri Damiani. "Epistula XXVIII." *Die Briefe des Petrus Damiani*. A.c. K. Reindel, vol. 1, München: Monumenta Germaniae Historica, 1983.

Consuetudo Camaldulensis. "Rodulphi constitutiones." "Liber eremitice regule." Edizione critica e traduzione. A.c. Pierluigi Licciardello. Firenze: SISMEL—Edizioni del Galluzzo, 2004, pp. CXLV-131 con 2 tavv. f.t. "Edizione Nazionale dei testi mediolatini, 8."

6. Select Bibliography

Bargellini, Emanuele, ed. *Camaldoli Ieri e Oggi; l'identità camaldolese nel nuovo millennio.* Camaldoli: Edizioni Camaldoli, 2000.

Belisle, Peter-Damian. "Primitive Romualdian/Camaldolese Spirituality." *Cistercian Studies Quarterly* 31:3 (1996) 413-429.

Belisle, Peter-Damian, ed. *The Privilege of Love; Camaldolese Benedictine Spirituality.* Collegeville: Liturgical Press, 2002.

Blum, Owen J. *St. Peter Damian: His Teaching on the Spiritual Life.* Washington: CUA, 1947.

Caby, Cécile. *De L'Érémitisme Rural au Monachisme Urbain. Les Camaldules en Italie à la Fin du Moyen Âge.* Rome: Ecole Française, 1999.

Cacciamani, Giuseppe M. "Le fondazioni eremitiche e cenobitiche di S. Pier Damiano. Inizi della congregazione di S. Croce di Fonte Avellana." *Ravennatensia* V (1976) 5-33.

Calati, Benedetto. *Sapienza Monastica; saggi di storia, spiritualità e problemi monastici.* A.c. A. Cislaghi e G. Remondi. Roma: Studia Anselmiana, 1994.

Centro di Studi Avellaniti. *Ottone III e Romualdo di Ravenna.* Verona: Gabrielli, 2003.

Centro di Studi Avellaniti. *San Romualdo. Storia, agiografia e spiritualità.* Verona: Gabrielli, 2002.

Della Santa, Mansueto. *Ricerche Sull'Idea Monastica di San Pier Damiano.* Camaldoli: Edizioni Camaldoli, 1961.

Giabbani, Anselmo. *L'Eremo: Vita e Spiritualità Eremitica nel Monachesimo Camaldolese Primitivo.* Brescia, 1945.

Hale, Robert. "Camaldolese Spirituality." *The New Dictionary of Catholic Spirituality.* Collegeville: Liturgical Press, 1993, 107-110.

Hamilton, Bernard. *"Orientale Lumen et Magistra Latinitas*: Greek Influences on Western Monasticism (900-1100)." *Le Millénaire du Mont Athos, 963-1963. Etudes e Mélanges* I. Chevetogne, 1963, 181-216.

Leclercq, Jean. "San Romualdo e il Monachesimo Missionario." *Momenti e Figure di Storia Monastica Italiana.* A.c. V. Cattana. Cesena,1993, 259-274.

Licciardello, Pierluigi. "Ricerche sui Rodolfo priori di Camaldoli (1080-1180)." *Vita Monastica* 220 (2002) 48-67.

Matus, Thomas. *The Mystery of Romuald and the Five Brothers.* Big Sur: Hermitage Books, 1994.

Merton, Thomas. *The Silent Life.* New York: Farrar, Straus, and Cudahy, 1957.

Meysztowicz, Valerien. "La Vocation Monastique d'Otton III." *Antemurale* 4 (1958) 27-75.

Phipps, Colin. "Romuald—Model Hermit: Eremitical Theory in Saint Peter Damian's *Vita Beati Romualdi*, chapters 16-27." *Monks, Hermits and the Ascetic Tradition.* Ed. Sheils. London, 1985, 65-77.

Roggi, Clemente. "Vita e costumanze dei Romualdini del Peréo di Fonte Avellana e di Camaldoli." *Benedictina* 4 (1950) 69-86.

Sansterre, J.M. "Otton III et les saints ascètes de son temps." *Rivista di Storia della Chiesa in Italia* 43 (1989) 377-412.

Tabacco, Giovanni. "*Privilegium Amoris*: Aspetti della Spiritualità Romualdina." *Il Saggiatore* IV (1954) 1-20.

Tabacco, Giovanni. "Romualdo di Ravenna e gli inizi dell'eremitismo camaldolese." *L'Eremitismo in Occidente Nei Secoli XI e XII.* Milano, 1965, 73-121.

Vedovato, Giuseppe. *Camaldoli e la sua Congregazione dalle Origini al 1184; Storia e Documentazione.* Cesena: Badia de S. Maria del Monte, 1994.

II

THE LIFE OF THE FIVE HERMIT BROTHERS

Bruno-Boniface of Querfurt

Prologue: The author supplicates the divine assistance.

Help me, O God, so that I who am modestly talented can tell of great deeds! May the words well up with understanding and feeling! Let my mouth strive to speak about the holy deeds of saints who, after having pure hearts and doing good works, received at last the gold of bloody martyrdom [*purpureae passionis aureum finem*]. Now, good Jesus, do not condemn me if I dare to mention their justice, while I am a carcass of a foul dog[1] on a dunghill of the crimes oppressing me, and alas, like a dirty sow playing in the thick muck of my own sins. If I, poorly equipped and a nonentity in deeds, speak poorly about good things, know, my judges, I beg you, that I would be a monster of aberrant behavior if I did not want to sing best, or at least bark. I would be condemned if, knowing and seeing these holy matters, I were to remain silent. And certainly, while we dip with the mind's quill into what we have to say, we have little time to think or do evil. Sometimes it helps less to talk about good things, but it always helps to write about them. If an ass[2]

---

1   Cf. 2 Sam. 24:15; 2 Peter 2:22.
2   Cf. Num. 22:23 f.

speaks of the Lord's power and mercy, why should not people speak of it, in the spirit of being guided by a child[3] as prophet, counseling salvation to those who want to live correctly?

Having laid out my intentions in the preamble, let us now turn to the facts. At this point, the work is in God's hands. The word comes from heaven—help from the Lord who made heaven and earth, who fashioned both sinner and saint. I want you to bless me, Lord; I want you to help me. Help me, you who restore innocence so one can speak and act well, and preserve for me, a miserable sinner, a better life in the end, O eternal Savior of the world. You, our God, have raised up for me a horn[4] of salvation; hasten to help me. Helper of humanity, O kind Jesus, speak; speak, my God, and come to my help and mercy. Say this: "I will finish my work with you, perverse sinner. Fear no longer what is right. After a few winters, I, your desired redemption, will come to you in due season."[5] So, because I now have the pure and fragrant life of the holy saints in my hands, help me, Lord, as you wish, through your goodness; help both my lives, eternal salvation of God omnipotent. Give me strength to speak well and, God willing, to work well. Let not my enemies mock what I have begun to build that you may bring to conclusion, when they have seen me in the abundance of your mercy and the fidelity of your salvation, O holy Galilean. May your apostle Peter and the martyrs speak in my favor. O great Savior, have pity on me for your sake, as I face the danger of the sea. Put an end to my anxieties; say to my soul: "I am your salvation."[6]

---

[3] Cf. Is. 11:6.
[4] Cf. Lk. 1:69.
[5] Cf. Gn. 18:14.
[6] Ps. 34:4.

Here begins the Passion of SS. Benedict and John and their companions.

1. Introducing St. Benedict of Benevento.

He to whom the word "welcome"[7] refers is this saint who came from Benevento—a term meaning he has come along well and lived well. Benedict began meditating on Christ [*Christo philosophari*] from childhood. Gifted with good intellect, he studied sacred Scripture, happily passing through adolescence and preserving himself from bad habits. Because he was not yet of age, his anxious parents made a mistake and, since it seemed too long to wait for their desire to be realized, he was ordained priest by the local bishop—something he was not empowered to do. Because the bishop was offered money for the ordination, he himself [Benedict] made amends with a suitable penance. He not only lived laudably with a group of canons, but touched by God's Spirit, he also abandoned the world and all its show. Since the early years of adolescence, he committed himself to an admirable continence and preserved his virginity with great zeal, for which he knew his reward would be great in heaven. And so, when it pleased God that he should become a monk, he embraced the *Rule* as mother in Holy Savior Monastery above the sea, where he voluntarily submitted himself to harsh command and bitter service, and where he came to know this nurturer of God's servants, the bearer of great future sweetness. Later, shining in a wonderful lifestyle among the monks, he had progressed in a few years to the point that, with his abbot's permission,

---

[7] Bruno-Boniface is using puns here in Latin: *bene venisse...bene isse...bene vixisse.*

he could live an eremitical life in a cell. The resolute fervor instilled in him by the Holy Spirit did not let him bear the brethren's weaknesses and superficial talk, and forced him to ask for the desert. Then, leaving his native place, he went to that mountain about which the pagan song speaks: "Look how pure Soracte is for its abundant snow." That is where the devout [Pope St.] Sylvester also hid himself when he was fleeing persecution, abandoning himself to readings, as well as where he received the good news that he should joyfully return to Rome in order to baptize Constantine. On that mountain, Benedict would later say, he lived for three years a life so severe and so rigorous an abstinence that almost no temptation managed to overwhelm him. His abbot later praised him and called him back with mercy and love. He also prepared a cell for him not far from the monastery, in which he lived the same eremitical life, but more easily so and successfully in the sweetness God gives to those who love him at such a level.

2. *Benedict becomes one of the disciples of Master Romald [sic]. Emperor Otto III participates in the Romaldian movement and proposes a mission to the Slavs, with a "threefold advantage"* [tripla commoda].

Now, at Montecassino lived an old nobleman named John [Gradenigo] who, along with the doge of Venice [St. Peter Orséolo], had wanted to live the monastic life. Drawn to a better kingdom, he abandoned earthly power with its riches and took on the monastic habit [at Cuixá] with such perfection that, under the guidance of a spiritual father, he undertook at once the eremitical life. But after the abbot of the monastery had died, and the doge of Venice had ended his time in God's service wearing the habit he had received, this old nobleman John continued in an excellent way to persevere in the solitary life, preserving a life wonderful in the exercise of virtue near Montecassino. Benedict began going to him and remaining in his holy company, and in order not to be wandering here and there as he pleased, thought prudently to live in John's cell. Old John, a true lover of humility, admitted that, though he had taught him salvation, all the counsels of life and heavenly words he offered came from the opinions and perfection of Master Romald, saying: "This Romald, the greatest in our times, lives sublime realities with great humility, not out of his own presumption but according to the *Conferences* of the hermit fathers, and taught us the right way." Young Benedict was enflamed whenever John praised Master Romald, since John, admired for already being a master in this life, was confessing that Romald was his Master. Now Romald was at the right age and was admired in that province for his uncommon virtue. Not many days later, Emperor Otto (the last Otto, and second to none in piety) took him forcefully out of his hermitage and named him abbot of Classe. Seeing that he now had less quiet and purity, Romald threw down his pastoral staff in the emperor's presence, so as not to ruin his life. He had been unsuccessful in winning over the others and wanted to distance himself as much as possible from those who knew him well, so he could at least save himself in some secret place. He had not won over any souls in that monastery due to the restlessness caused by outsiders. Without delay, he went to Cassino as a fugitive, the place serving as source and origin of monks who follow the *Rule*. To justify his trip there, he had the good motive of visiting and speaking with his old friend John, whom he had not seen for a long time. Among his many virtues, John was particularly noted for never speaking or giving ear to words of detraction. When the news reached him that Romald, the father of hermits who live according to reason and follow the *Rule*, was coming, Benedict mounted a horse and ran in all simplicity to meet Romald, as though a fortune had been spontaneously offered him. Finding him, he could not leave his side—loving him so much that he could not be separated from him, even when Romald scolded him and punished him severely. Benedict was happy to have finally found the Master. He believed nothing was right or holy unless Romald taught so; he mortified his passions and eagerly followed the counsels of the harsh teacher. Master Romald praised Benedict to such an extent that he said he was like a rock in his fasting and vigils, and was correct in touting him before me and all the others for his simplicity of obedience and the chastity of his habits in which he traveled joyfully as a witness to God. When autumn arrived, carrying sickness, Abbot Romald became gravely ill and was close to death. So he might recover, Benedict devoted himself in unswerving goodness to serving Romald in the midst of all the other attendants. Once he got better, Romald continued his voyage to Rome, which was itself a sick place. To serve him faithfully, Benedict, flower of youth and man of desires, joined him in obedience and humility. How could he abandon an old man who possessed the grace of perfection? He had such an insatiable desire to be with him that he felt nothing hard or bitter, but burned ardently in his bones with the love of God. When Emperor Otto, defender of the faith, returned to Rome from visiting the tomb of St. Adalbert, where he had gone on pilgrimage, the citizens of Rome received him with false joy, but great pomp. A large thunderstorm accompanied his entrance and, to add to the danger, dreadful thunder broke out and presaged mournfully, with an unusual cloudburst of sudden rain, what would come to pass. Then Abbot Romald, who wanders like a gyrovague to many places when he travels, but always succeeds in receiving sons with the finger of God, won over two whom the emperor loved—Benignus [St. Bruno-Boniface] and Thomas [Tammo]. Full of joy, he returned with them to serve God in golden solitude. Studies of Christian philosophy began to flourish in that hermitage and, with the descent of the Holy Spirit, the brethren's hearts were strengthened and, in the fear of God, produced foliage of virtue and fruits of holiness. The devil raised hostility against the peace of God's servants because Rome, quite near the hermitage, threw out good Emperor Otto, who did not deserve such treatment, angrily rejecting him and forcing him to go to Ravenna. But how could he leave without visiting the hermitage, since for many days he had entertained the thought of leaving the world with a love of God that burned more brightly in him than in many a monk? Whether by night or daytime, he visited the solitary hermits in God's silence and, because he grew in spiritual realities, this "rare bird" carried himself in such a way that, except for those he himself deemed worthy companions for such an undertaking, no one else in the palace knew about it, even though it is rather difficult to keep a king's movements secret. But, as they say, "Where the corpse is, there the eagles will gather." Unable and unwilling as king to remain hidden, the people followed him. This disturbed the contemplative life very much and, whether he felt called to come to us at the hermitage or we were summoned to him, the hermitage so reduced lost its order, as surely as he had lost Rome, and Rome had lost the world. The king had made a solemn promise spontaneously to renounce for the love of Jesus Christ his kingdom and all its riches that he did not really love and considered as nothing. Because adversities that usually move people towards salvation were pressing in on him, he manifested in words what was in his heart before witnesses in the presence of God and the angels, so that every word could stand on the testimony of two or three: "From this moment, I promise God and His saints that, after three years' time during which I will try to correct the errors of my reign, I will renounce the kingdom for one better for me and, distributing the money I inherited from my mother, stripped of all, I will follow Christ with all my heart."

One of those present spoke for Abbot Romald and the others, by virtue of his long life experience: "Persist in this plan, O king, and if life's uncertainty does not let you fulfill it, hold it before the eyes of one who knows the future and judges men's outer works by their inner hearts."

For this reason, the glorious emperor wanted to send from the hermitage to Slavonia, some brothers who, fervent in spirit, would go to a beautifully forested spot in Christian lands next to pagan territory, build a monastery, and offer to seekers of God's way *a threefold good: a nice cenobium for those newly come from the world, golden solitude for the mature members thirsting for the living God, and the preaching of the Gospel to pagans for those eager to depart and be with Christ.* Meanwhile, in order to have a twofold good, where it was not yet possible to have the third, as we were beginning our eremitical life [at Peréo], Otto decided to build a cenobium with holy intention for the salvation of many; but because of our sins, our undertaking took a mistaken turn for the worse—as one sees in the end—and he lost the hermitage while failing to build the monastery. Seeing what had happened, many blamed Father Romald and were scandalized, not knowing his extraordinary heart, which desired the emperor's salvation and the usefulness of a monastery for winning souls. Romald, contemplative spirit and true servant of God, had a singular propensity to do the opposite of what people wanted, respecting himself and preserving his own virtuousness while succeeding in having others scorn, insult, and defame him. Romald intended to name as abbot young Benedict, whom he had loved so much for his perfection and wonderful virtue, either for us at the hermitage or at the new monastery the emperor had begun to build. Indeed, Romald, the guardian of humility, thought himself more an abbot of souls than of bodies, while the crowd of brethren considered him indispensable. Because he did not want to become their abbot as the brethren wished, he needed to name someone else abbot. For this task, he— in whom the Spirit of God dwelled for the discernment of persons—found no one better adapted than Benedict. To him applied the saying, "Thoughts of the celestial city dwelled in his breast; the virtues of the Kingdom of God shone through his way of life." The brethren agreed, happy to have Benedict as their abbot. He, in all humility, presuming nothing about himself, said: "It is very difficult to accept the responsibility of directing souls when one cannot watch over one's own soul. Those entrusted to directing souls and correcting the actions of others must have sobriety of life, maturity, holiness, and wise discernment." Since he was charged in helping me, unworthy as I was, to understand the heavenly realities through his care, I had to live in his cell. He wanted me to ask the emperor not to make him the abbot. And so, the childish willfulness of Benedict rendered Father Romald's intentions useless, and another was consecrated abbot, as similar to Benedict as sand is to silver, or mud to gold. Once the blame seemed clear, the Master became furious and Benedict was whipped naked in the cloister, he who had in this case been wrong through humility, while I had deliberately suggested to the emperor that he not name Benedict abbot. I, who used to hear him call me "my brother" in the privilege of love during the pauses of our recited hours, suggested to Blessed Benedict that we depart to evangelize the Slavs, affirming that I was ready for such an undertaking. I said: "Our present location is stinking and the swamp, hostile. Who isn't sick here, from top to bottom? Is it not as though a sign from God that in such great sickness, no one has as yet died? I ask (myself), what can we do in the cell with our hands, when our feet cannot convey us to the Church on Sunday to receive Holy Communion? What fruit can we gather from wholesome reading or what prayer issue from our senses when our sick members cannot rise from bed? One cannot fast when in the grip of sickness, nor practice the other virtues when concentrating on patience as the only one necessary. Before we needlessly die in this swamp, let us leave for a place where we can do one or the other. Now, as the will carries God-seekers to the hermitage and we are not afraid to die, would we fear dying for Christ while evangelizing the pagans? Do not say, 'It is pride for sinners to seek martyrdom,' since many unbaptized people, fornicators, and idolaters receive this grace, and especially since we would not be seeking holiness, but the remission of our sins that are washed away by baptism, and totally extinguished in martyrdom." Persuaded by these and similar words, the highly blessed one began to desire it. In virtue of his journey toward another humility, he continued in his unwillingness to become abbot. If he had taken on this charge, a person such as he could have done much good for the cenobites and the hermits. And so during the rest of that year, in which they suffered and became seriously ill from the swamp, the brothers remained in the hermitage. Emperor Otto, a man of good will, built them a circular chapel beautifully decorated with marble columns and dedicated to his dear St. Adalbert, martyr of God. He spent one hundred pounds of silver on its construction.

3. *The breakup of the community at Peréo. John and Benedict missioned to the Slavs. The humble appearance and solid virtues of St. John.*

Wanting to avenge the offense Rome committed against him, the emperor—if only he had never undertaken that expedition during which he conducted himself badly against St. Peter—stopped off on his journey to celebrate the dedication of this basilica with great pomp, since he had a crowd of bishops with him. Here, as usual, the people who were following Otto filled the hermitage. Two of the disciples who spoke Otto's language [Bruno-Boniface and Tammo] and could not bear the snares and obstacles of the heart, obtained through him the reluctant permission of Fr. Romald, not without sadness, to transfer [from Peréo] to another more hidden hermitage where, away from people and the agitation of relatives, they could live under the authority of one of his disciples. However, neither the young monks themselves, nor the king who obtained the permission with good intention, nor the disciple who welcomed them out of imperfect love, would go unpunished for this sin. So when they left the hermitage, the disciples lost him and the same Master Romald lost his disciples. He set sail for Istria, his homeland, to beget new sons.

Near the swamp, whose stench usually causes dangerous and high fevers, sat the man of God, Benedict, by a fire in front of his cell set far into the woods, sick and unaware of all that had happened. It was as if he were the other half of my soul, and I, Bruno, told him that through a big mistake I had abandoned the Master, and that I did so to avoid damage to my weaker soul. Knowing this, the holy man said: "You have made a great leap, my brother. We are like two who should be one person, but you have abandoned the Master without my knowledge and you may never again find what you have lost. And as hard as it is for me to abandon the Master, with your departure I certainly cannot stay here." Benedict fell silent and, after a while, calmly said: "Give me my shoes and let us leave here." Then he added: "Does none of that former desire and will remain? Where is the king's noble plan, his secret project in his confession of Christ that he promised before God's angels to leave all for the love of eternal life? What man voluntarily wants to preserve will be lost at death, even against his will. Where is his abandonment of the kingdom to a wise successor so that, stripped of all royal honors, he might start out for holy Jerusalem, wanting to become a monk and contemplate [*philosophari*] in a distant hermitage, far from the beaten track?"

I, the son of negligence, whom Benedict loved much just as I was, responded: "The emperor desired greatly that you might precede him into the Slavic lands; his decision is still presently firm. Do not doubt that, if I remain alive, I will follow you. But I remain in this unhappy land in order to see what developments take place from the decisions of the imperial will." We were leaving the woods in the direction of the church, and we found the emperor just rising from his meal. With his accustomed humility, he went to the Master offended by the separation of his disciples. Against all we might have hoped for, he easily obtained permission to send good John and (as it seemed in people's estimation) the even better Benedict to Slavic territory. John was shorter than Benedict, coming only up to his shoulders, but he was superior to everyone else in the hermitage for his fervor, always growing in humility. He was a quiet man, moderate in that no one ever saw him angry. Averse to vainglory, he hid his sobriety behind a smiling face and, surmounting his years with great wisdom and innate patience, he had gained the reputation of having three eyes in place of one (for he had lost an eye to smallpox). Choosing the better part from youth, he considered pleasure his enemy; never fleeing a task, he engaged in battle his flesh and blood. Having entered a monastery as a lay brother, he succeeded in living without reproach, taming the hearts of rougher brothers, and rejecting all unbecoming conduct. Well received by his abbot, he sweetened whatever he did with humility. Kind and patient, he learned fervor with his great love of God and neighbor. In short, he matured and acquired experience. He suffered freely every bitterness and difficulty for love of Jesus Christ, on the apostle's example: "For me, to live is Christ and to die is gain."[8] And the psalmist: "Great peace is theirs who love Jesus, for

---

[8]   Phil. 1:21.

whom there is no obstacle."[9] And again, "My heart and flesh exult in the living God."[10]

4. *St. Bruno-Boniface bids Benedict farewell.*

Then Otto boarded a ship on the river and turned toward Ravenna with a group of monks—good and bad—at his royal side. Preparing the way for Benedict and John with great detail and the love of Christ, the emperor ordered whatever was necessary. He sent the two holy brothers, kindred hearts, to Slavonia across the Alps. From the night before until dawn— and this I cannot mention without tears in my eyes—I walked at celestial heights with Benedict. Beyond feeling my love for him, I was profoundly saddened with him, and I confess that our discussion was sweet for me in my wretchedness. And I must not be silent about how he, who usually called me "my brother" lovingly, was prophesying about what would happen to me for my sins, and called me "Lord Bishop" often with the same love. And this is a great source of fear for me because just as virtue can beget fault, so often fault can beget virtue. While the spirit of wandering had taken control of my thoughts or persuaded me, the spirit of holiness that had abandoned me turned him toward Slavonia. As the psalmist says, "Salvation is far from sinners."[11]

5. *"They went forth like twin stars...[for a] noble fortune in the land of the Slavs."*

In a vision of the night, when sleep can hold men captive, the bishop who had ordained this Benedict priest saw himself

---

[9] Ps. 119:165 adapted.
[10] Ps. 84:2.
[11] Ps. 119:155.

pouring a great quantity of oil over the venerable man's head. Later someone—I cannot say who—saw Benedict take the chalice of salvation and drain it all in one draught. These are the two things we desire when we sing the verse: "You have anointed my head with oil; how splendid is your overflowing chalice."[12] But considering future realities, prophecy, and similar things about salvation did not interest Blessed Benedict because, worthy man of God that he was, he was guided by the Holy Spirit to place all his hope in God, who had created all from nothing in His work of salvation. But I, who lingered in his embraces, kissing him on both cheeks all along the way as I followed him, discovered the only thing that my heart produced on my lips among the many things one could say at such a last meeting (oh, that I had been worthy to shout out: "My Lord!") was: "My dearest brother, I beg you through our shared hope, Jesus Christ, Son of the Virgin, remember that you know I am with you, and you with me. When you are praying or singing Psalms, always pray and beseech the living God that He will bring that unique desire He gave both of us to perfection for His name's sake, and that we will not delay until you and I, sinners, will see through God's mercy the blessed day on which we will shed our blood for a just cause and gain by God's power the remission of all our sins. In a way, this is not very different from what is written: 'Whoever seeks the salvation of his soul, seeks in Jesus' name.'" This is how I, a sinner, left a pledge of my love to the saint and, holding on to him and impressing it upon his ears, that I would surely follow wherever in the world he might go. Among other things, he asked me to

---

[12] Ps. 23:5.

study the Slavic language. And Blessed Benedict warmly recommended and repeated the admonition that I not leave without the apostolic license (to preach). With these words, my Lord Benedict disappeared from my eyes, and I would never see him again in this life full of toil. They went like twin stars to receive the Kingdom of God and a noble end in the Slavic lands: the man of God, Benedict, who burned with a love of Jesus like wood in a fire, and whose unique and simple intention was eternal life, with the one pure love of God's wisdom; and the man sent by God, John, who although he did not have a particularly holy fervor in the love of Christ, nonetheless was a serious person, patient, not easily swayed, and master of himself. Though less skilled in the interior life, he was more skilled in the exterior. He would begin something slowly, but with a good spirit, and see it through to the end. As far as the best practices [of monastic observance] are concerned, he was a true servant of God.

6. *Duke Boleslas "the Brave" Chrobry warmly welcomes Benedict and John to Poland.*

And so, they made the long passage across the Alps. After having a difficult trip, they came to the end of their journey, having seen many similar regions and having met the lord of the area, Boleslas (which is translated "greater in glory"). They had entered the province of the Poles, of unknown language. He was the only one of all those of our time who was privileged to send the martyr Adalbert, that rare bird, to preach, and to have him die in his kingdom. He welcomed them as the servants of God they were, with great desire and a grateful heart. He showed them the greatest courtesy and built them a quiet hermitage, generously provided for, in a suitable place for this type of life, and placed at their disposal life's necessities so they would not have to work.

7. *Emperor Otto III, bent on revenge against Rome, is struck down by the plague.*

At that same time, in the beginning of winter, Otto inauspiciously undertook his secular journey against the city of Rome with the forces of his reign and a chosen group of brave men. Alas, pious Otto died without children. He died in an unexpected way in a small outpost. Having accomplished much good, he made a mistake in this case because he forgot that the Lord said: "Vengeance is mine; only I will repay."[13] He did not honor God and His dear Apostle Peter who holds the key to heaven, as it is written, "Honor your Lord," the Holy One of Israel. Now since Otto had especially loved Rome he spent money and honors among the Roman people, but he vainly thought as a young boy that he would settle there permanently and renew the city's magnificent ancient splendor. And he did not have to look far for an example, for the psalmist wrote, "The thoughts of men are vain."[14] This was the king's sin. He no longer wanted to see his own native land, pleasant Germany. His desire to live in Italy was too great, a place where a terrible defeat seized his armies with thousands of sicknesses and deaths. His chaplain and companion, the bishop, died at his side, as did a large number of his servants, many soldiers, and excellent people. The sword raged against the blood of nobles, dripping from the massacre of those dear to him, and dreadfully wounding Otto's heart.

---

13 Rm. 12:19.
14 Cf. Ps. 93:11.

Neither the empire nor his sad wealth nor the army he had gathered served him now. The spear and the sharpened sword could not save him from the grip of death, the only one who does not know how to honor kings. He was a good king on a mistaken path, who thought he could destroy the imposing walls of great Rome, whose citizens did evil for good, that city in which God has fixed the apostolic see. It was not enough for him to conquer his native land and pleasant Germany, but also the land of Romulus, that feeds on the death of its dear ones and is still very pleasing in its adulterous beauty. Surely, as the ancient kings and pagans customarily recognized, whoever abandons his own will with difficulty exerts himself uselessly in restoring the dead splendor of old Rome. He read but did not understand, because the love of passing things will blind men's minds. Filled with the Holy Spirit, our most holy Father Benedict could not lie. When asked, he responded with prophetic inspiration: "Rome will not be conquered by the peoples, but will decay from within." Setting aside that true statement, he went ahead with his desire. At first he uselessly attempted to renew its splendor; then, with fickle reasoning, he tried to seize and destroy it. Not much later, the Romans were ungrateful for the benefits often given them by Otto. They forgot the great amount of money he spent on them, that he might as well have thrown into the abyss. He loved them, but they did not love him. They were irritated that, moving beyond the habits of preceding kings, he wanted sincerely to remain with them, and they came close to killing strong Otto and his German followers. Since the merciful God did not yet wish it, they shamefully forced Otto outside the miserable city he loved. Because he unleashed the excessive fury of the vassals, Otto left, unhurt but humiliated, and moved to the famous fortress of St. Peter. He wanted to revenge this pain (alas, for his sins), but death rose up and took him at an unexpected moment. Indeed, he threatened beyond what is licit to any authority, or better, he considered himself allowed what he was not—swearing and insisting categorically that he would settle for nothing less in this dangerous enterprise than the city's desolation and being vindicated of his enemies. While he was quick to anger in a worldly way and slow to convert as he had promised God, the hesitant, good emperor lost the good, and excited by the work, brought to completion the evil only in his thinking. As the saying goes, "Man proposes, but God disposes," and "Woe to one who wills the good and is not quick to do it, because he will soon lose it." But the bitterness of the death that prematurely took him expiated mercilessly enough whatever evil he committed in his youth. In the same way, he held to his firm decision to convert, as he had promised his elders. Lined up in double file, they filled the house where he lay dying, and his open confession of his sins purified the misdeeds of his youth and rendered his soul whiter than snow. As it is written, "We believe that sins are surely cancelled by repentance, even if one repents with one's last breath on earth, and that sins are annulled by a public contrition." He shed many tears, and everyone began to cry with him before the saints' reliquaries, including a precious relic of the saving Cross on which Jesus the Son of God died. With both fear and great joy he received the Body and Blood of our Savior, because from the onset of this great sickness he devoutly partook daily of the sacred Eucharist, on which complete salvation depends. Then, at the point of death, without ever losing consciousness, he divested and wounded his friends' souls when he breathed his last with a delicate gasp, under the Savior's mercy, for which he had always hoped. Alas, bitter death! Premature death, that plucks flowers in the whole world, found none more beautiful than he. His vigorous appearance, his face worthy of an emperor, was covered with spots. Whoever formerly saw it and could not have his fill nor see enough of him, now saw that he had lost his previous beauty to such an extent that everyone was repulsed. So he paid for his crime, while Rome remained unscathed. He was swept up into heaven before malice could alter his soul. He suffered death still in the flower of his youth, because our guilty world was absolutely unworthy of such a great king. What if he had been able to live to adulthood, where the letter "Y" of Pythagoras shows the right branch?[15] If opinion does not deceive, he would have been a just and most beloved emperor, beyond any that human eyes might behold. But what God wished and permitted is better, whose judgments are always holy, even if they seem uncertain to us sinners. Those who were present say that he died emitting his breath so sweetly that he seemed like someone falling asleep. We believe that the souls of the faithful called in such peace, according to the writings of the holy doctors, surely enter beatific light and peace. And even if the pain of purgatory demands account, his works and good intentions help us conclude that Otto will soon be in God's Paradise, as a humble servant of the saints and a true son of the angels who never sin. Although one might have considered him less virtuous before God, since he was a beautiful youth who had not married, and though his fragile flesh had led him into some

---

[15] Evidently, Bruno-Boniface is alluding to the usage of the letter "Y" as representing a fork in the road, where one has to choose one or the other path.

vain enticements, still his vigils, sackcloth, and fasting, his hidden almsgiving, healthy *lectio divina*, and the gentle prayer in which he took refuge, always lifted him up to our Redeemer's mercy. But it avails nothing if, as it is written, "One builds while another destroys; one prays while another curses."[16] It is undeniably true that, like those who want to please God more and do not succeed because they are unable, he made mistakes through excessive vanity. But that did him no harm, as far as he was displeased with himself in each case. As they say, "The consciousness of one's own misery is no small access to God's bliss." With the comfort of divine clemency for his weakness, he desired better things—the three greatest goods—any one of which suffices for salvation: he wanted with all his heart the monastic habit, the hermitage, and martyrdom. He did not want to master spiritual minutiae nor take on the spiritual journey with caution and gradually, but with greatness of character and a sudden change, he decided to renounce supreme authority and the greatest honors. Still, they often reproved what he did, for what he considered virtuous was often a defect displeasing God; that is, through human frailty, he undertook duties other than his own, neglecting the laws and justice he had been entrusted to administer to the poor throughout the kingdom. As far as promoting justice is concerned, Otto rarely functioned as a king, and even less so on a personal level. He was always seeking the spiritual realities of monks; he was very humble, with strong faith, and open-handed in giving. No one of sound mind could deny that he accomplished much. His mind and heart were not fixed on this world, and in his great love of

---

[16] Cf. Sir. 34:28-29.

God he sought wholeheartedly that future, as though he had no permanent city here.[17] He seemed an emperor in human eyes, but in his Creator's eyes, he already carried within himself the monk's reality. He considered useless all the luxuries that drag people to death—gold, silver, a kingdom, and regal powers; it is as if he had already renounced these things. His death seemed to fulfill an oracle of the Cumaean Sibyl, who had predicted many truths about the Savior's coming, the redemption, and last judgment. Among the Roman predictions regarding kings, she said of Emperor Otto: "The king born to purple will die in front of the city gate, in a land not his own." This corresponds to the truth, because the emperor's death re-echoed in a rebellious land and in a closed city. Such was Otto: father of monks, mother of bishops, son of humility and mercy, genuine servant of religion and the true faith, rich in good will and poor with virtue's perfection, lavish with material goods without exception, victorious over youthful sins. He neglected his homeland out of love for heavenly realities. He was fond of golden Rome, but God's anger was brief, and long was people's funereal mourning over him. Assured of salvation, his soul has a better life in Christ Jesus.

8. *Otto is mourned by Benedict, John, and Boleslas.*

The news of Otto's death wounded the holy men, Benedict and John, who had suffered the effort of a long, wandering journey for love of him and his salvation; they felt untold agony in their hearts. Among other good qualities he had was the noble custom of admiring good people, even while,

---

[17] Cf. Heb. 13:14.

in his youth, he also admired petty and worldly persons. He strove to love anyone he considered better, whether layman or cleric, especially if he was a servant of God. Nobody wept with greater sorrow at Otto's death than Boleslas, for whom the young king had wanted to do much good, because the holy Benedict and John had built their hermitage near him. If Boleslas is still faithful, he must preserve Otto's memory in his heart more than others.

9. War within Christendom. The worries and uncertainty of Bruno-Boniface, Benedict, and John.

After the emperor's death, the Christian world turned on itself deeply, as never before, with wars and rumors of war, like the sea in a storm, all due to our sins, just like the situation today. Meanwhile, all the pagans were at peace and could fight against Christians without cost, while the Christian kingdoms began to fight among themselves with fierce hatred in a cruel and ceaseless struggle. But as wound followed upon wound, a greater sadness than this came upon me: with the loss of peace and quiet due to war, I could not go to Rome to seek permission to carry the Gospel to the pagans. The aforementioned saints were amazed that I had not yet arrived with the permission. My negligence was a reproach to me because I continued to linger, having fearlessly sinned by lying and brazenly promised something I now refused to fulfill. They increasingly told themselves that they would not have thought about coming to this place, if I had not persuaded them to do so and succeeded in filling the emperor's head with such a plan. There were many beautiful solitary areas in which they could live the eremitical life in their own land. They had not been attracted to living in a hermitage in an unknown land and doing all this hard work for solitude, but they had sought the advantage of an angelic life by which they could insert themselves into paganism and evangelize the pagans. Benedict, in the flower of youth, especially wanted very much to do every good thing and forced his way into the Kingdom of heaven by violence, with great fervor for a better life. With its armed conflict, the world did not have any greater stress than these same saints did in their care for their shifting thoughts. The causes of the world's struggle were vanity and pride, while in the saints' hearts they were God and truth. They only feared dying without glory and usefulness, before fighting in some legitimate way in the service of God's Kingdom, with all the great tribulations considered indispensable for entering the Kingdom of heaven. They thought how death, thrust into their midst, cruelly killed the emperor's conversion and impeded his good works, and thus warns us who remain behind not to fall asleep. They spoke like this and stirred up their joyful souls. I heard this testimony from one of their disciples who is still alive. They expected me to arrive any day, bearing the venerable permission of the Apostolic See, enthusiasm for which same See had brought these noble spirits there. But many sins restrained me, guilty of transgressions and not fully converted, and I could not come to such a point. For my evil deeds were many, and even my good deeds were weak and tainted by evil, as it is written: "With hand joined to hand, the wicked will not be innocent." And the psalmist writes: "His ways are corrupt at all times."[18] Even when I was in the hermitage in Latin territory, I accomplished less good, but I correctly feared leaving the place in a hurry. As they say: "In whatever place you are, do not leave it too

---

18   Prv. 11:21 and 16:5; Ps. 10:5.

quickly." And even if the devil, making sport of me, had found in me no saving work, I was still being sent on to others. The desire admonishes me even now. For agony held me back, and I feared much that some diabolical thought might win me over if I were to abandon the cell in hope of better things—abandoning the way without finding any of the riches I had sought. As it is written: "There are ways that seem right to men, but their end finally plunges into the depths of hell." [19] Just as the other saying goes: "A man toils for himself and attains his own perdition."

10. Bruno-Boniface obtains papal authorization and heads north to preach to the heathen. Meanwhile, Benedict leaves John and goes in search of Bruno-Boniface.

Meanwhile, one day a certain person came seeking advice and visiting the brethren. He was led by the Spirit to my cell and, amidst the matters he had come to ask me about, he began to tell me in a mournful tone about a miserable crime: "Not long ago at Rimini, everyone rose up against a nobleman you know, the monk Rothulf. A worldly-wise man, he assisted Bishop Leo and devoted himself to gaining the favor of the king and accumulating a lot of money from the local people. He fled, but he could not take advantage of the sanctuary of the saints. Blind with anger and fury, the people dragged him out of hiding, not simply away from confession but even from the very altar of St. Gaudenzio. Not content with simply killing him, they first cut off his hands, arms, feet, and legs, then tore apart his whole body,

---

[19] Cf. Prv. 16:25.

reducing him to mere pieces, like a pack of dogs." I was horrified more than you can believe. "Alas," I said, "were we not sitting at table together the other day, thinking not at all about dying, but eating of the same bread and fish? I held him close to my heart, even if he broke the laws in worldly affairs. I always thought that the time would come when I could win him over to God. What can we do, brother? Truly the life of man on earth is warfare. Those who are full of life and with us today are swept away. And we are not even concerned, as if we must never leave all this, and we miserably love our unstable life, with its bittersweet, passing things." Having told me these things about the murdered monk, he left, and this thought began to torment me: "Why wait any longer?" I asked myself. "Delay no longer, but get moving. I would rather die in a pagan land, proclaiming the Savior, than to die here in this swamp someday of malaria, without producing any fruit." And yet, heedless again, I was disturbed by my wicked lingering and responded to my spirit just as the holy man Benedict used to answer me when I would express some new thinking: "I do not believe you!" And quoting the prophet, he would add, "Wait and wait again a little more, a little more."[20] But after a few more days, encouraged by my abbot, I finally reached Rome with a willing heart, but lingering feet. There I received permission from the pope to evangelize.

After much exertion on a journey by land and sea, I arrived at Regensburg, formerly *Radix bona* in Latin. Here I saw that the wars continued and the street was full of enemies. So I deflected my itinerary away from the Slavic

---

[20] Is. 28:10,13.

region, where the two holy brothers were awaiting my arrival with much anxiety, while not even the shadow of memory of my promise and of the sin of fraternal deception remained in my heart. Having abandoned the idea of going to the Prussians, where a more just cause would have drawn me since the murder of the new saint, Adalbert, I began with clumsy work and weak capabilities to carry the Gospel to the Black Hungarians, toward whom I embarked in the direction of their eastern borders. I said in my heart, "I will not close my eyes in sleep nor rest my head until I have found Christ." To Him our life must be available both day and night, because at night our nocturnal fears rob us of our sweet security. So that our heart may be strong, with God's help we must always enflame all our thoughts and deeds. I do not know if my Maker will take me away soon. At that time, I was, as it is written, "far from my salvation,"[21] but the time was near for the Lord God to repay his servants who would bravely suffer death. I was not worthy to join them, like a dog unworthy to be among the holy or a pig unfit for pearls. This was not through any injustice, for I had chosen not to go to those who were waiting for me day and night in great discomfort. I was not fit to be a saint among saints or chosen with the chosen, like a poor miserable Sarabaite[22] enclosed in my own will, and a thorny, vainglorious hypocrite, because I gave my honor to strangers and my years to the cruel.[23] I am taken up with passions as my law, and I like to wander through the world

---

[21] Cf. Ps. 22:2.

[22] Bruno-Boniface refers to the type of monk in the *Rule of St. Benedict*, ch. 1, who are self-willed and individualistic.

[23] Prv. 5:9.

with my desires, ready to serve many lords, so that I do not find God's salvation, but go wandering in the streets of my heart. As it is written, "With the perverse, you show yourself perverse,"[24] and again, "The worm is his sweetness and his mercy is forgotten."[25] It is really dangerous to rely on the merits of the perverse.

But Benedict was not at all like that; he held fast the truth and was mindful of his promises. Since I had not wanted to go to him, Benedict took ten pounds of silver to make the initiative of going to find me in a difficult journey inspired by God. The one whose fervor had drawn him straight to the hermitage from novitiate, the already often-mentioned John, was competent to watch over the place and maintain it in divine service and sound doctrine. He was more patient to stay at home and less desirous of evangelizing. He was not usually fazed by such questions as usually came up, but faced them with serenity and equanimity, making allowances for that holy restlessness of blessed Benedict and sharing charitably with the great grief and toil that Benedict felt in his heart through the depths of compassion. I believe that it would be difficult to find a similar fervor for Jesus Christ among God's chosen, and certainly not greater than Benedict's, who sought only to please the Lord God in his life and had no peace until he fully accomplished what he had to do, no matter how hard and rough. He knew how to be pleasing in God's eyes, as it is said: "I do not consider my life more precious than myself."[26] This, then, was his only thought, day and night: that he obtain permission to preach

---

[24] Ps. 18:26.
[25] Job 24:20.
[26] Acts 20:22-24.

the Gospel or, permission granted me, that he find me. And so those holy sentiments of blessed Benedict, the depths of tribulation and anguish, mercilessly and continuously kept him in tears and sighs. Blessed John, that other saint, humbly bowed his neck to God's judgments and patiently endured with wisdom and successfully restrained his spirit, tamed by God's gift. If something could not be as he had wished, he wished it to be whatever it might be. Only Benedict wavered, impatient with time's passage, and struggled within himself, lest he be cheated of his holy desire and lose the hoped-for precious goal for which he had abandoned homeland, where he could have been more useful. Instead, he had crossed mountains, rivers, and valleys and entered a land whose language he did not know, although by now he had begun to understand and speak the Slavic language. Because they both agreed, Benedict and John decided to shave their heads completely and to dress in the local attire. This would appease pagan eyes exteriorly and not shock them with their strange clothing, nor give them any reason to distance themselves from the brothers. Showing themselves as similarly dressed, Benedict could find more easily a place suitable for preaching and, at an opportune moment, with the discretion that is always necessary, could turn them toward the way of salvation.

11. Benedict travels as far as Prague looking for Bruno-Boniface.

So Benedict left the hermitage, where he had profitably stayed like a happy farmer, and set out with all the desire of his heart to find me. Happily, he began to travel until, leaving Polish territory behind him, he entered the borders of a harassed Bohemia and came to the greatest city in that area, noble Prague, as a newcomer. There lies the martyr Wenceslaus, King of that land, who showed his own holiness through miraculous signs of compassion. While he had loved heavenly realities and despised earthly ones, his cruel brother, in contrast, killed him as an innocent lamb. In this city there was also a bishop who was a noble creature whose equal could not be found today, but the injustice of the godless did not want to listen to him, and they forced him to flee by their sacrilegious behavior. They forced holy Adalbert to take the monastic habit in magnificent Rome, called the "garden of St. Peter" by pious pilgrims. Pressured to return against his will because they needed a shepherd, he was forced to flee a second time when the people did not follow through on their promise to change their ways. Persecuted yet a third time by their filthy intrigue, he finally heard them say openly, to his greater glory, "We do not want you as bishop." But because all things cooperate for good for those who love God, the just Adalbert did not grieve over whatever befell him. While he introduced Christ to pagan ears, Adalbert died under seven blows, becoming precious through his desired martyrdom as a source of grace and immense glory for our modern times. He was a good bishop and an even better monk, an angelic man with a beautiful, expressive demeanor. After his happy triumph, those who would not listen to the bishop, who genuinely urged them on and lived in a saintly manner, now tore apart their bodies with their own hands and killed one another. Once they had cut off the heads of their innocent brothers, they could not avoid the furious sword themselves. They repented too late of not having now what they could not have because they did not formerly want him and drove him away by their contrary ways. So the bad Christians did not provide for the saint a good undertaking, but gave their pastor leave to go to the pagans where, preaching, he brought them eternal life. He suffered temporal death at their hands. As is sung in praise of the just: "Precious in the eyes of the Lord is the death of his saints."[27]

When the just Benedict entered guilty Bohemia and its ruined metropolis, he wanted to travel the streets on foot to reach me, whom he loved truly and tenderly. That would have been easier, though more tiresome, than by horse, because war had blocked the way everywhere.

There was a great wintertime of war agitated by many forces, and the streets were impassable, so that even the messengers themselves, guaranteed safe passage by ancient law, did not find the streets safe. For this reason good King Boleslas, who had financed this undertaking, now sought persuasively to dissuade blessed Benedict from setting out into such a difficult situation of opposing forces and running into enemies. He was afraid of losing so just a man. He loved him, and he would rather have aggrieved the saint a hundred times than deprive himself of so great an advocate. Seeing his route blocked, Benedict became very sad (an inclination of his temperament), because his love for me was his primary motive. Showing how much he cared for me, he wept bitterly because he could not now see me. A flood of tears accompanied his sorrow, dampening his sad face with its flowing torrent, as he thought about what he had set out to do. He blamed himself for the present situation, in which his desire could neither be realized by remaining at home

---

27 Ps. 116:15.

nor by going outside. He told himself that he had to endure
it, because he had not had any foresight. He had left a land
where he could have won over many, looking for what he did
not find and losing what he had. It had all come to nothing.
He had come into that region with good intentions, but all
he had done proved useless. Now he had enemies and little
hope. As it is written: "If you have rightly offered and not
discerned rightly, you have sinned."[28] And again, "I want to
do good, but I cannot do it."[29] And still again, "Many can
begin, but few can bring to completion." Benedict was angry
with Lord Boleslas, who did not want him to go, because he
himself was unafraid and considered all the talk about wars
and enemies useless. He also accented my own sin, since I
was then nearby and could have fulfilled the promise I had
made. This was true, but at that time I did not wish to see
him. Indeed, a sinner always dislikes seeing saints. How can
I ever face up to the heavenly Master, despicable as I am,
loosening the bit and following my own will faster than a
horse? I decided to interest myself in spiritual undertakings
and did so, but without renouncing worldly comforts. As
a wavering servant, I wanted to cultivate the love of Jesus
Christ without holding the deceitful world in contempt. As
it is written: "You have lost the senator, but you have not
achieved the monk"; "Woe to the sinner who follows two
paths"[30]; "No one can be delighted with the world and reign
with Christ."

---

[28] Gen. 4:7.

[29] Rm. 7:18.

[30] Sir. 2:14.

12. Benedict returns to the hermitage in Poland. He sends out a brother (St. Barnaby) to try to find Bruno-Boniface and to return with a papal rescript.

Holy Benedict returned to Brother John, expelling the various pains in his heart, weeping much, and filled with profound sadness because his efforts had been ineffectual. There was one brother who, for the love of heavenly things, once served under their teaching in the hermitage, and who is now abbot of that same holy place, presiding over the study of spiritual discipline. Benedict sent him to Rome, the mistress of the world and mother of the churches, since King Boleslas did not object to this brother traveling. This was for his consolation, on fire with celestial longing to obtain the apostolic permission. He ordered him under holy obedience to try to find me, who had been their inspiration to travel to the Slavic lands. If he found me and I had obtained permission, he should hurry back directly; if not, he should ask me for a companion to travel to Rome and get it, bringing his journey to a conclusion. Just as while hoping for what is certain, a lover's wait is brief, so it is long when things are fearfully uncertain. He hoped to temper his recent pain and the intensity of his bitterness by setting a date by which he would return: he would either return by the feast of All Saints or by the feast of St. Martin at the latest. But he forgot, I believe, in the urgency of the moment and the violence of his suffering, that the holy *Conferences* of the Fathers agree with the *Rule* under which he lived, namely, that the monk ought never assert any plan as certain. So blessed Benedict sent the disciple on the road from the hermitage. Because of my wanderings, the brother did not find me, who had frustrated Benedict's desire through my laziness, so he proceeded directly toward Rome to obtain the permission of the apostolic authority.

13. Benedict and John, together with their novices Matthew and Isaac and their cook Cristin, die nobly at the hands of robbers. Their bodies remain incorrupt.

At the same time, Benedict did not live on in an embittered spirit but returned to the sweet desire he always lived. He disposed himself, as the strong man he was, to focus on the desirable and precious comfort of the future and not to dwell on the bitterness of the present. For him, there was but one good among all the many goods, only one happiness among the multiplicity of beautiful joys that capture and enkindle mortal hearts and force them to run in vain, namely, the holy fear of God. This fear possessed his soul forcefully, and he knew how to invoke the living God in the midst of every tribulation, countering every wrong desire with a perfect contempt and renunciation of the world. He knew that he possessed nothing on earth except himself and he wanted nothing on earth except God, always keeping the remembrance of eternal glory before his eyes. This is life for the wise man: remembering the night of eternal punishment and keeping always in mind the happiness of the future Kingdom. This guides our journey, with golden discretion and meditation on all the virtues leading us to heaven.

All summer long until the feast of All Saints, they kept their minds fixed on prayer and fasting, waiting according to the Apostolic saying, "until you are clothed with power from above."[31] And there was such harmony between the holy brothers that whatever one wanted, the other wanted as well—whether regarding the cell, or work, or clothing, or lifestyle, or prayer. If one wished something, the other sought not to disagree, out of fraternal love and to avoid bad feelings. Their only thought in arranging their life and customs was to love God above all, devoting themselves to prayer and purity of heart, as it is written: "They all had one heart and one mind."[32] And as the psalmist writes: "Behold how good and how pleasant it is, brothers dwelling in unity."[33]

When the brother sent to Rome to find me did not return on the assigned date, the holy brothers Benedict and John, who loved nothing of this world, became distressed again about the salvation of souls. As it is written: "The corruptible body weighs down the soul, and an earthly dwelling humbles the mind with many thoughts."[34] Their great love for the secure happiness of the heavenly Emperor saddened them, not their thinking about the uncertainty of human events, the delays, or the double loss of the two brothers—me and the one sent to find me. They did not know if they would ever see us again in this life; and of course, they did not. They considered it their own fault that the brother sent to Rome was lost, and they beseeched God's mercy for his return and mine, saying: "Since you are my patience, my God, and my mercy." So, suffering bitter remorse, the servants of Christ began to piece these things together with a commendable complaint: if men can toil for perishable goods, why should

---

[31] Lk. 24:49.
[32] Acts 4:32.
[33] Ps. 133:1.
[34] Wis. 9:15.

we not cheerfully toil to gain the truth of heavenly realities? This problem, this situation, never allowed them any rest. It relentlessly upset their spirits every time they saw someone or came together to speak, since they were ever together with the sincere feelings of the heart. Why had I not yet come, as I had promised? Why had the one sent to find me not come with the permission?

For so long a time, they told themselves, they had waited in vain. They had sweated hard to learn the Slavic language, so that the pagans might better reach salvation; they had stopped shaving and grown miserable with their long beards and completely shaven heads. With good intentions, they changed into their clothing and accustomed themselves to the ways of the people, believing that the pagans would accept them as fellow countrymen and not see them as different from themselves. For us, they said, the way lies open for preaching, as well as for martyrdom: no matter which, since one conducts us to the good and the other leads to salvation. But now here we are, without the holy permission of the apostolic notification, on which decision depends this whole undertaking. We sinners are not worthy to receive it. But it is also true that "the poor will not always be forgotten, and the patience of the poor will not perish forever."[35]

There were also two other blood brothers living at the hermitage in formation, Isaac and Matthew, like regal offspring beautifully similar to their noble fathers from Italy, though they were Slavic. These two brothers had sisters who dedicated themselves to God in a monastery of consecrated

---

[35] Ps. 9:18.

virgins. And the two brothers in the flesh became even better brothers in the Spirit.

Meanwhile some thieves, conspiring sacrilegiously, planned to steal the ten pounds of silver from Lord Boleslas that they had come to know about and, under the cover of darkness when night could help hide their crime, kill all the servants of God in the forest. They could then divide among themselves all the money they thought they would find near the brothers. While the evil thieves were perversely thinking about all this, it so happened that it was a feast day. Those holy monks, who loved what is unshakably true and good, had gathered in holy vigil to sing the nocturns of the good and generous Saint Martin, according to the universal Christian rite, and to celebrate Mass, the sacrament of redemption. That same night—according to their servant who had gone home—they were very anxious and depressed more than ever. They sang the mournful verses of the ancients with their usual plaintive moaning: "It is in vain we left our homeland, came to a foreign land, and beneath another sun labored hard to learn a new language. We have found no trace of the brothers who were coming and no sign of apostolic obedience so as to do battle with the weapons of Christ and shake up the deepest paganism. As it is written: 'Has God forgotten to have pity or in his anger shut up his mercy?'[36]"

O the depth of the riches of God's wisdom, knowledge, and mercy! They did not know what was about to happen. Because they still had no news, they went around dispirited and groaned in anguish, though even if they had acquired the apostolic permission, the blessed martyrdom their hearts

---

[36] Ps. 77:10.

yearned for so ardently would still have been no closer. The good Lord, who brings much good out of man's evil, was getting ready to grant them their hearts' desire, just as He listens to those who ask in His name. He never lies to His saints, as it is written: "If he has delayed, wait for him because he will surely come and will not delay!"[37] And again: "Can a mother forget to have pity on the son of her womb? If she should forget, I will not forget you."[38] And still again: "For a while I abandoned you, but with great mercy I will gather you."[39] Thus says the Lord God, hope of the saints and their tower of strength, who does so many good things and is excellent in all His works. He is supremely beautiful and dazzling, and wonderful in His saints.

While they were sleeping in the dead of night, as they rested their weary limbs in a deep sleep, the wicked ones approached, eager to do their wickedness—their hearts pounding to commit their crime. With mind quickened, lips trembling, nostrils flared, and blood coursing through their veins, they were ready. With quick feet, chattering teeth, hushed voices, and inflamed with an absurd anger, they carried their weapons in sweaty palms—eager to effect their greedy plan. They came like dogs smelling blood or wolves after prey. They wanted to do harm, and they did evil in God's sight, but it turned into good. These evil men came in the night like thieves to end the lives of the innocent. Certainly, Benedict had received the money to fund his great journey. But as soon as he saw his way thwarted, he who had never abandoned his heart to hope in money immediately

---

[37] Hab. 2:3.
[38] Is. 49:15.
[39] Is. 54:7.

returned the funds he did not need. But the evil Christians thought they would find the money. It is said of them: "This is all they see in the whole world." Unlike pagans, who for religious reasons usually hesitate to put to death the just, they were ready and willing without fear or qualms to act differently from what is written: "Do not hope in iniquity, and if riches abound, do not set your heart on them."[40] But one of this crowd of sacrilegious men, whose deed accomplished the noble death of the poor brothers, knew them well, for he had worked in their service at one point. He was the leader of the raid, so he was hoping to get a bigger share of the loot. He came to them armed with a hidden sword. But before he entered the room, he drank two cups of strong drink with Satan's blessing, so his heart would not be too frightened to commit the sacrilegious crime. Holding a candle in his left hand and a lance in his right, he suddenly came upon the waking saints as a deadly executioner with a terrifying grimace.

The gentle brothers sat up in their beds. Because necessity breaks the rules and the concern for guests permits the breaking of silence, and since Christ was always on their lips and in their hearts, they began to whisper among themselves. This executioner later repented of his crime and described the scene. Perhaps they spoke that verse appropriate for the conclusion of the monks' chapter, "Precious in the eyes of the Lord is the death of his saints,"[41] since their precious death was imminent. But because of the immediate danger, in my opinion, I think it could have been the *Confiteor*. But

---

[40] Ps. 62:10.
[41] Ps. 116:15.

the executioner said he just stood there, dead in his spirit, wanting to kill them and afraid of doing so. After they finished their whispering, John, the son of patience, ready to sanctify himself quickly in martyrdom, and the one who knew the language better and usually answered whomever came to them, said: "Friend, what have you come for, and what is the meaning of this armed band?" The astonished aggressor, who now does good and repents of his evil crime, answered: "The lord of this land, Boleslas, commanded us to bind you without mercy." Smiling, the saint said: "The good old man, who loves us much for the love of God, never ordered such a thing. Why are you lying to no purpose, my son?" The assassin answered: "Actually, we want to kill you. That is why we have come." And holy John replied: "God help you and us." Blanching at those words, the murderer brought out his sword and struck two blows to John's body. He had already carried a third wound—not so glorious as the others—throughout life in his eye, owing to the after-effects of a sty. Then he quickly turned to the others and struck blessed Benedict, that precious pearl, a hard blow in the upper middle part of his skull. Like an overflowing torrent, a great spurt of blood stained the walls crimson, and one can still see today the beautiful stains in that part of the house. Naturally, the brothers were sadder than ever as they neared death. As it is written: "May my soul die the death of the just."[42] But even our Redeemer, salvation itself, our holy mercy, our God, confessed to His beloved followers that He was tired and sad as He approached the Passion He underwent with inestimable love for humanity's salvation, to

---

[42] Num. 23:10.

save the lost. In the beginning He was the Word, in whose hand was the soul of every living being, and so that mercy moved Him to bear our sins. He said: "My soul is sad unto death."[43] Setting aside certain witnesses, there is that holy Israelite, the truly good Adalbert, whose recent martyrdom rendered a miserable epoch blessed. When the Prussians expelled him from their territory, refusing to listen to him or kill him, he fell into the deepest sorrow and blamed himself for not winning them over. According to those with him, he was never imprudently diverted in his sadness of heart until, in spite of themselves and by God's bestowal, the Prussians turned their malice to his favor. So it also was now. Although the brothers' sadness had grown immeasurable just a little before, God, the holy and faithful lover of mankind, who grants with an abundance of mercy more than we could ask or understand, gave the desired martyrdom to their satisfied souls at home. Though it is very dangerous to rush into it rashly, it is safe and holy to seek martyrdom in prayer.

One of the two Slavs who had joined the blessed masters Benedict and John by holy profession, Isaac by name, was the third to die. He was a robust man, who awoke abruptly and kept repeating loudly the noble outcry: "Help us, O God! Help us, O God!" As it is written: "The Lord's name is a mighty tower; the just flies to it for refuge and is saved."[44] He stood up as though to pray and received the sword's violent blow in the middle of his legs. As it is written: "The eye seeks what is loved; the hand wards off pain." Raising his hands as though to say, "skin for skin", he received a second merciless

---

[43] Mt. 26:38; Mk. 14:34.
[44] Prv. 18:10.

blow on his blessed hands. Hoping to reach his longed-for goal in his awaited death, Isaac realized that, through the bestowal of Christ who is the salvation of all who believe in Him, he would receive at home the martyrdom by which one removes the great load of sins once carried. He showed the great joy in his heart with words like these: "It is a blessing for us to have found such a good night and so happy an hour, given us, not for our merits, but only out of the Savior's mercy." As it is written: "My heart will exult in your salvation; I will sing to the Lord, who has been good to me." [45] And then he said: "May the Lord bless you, because you have done good to us." As it is written: "Bless those who persecute you and pardon them,[46] because they do not know what they are doing." [47] Having said this, Isaac had his throat slit with a third blow and expired. When the Godless men heard him blessing them who had come only to do evil, they were struck by such goodness, his kind and serene patience, and began to feel disgusted and penitent, as if to say, "Woe to us! We came to kill such men, who show joy at being killed and, something unheard of, bless those who slay them. But we cannot undo our actions and must kill them all. So that our crimes will not become known and punished, we must finish what we have begun." And this is precisely the misfortune of such people, because God watches all from on high. Since they have no fear of corporal punishment here, they do not think about the consequent intolerable punishment of their souls later on. As it is written: "It is a terrible thing to fall into the

---

[45] Ps. 13:6.
[46] Rm. 12:14.
[47] Lk. 23:34.

hands of God Almighty."[48] Alarmed at what was happening, Matthew tried in vain to flee outside. They struck him with a lance near the church, where he fell prostrate on the earth, as if he were in prayer. Cristin, their cook, whose brother was spending that night in the village—as it is written: "One will be taken and one left behind"[49]—tried to defend himself with a staff. He called in vain for the brothers to help, not knowing that they had already been murdered—the dead cannot hear. Cristin was a loveable and pleasant person who had remained faithfully in their service, and now he became the fifth to be killed with an impious blow and joined the other four murdered saints. This was much to his benefit, because from the fifth wound flowed blood and water that remitted the sins of men. He who is good wished to grant to the last what had been given the first. Each one is saved through His mercy, not through his own merits. The assassins thought they would find money, but to their dismay, they found nothing. They divided the Mass vestments among themselves by the sword, but they did not touch the excellent books that the brothers had brought with them from Latin territory as gifts from the emperor. But they did take the altar frontal containing the relics, and they burned incense wrapped up in an oilskin cloth placed near the church walls so that, burning down the whole church, all the little rooms of the narrow enclosure would be reduced to ashes along with the holy corpses. That way, an accident would seem to have happened rather than a deed of thieves or assassins. But God and man think differently. The church did not burn, and the

---

[48] Heb. 10:31.
[49] Mt. 24:40.

saints' bodies were buried in peace. And the guilty parties, by God's decree, could not hide, even if no victim lived to tell the tale. Late in the night, they repented of their deed and fled much faster than they had arrived. To intensify the condemnation of their guilty conscience, from the time they went outside after killing the saints, they heard the sweet melody and sound of singing inside. We know this from their own true and decisive testimony, because they are now serving in that same monastery, trying to repay their debt as well as they can. After an unevenly matched fight, the wicked fled, and the souls of the martyrs, whose excellent life had come to a good end with an unexpected salvation, were presented as innocent and upright before Jesus Christ, the eternal and true God. In that massacre, they all lay down differently from the way they had slept, even though no one had resisted except young Cristin. Each knew the joy of a noble death in the Holy Spirit. Matthew lay by the church, where he had fled from the evil. Cristin fell on the square, while defending the innocent. Rising on his feet at the unusual awakening and struck three times with a sword, Isaac lay prostrate as though beseeching pardon. John had fallen out of bed onto his knees as though in the *orans*[50] position. Only Benedict, the leader of the divine band, lay as if asleep, having restored his spirit to the Lord, dying gloriously. Once they had committed their crime, they still heard voices singing songs to God inside, so they entered to see if anyone might still be alive. Holy Benedict was dead, along with all the others, but had covered his head with his hood and changed position, now facing the wall. But one of the assassins opened the

---

[50] i.e. with outstretched arms

door and rushed inside, fearing they had not finished their crime—that the brothers were still alive, and that they would be punished. Trembling, he touched their rigid members and looked at their pale features, finding no traces of breathing. Just as the great saint Denis the Areopagite carried around his own decapitated head, while angelic voices sang melodies, so through His mercy, our little Saint Benedict could change his position, place his hood over his crimson head, and not be found breaking the rule.[51]

A rosy day dawned on sad mortals. The courtyard was still closed, so none of the nearby villagers who came there dared to enter. All were wondering what had happened inside, since no one had come out. Finally, one peeked through the thorn hedge and saw the body of Cristin lying in the middle of the courtyard. He was the innocent servant of the innocent, a lad who was accustomed to be at the brothers' service. God allowed him to be crowned with them in the fullest joy, because he loved the holy brothers. Without delay, the amazed villagers competed with one another to rush in to see this dreadful scene, but they did not dare touch the saints' bodies with unclean hands and impure hearts until all the facts about the night's sin might be brought to light. Not until the third day was the deed reported to the local bishop, who gathered a discreet number of clerics and those consecrated to God for the appropriate funeral rites of the holy innocents. The nearby forest furnished the wood for their caskets, and the bishop ordered a large grave dug inside the church that could contain the bodies of four—twice over. Then old Bishop Unger, rich in

---

[51] Bruno-Boniface piously asserts that Benedict covered his head in deference to the rule of night silence.

good will, came to the holy place, celebrated the sacrifice of the Mass and funeral rites with the clergy, and then approached the saints' bodies with hands and heart in supplication.

Then he saw that champion Benedict, the precious stone among all the others, the golden star and sweet splendor, whose passion to battle with God was steadfast until he had them all baptized with martyrdom and blessed with the Lord's hand. He lay stretched out in the principal corner of the house, to the right of the entryway, turned on his side and facing the wall—in the same position he had assumed, with great love, upon his happy death. His noble head was turned toward the south and his feet to the north, like the wind in the *Song of Songs*: "Arise, north wind; come, south wind and blow upon my garden and spread its perfumes."[52] That is to say: "Begone, Satan, and come, Holy Spirit, fill my soul and make its fragrant virtues appear." All the others slain with him were lying differently as they had fallen, or rather they now seemed to be at prayer. The noble head of Benedict had not only reddened the walls, but they even found the holy man's hood full of blood, as it is written: "He washed his robe in wine and his cloak in blood."[53] Later, the bishop accompanied the saints' bodies to the tomb with prayers and the customary antiphons. They were placed in a single grave, two by two, on the same day the Son of God, our Redeemer, rested in the sepulcher after He had redeemed a lost world through His passion, and God's salvation slew our death by His death. The noble Benedict, that flower of youth, was in the middle of the church, along with the glorious shoot John.

---

[52] Song 4:16.
[53] Cf. Gen. 49.11.

They placed the other two, whom God's grace had rendered novices of His holy service and worthy disciples in glorious martyrdom, along the walls. As it is written: "The virtues hold to the mean, but all praise is sung for the disciples at the end." Cristin, the young man in the saints' service, was buried in the cloister, since he had not reached the same degree of holiness and had wanted to defend himself with a staff. As it is written: "Do not yoke the ox with the ass," that is, the wise with the foolish. But not too long afterwards, they exhumed Cristin and found his body completely intact, as though he were still alive, and without any bad odor present. Suddenly there was a rainstorm that flooded the ground more than usual, and the men working in the cloister fled, interrupting their work. So the monks took him in their own hands, carried him into the church, and buried him there, since he was not separate from the others while still alive. As they say: "There is no distinction between Jew and Greek, slave and free; all are one in Christ."[54] They opened the holy monks' tomb in order to place the servant there. Although enough time had elapsed, the saints' flesh gave off no bad odor normal for corpses, let alone the thick stench that the putrid flesh of sinners normally gives off already after the first day.

14. John's corpse turns over.

We must not pass over in silence the fact that, late one night, when two boys were reciting the Office and singing the appropriate Psalms, holy John, who was laid in the middle of the church with his brother, turned over on his other side. Terrified, one of the boys fled, but the other saw it as an angelic

---

[54] Cf. Rm. 10:12; Gal. 3:28; I Cor. 12:13; Acts 10:34.

event and continued to sing the Psalms. He is now a monk and serves as deacon in that same church. So it happened that what Benedict had done when he was murdered, that is, turning on his side, John now did in the tomb.

God has granted many signs and wonders through the merits of the saints. This was the first of them, after the life of the congregation had been re-established there.

15. *A burning candle appears at the tomb.*

One Saturday, after the customary instruction reminding the monks of divine charity, all the brothers saw a candle burning with a bright light on the tomb of the saints, and no one had placed it there. This happened many times at different intervals, as if showing the light shining in their souls in God's presence and the joy of heaven. It proved to mortal eyes that they live in the land of the living. And if this event of the burning candle perhaps seems ordinary, I will refer now to another event about the saints' light. There were many witnesses from a neighboring village, some of whom are still alive.

16. *A midnight light over the church.*

When the great and powerful armed forces of the king of Saxony moved against that village, and no one doubted that the whole area was in danger, a large bright circle appeared above the church in the middle of the night and flooded the whole courtyard with light, remaining there for an entire hour.

17. *The light reappears.*

Similarly, a year and eight days after their martyrdom, another light phenomenon shone brightly above the same church. From the first experience, people understood that the land was under the saints' protection, and the armed forces of the king left it intact, free of the consequences of planned destruction. From the second light phenomenon, they grasped the holiness of the martyrs, whose patronage was sought with devotion and mercifully reached all the land from that monastery, where a heavenly treasure lay beneath a poor and naked tomb.

18. *A light and voices near the church.*

Another time, a monk and a layman were sleeping near the church, when a great light and the sound of singing voices terrified both. And they heard the voice of one reading the Gospel of the Living God that ends: "Enter into the joy of your Lord."[55]

19. *Brother Stephen is healed of paralysis.*

There was one there who now serves as deacon in that church. He was unable to go to the church, because he had long suffered an ailment that desiccated his bones and prevented movement. One night when he was asleep, pious Benedict and blessed John appeared to another brother in heavenly splendor. With shining faces, they said: "Rebuke Brother Stephen, who has failed to show up at church for many days. Why is he lazy? Does he love staying in bed so much? He should get up and participate in God's service with his brothers." The next day, the brother who had this vision saw Stephen walking quickly, while the day before he had been near death in his illness. He was amazed that

---

[55] Mt. 25:21.

the sleeping brother had regained his health and now could enter the house of prayer in perfect shape, after the invitation from the heavenly doctors. It was as though he had never lost the strength of his weary body. This clearly indicates how merciful salvation is present to all the needs of those who serve God day and night, having honored the holy monks. As it is written: "First seek the kingdom of God, and all these things will be added unto you,"[56] that is, all that you need.

20. *Exorcisms.*

There are no official data about the extent or exact number of people freed from demonic forces. Nor can we recount all the ways they were freed, thanks be to God, through the merits of the martyrs.

21. *Barnaby returns from Rome with papal recognition for the cult of the martyrs.*

We hesitate to admit that we are too lazy to count how many people have been freed through their goodness from iron chains and wooden fetters: leaving them intact or breaking the iron, but in any case, undoing every constraint. Clearly these immortals care for those who are striving for salvation without counting the cost, however serious their situation. They take care especially of those who serve more intently, or who, despite a weak conscience, rejoice all the more for their own salvation now that God has crowned the new saints. As it is said: "The sins forgiven her are many, because she has loved much."[57]

---

[56] Mt. 6:33.
[57] Lk. 7:47.

Meanwhile, that brother whom the saints, while still alive, had sent to the Apostolic See returned with the permission and discovered that the story had reached a happy ending. The saints had been martyred and taken into heaven. But I, whom Benedict in his goodness and great charity used to call "my brother", had already—unknown to them—received the apostolic permission. Now that the Redeemer's merciful will was accomplished in His saints, that brother returned to Rome to announce the martyrdom and was interviewed by the pope personally. He decided, without hesitation, that they should be considered holy martyrs, and honored as such. I, the gyrovague, could not be found. The brother had gone back to Rome not only to announce their martyrdom, but also to learn about me. There were great disagreements with the king of Saxony, who feared that allowing the brother and good Bishop Unger to leave his territory might prove harmful, so he sent the brother to Magdeburg, where he remained a prisoner in a monastery.

One night, while he was trying with difficulty to get some sleep amidst the wandering shadows of night, the holy John and Benedict appeared to him like two stars, rebuking him, because he was still there unwillingly after a few days in that dreadful prison. They said: "You have lost one of the two you left behind at the monastery, and you will lose the other if you do not return quickly. The brother understood that things were not going well at the monastery, where he had left two clerics in charge until his return. Not doubting this heavenly help, he immediately fled in the silence of the night, once the saints had told him to return at once. Passing through the enemy, he was able to arrive home safe and sound, as the archangel Raphael said: "I will guide him and bring him back safe and sound."

22. *A wayward cleric's flight from the cloister is checked by "good master wolf".*

Again, one of the clerics had left the house, as often happens in these times. As they say: "Men will be lovers of themselves," and "The charity of many will grow cold."[58] He was a prisoner of his own fickle, disturbed mind, missing his relatives, so he left the sacred place without any fear. As he was on his carefree way homeward, a wolf with snapping jaws crossed the road and turned on him furiously. In terror, his blood melted within him; he lost his voice; he could not move; his whole body began trembling; his hair stood on end; and his feet began to totter. Thinking himself near death, he wished that he were still there from where he had taken his sweet flight a little while before. Similarly, people fear a thunderstorm or an unforeseen death that spares no one, and so they wish they had been better, done those good deeds left undone, and done better what deeds they had done for the love of God. And so, they begin promising to do better, even though it is too late. Now, taught by good master wolf, the lad thought in his heart of hearts where God sees all and weighs every person, that he would prefer to escape the beast's bloody jaws and monstrous clutches and return whence he fled. He promised with total devotion that he would never again abandon the life without the certainty of doing a better thing, and wanting to return joyously to the happy threshold of the holy martyrs, invoked the names of his patrons a number of times. They spare those they love, and they know how to make them benefit even from the danger of death. So he could understand this, the wolf left the martyrs' servant much more

---

[58] 2 Tim. 3:2; Mt. 24:12.

quickly than it had arrived, as if that dull animal had heard their injunction, "If God is with us, who is against us?"[59] and, "Tell me, O nature, where are your laws, after such events?"

He did not delay in returning to his spiritual father to make amends, after giving up, by the help of the saints, his plan to flee. It pleased the senior monk to hear the younger monk saved from the wolf tell about the saints' miracle enabling his return: "While I was fleeing toward my beloved relatives and going along perfectly calm, thinking only about them, I met a ferocious wolf. Fully aware that my life was about to end, I invoked the saints' patronage with all my heart, promising to return without hesitation and so save my life and my soul." So simultaneously, but in a different manner, they shared that joy of a son restored safe and sound to his father, to the glory of the grace of the living Son of God. As it is written: "All shall know me from the least to the greatest,"[60] and, "As the life of the father is mine, so is the life of the son."[61]

23. Frivolity at the site of the martyrdom brings a terrifying rebuke.

Meanwhile, after the saints had been buried, the priest who had been in charge of celebrating the Mass at the time for the Divine Office entered the place where the saints had been murdered. He began to eat and drink with his attendants, and to spend the night there in pleasant merriment. At a certain point, they felt a great thunderclap of intense strength shake the whole house like an earthquake, with the noise of a great

---

[59] Rm. 8:31.
[60] Jer. 31:34.
[61] Ezek. 18:4.

crashing sound. The first jolt made their hearts skip and their blood melt, so the boys stopped playing and were silent. After a little, they lost their fear, since they were with that priest, and they began to play again. Then it was as though God were indignant with such wicked audacity and arrogance as drunkenness, vulgarity, and rambling on with cracking jokes, in a place where the angels had just intoned heavenly melodies over the blessed conclusion of earthly events. Suddenly, the former jolt repeated itself with a roar, as if to threaten a terrible punishment in its dangerous rumbling. And as though it did not wish to endure their disgrace, that same house rose off the ground and its foundations and suspended itself up in the air, threatening to vanish, because it could not endure such futile trafficking where God had accomplished His truth.

This was the first sign of their holiness that took place after their burial.

24. Unseemly laughter cut short by pain.

One Sunday, an elderly priest named Moses, who had become a novice, confused the customary order of precedence when giving the kiss of peace to the brothers. The caretaker of the church, who was standing near the saints' tomb, smiled uncontrollably (a fault typical among undisciplined brothers) at his incapacity. Suddenly, he felt a sharp pain, as though he had been stabbed in the heart by a sharp blade, and he began to fall down with his legs up in the air. Thinking himself wounded with a knife, he felt for it, but found nothing dangerous. Finally, it dawned on him as he moaned that he had sinned against God in the presence of the saints. Because such laughter in a monk is diabolical, it is a grave sin to be so easily moved to laughter anywhere, especially when at prayer or reciting the Psalms in the sight of the angels, before the Lord God who descended from heaven to earth to save humanity. Of Him it is written that He many times wept, but never that He laughed.

25. The saints, appearing to Brother Andrew in a dream, ask for clemency toward their killers and the building of a church.

There was a certain brother named Andrew, whom the Lord pierced to the heart whenever he heard about the noble deaths of the saints. So he renounced self-will and took refuge in their monastery, that the local lord had generously begun to build after naming an abbot for the house. Living there for an entire year in simplicity as a layman, and desiring with all his heart to remain in that sacred place, it happened one night, as he slept in his assigned cell, that he woke up as if someone had taken his blanket away. He leaped up at once and moved to the open window. In the diffused light filling the entire cloister, he saw this vision. The holy brothers appeared and began to walk, blessed John in front of humble Benedict, carrying a great light in his right hand and a book in his left. From his middle finger hung an enormous thurible, from which smoked the fragrances of various perfumes that filled the cloister. When the church door opened wide, they entered it. Brother Andrew, who held the keys, was frightened by this vision and thought the (novice) master had taken the keys from him and entered the church with them. He felt for them and discovered he still had the keys, so he became even more frightened. Then, wrapping his shaking body in full clothing, he went back to sleep. The two brothers joined in fraternal love appeared to him again to speak with him while he slept. Their faces shone and their clothing was as white as snow, accompanied by the same light and the same perfumes as the first time they appeared to him while awake. First, they sent him to the abbot; then Benedict suggested they send him to Lord Boleslas to give him these recommendations: "We have already appeared with signs and wonders, even to secular people. Why do you not believe us? By virtue of God's power and mercy, we have freed men from chains and fetters, either shattering them or leaving them intact. If reverence for God has not moved him, at least this fresh manifestation should make him free those he has harshly imprisoned. Similarly, he must not harm those men who, even if with bad will, gave us in death the possibility of enjoying these benefits, nor should he scatter their wives, children, and goods. It would be suitable for them to do penance and live out their lives in service of God near this sacred place. We willingly came into your glorious realm, and in your land we have found the superabundant mercy of the kind Savior. With all humility, you always supplied us during our lifetime with as much as we needed. Now you should finish the good you have begun. Do what we request: free the prisoners and be merciful to our murderers. You could build in other places, but we ask you to build a church next to our cell—a place where our community can gather on Sundays. If you honor our request, know that you will receive many graces from God, as we will lovingly intercede for you and be close to you." After these words, the dream ended, and they went into the church, and then to heaven. But the abbot thought that Boleslas was already somewhat incredulous and, because he might consider this a joke, did not allow Andrew to go to him and tell him the story. As it is written: "They trembled in fear where there was nothing to fear."[62]

26. *The saints reprimand Andrew for not having obeyed them.*

On another occasion, after he had become a monk, that same Brother Andrew had another experience. One day as he was moving earth that needed to be moved, there was a great clap like thunder in the clear sky, and suddenly the saints appeared walking toward him. He put down his rake and knelt down at their feet, half-dead with fear. They reproved him for not carrying out their order, telling him to leave the abbot be and go to Lord Boleslas with the same message he had heard in the dream. When later questioned, he confessed that he had not really understood anything but what he heard with his ears when he was severely admonished for not carrying out his task. When he tried to speak to the saints, their hands made it clear he was to say absolutely nothing, because "praise is not comely in the mouth of the sinner."[63] And it is very harmful for a man of unclean lips to speak to holy spirits. Then they said: "Open the church. If the brothers want to sing the Mass, we will listen." Andrew could not tell where the saints were then, and thinking they were still speaking over his shoulders, he saw some guests walking past in order to attend Mass. Coming to himself; he saw that when the secular guests arrived, the holy men disappeared. Quickly, he opened the gates and entered the church, prostrating himself before the tomb of the saints. It was as though he had heard footsteps behind the altar. After

---

[62] Ps. 14:5.
[63] Sir. 15:9.

this awesome vision, Christopher the priest clothed himself in white vestments. He was inspired by the fear of God as the sweetest perfume filled both the church and the entire cloister, and he celebrated solemn Mass with compunction. He later confessed that the thick smoke of aromas he smelled took his breath away, and that he had to struggle to finish Mass. Once again, with a loud clap like thunder, he saw the pyramid of the saints' tomb open, as though the cover were rising in the air.

27. Andrew's vision repeated for Brother Paul.

One day when the other brothers were at table, one named Paul stayed behind in church to make genuflections. He also had the good fortune of seeing the same vision as Andrew, the caretaker of the church. As it is written of the invisible God: "His conversation is with the simple."[64]

28. Wicker baskets woven by the saints will not burn.

Similarly, so God might manifest His goodness and show how acceptable to Him their life was, some rushes and some baskets woven by the saints were being burned in the center of a fire. Unlike everything else, the baskets would not burn, as the saying goes: "You tried me with fire, and no iniquity was found in me."[65]

29. A voice sings hosanna.

A Hungarian novice of good quality, prompt in obedience and simple in a life of great purity, saw during pitch darkness one night a great light like the sun illuminating the whole

---

[64] Prv. 3:34.
[65] Ps. 17:3.

church. And he heard a very gentle, high-pitched voice singing: "Hosanna, O Merciful One" [*Osanna pium*]. At the same time, he saw a cloud of perfume come out of the saturated church, so that the fragrant scent spread throughout the cloister. Realizing that he, a sinner, had been allowed to witness such a wonder, he ran and hid himself in terror and a flood of tears. All the brothers confirm it, including good Brother Antony, who first saw the wonder, and Paul, a man of great simplicity, whom we just mentioned. They say: "Now we are many and no longer have a grace like that. But at one time, our only joy and desire was to be and live in this holy place, without eating and drinking, as though we were in Paradise. Now we no longer see the incense because of our sins. At one time it spread everywhere, day and night, constantly, so one could see a thick cloud of aromas with the most delicate perfume, not only in the church, but also throughout the whole cloister."

30. The saints liberate a captive.

There was a man bound with hard iron chains, who found himself in great danger under sad circumstances. During the night, which carried out its duty of offering a little relief to the afflicted who forget about their suffering, he slept sweetly. He was visited from on high and chided because he did not get up. The two holy brothers, appearing as though they were one, ordered him to get up at once and follow them. Sighing, he told them he could not do so. Bowing, the holy men touched the iron lightly with their heavenly fingertips, and the chains broke apart and flew off. Sleep fled from his eyes; he was free and, moving his feet, he ran after the saints, whom he saw ahead of him. These two good saints help us in heaven when they pray for the salvation of men. And likewise now on earth, having unbound a man from bodily restriction, they sent him ahead of them and enjoined him under obedience to go to their monastery safely, without anyone following him, and there to give thanks. As it is said: "The Lord is my light and my salvation; whom shall I fear?"[66]

31. The significance of Thursday, 11 November, as the day of the martyrdom.

It is a fact that, whenever they showed themselves to people and performed signs, there were always only two who appeared, without the other three. Surely this is because the sole and unique glory that God's grace granted to all of them was principally the merit of these two, who lived well and desired even better. The saints were martyred on the same day that good Menna suffered martyrdom while uttering unheard of wonders in Greek. And likewise Martin, the precious confessor of the Lord, the jewel of priests, who bestowed in France great signs and favors, this day possessed Jesus Christ entirely in heaven. He had partially clothed Him on earth, Who is the life of the angels and the lover of mankind. The day on which the magnificent triumph took place was the same day of the week when God wondrously ascended into heaven, led the earth's captivity captive, sent down the joyous peace of the angels, and saved a lost humanity from death. This was the day when the Savior gave His Body and Blood to the redeemed, the chalice of salvation and the only hope of our empty misery. This was the day when the creator of

---

[66] Ps. 27:1.

heaven and earth washed the disciples' feet, giving them an example of pure charity, with the great privilege of sublime humility. This was the day when, in God's love, "two died with three, and three not apart from two."

32. The virtues and the triumph of Benedict and John are lauded. The "Brief Rule" of Master Romald. "They have gained for themselves Alleluia, *they have left us* Kyrie eleison."

These are the two brothers in spirit and in truth, John and Benedict, whose virtue was not measured by the amount of time they lived, but by the intensity of their fervor. They stayed awhile in the monastery, and even longer in the hermitage, mortifying their vices and passions. Similar in their obedience and humility, they were different in their patience and charity. Young in age, they were mature in their thinking. They cultivated dear fraternity, intent on eternal realities. They guarded their virtue with a disdain for the world and its riches, bearing salutary sadness and heartfelt pain. They were not soft and lazy like us truly miserable folk, who have accomplished nothing useful, but they grieved because, in these spiritual matters, they had not struggled as much as men should who are being prepared and perfected for the "better part" of Mary. They feared that this would be the just judgment of Jesus and the wrath of God, because it had not been with them according to what is written: "We have become a spectacle to the world, to the angels and to men."[67] They might instead just be entertaining the sight of those competing legitimately, without finding a place among

---

[67] I Cor. 4:9.

them. They feared that they did not have such a place because, though running willingly, they were not found worthy to find the good racecourse. As it is written: "It is not a matter of who wills or who runs, but of God, who shows mercy."[68] They wanted to raise up the dead pagans to the life of Christianity, thinking that the more souls they would save in God's sight and in His service, the more mercy they would receive from God who, in His love, did not spare His only Son. If in that event God, who gives freely every good thing, would wish to offer them the cup of salvation, they would willingly drink it. They desired it so ardently, not because it involved someone's sinning, but for the winning of souls acceptable to their King, for whose name's sake they spared no efforts. When their sorrow was most bitter, God came to them with unhoped-for salvation. Although they were unwilling to allow their hearts any rest, they received eternal rest after only a brief effort. With brutish intent, their agitated visitors did not spare the iron and unwillingly brought them, with a little suffering, a sweetness beyond measure or limit—freeing them from all evil and bringing them all good. So that nothing might be lacking in God's grace or in their glory, even their novice disciples and their cook were killed with them—all innocent. They had not joined them for profit or worldly advantage, but they remained faithful like their seniors in God's service. They also obtained what they had long desired: What they tried to get with great effort on the outside, spontaneously came to them at home. Without wearying themselves on the road, grace flooded them abundantly while they rested in bed. Because the Lord's mercies are very many, His graces are good

---

[68] Rm. 9:16.

deeds more precious than thousands of gold and silver pieces. His judgments are just, and celebrated in angelic songs as more desirable than much gold and sweeter than honey from the honeycomb.[69] Both of them were followers of Christ, for this was their desire in life; both were bent on heaven, and in death they attained what they desired, together with all their friends. For both of them, old age did not lie in length of days, nor was it computed by the number of their years, but old age was an immaculate life. The foremost, Benedict, detested evil as if it were poison. He never detracted from anyone, nor would he ever tolerate detraction. Guilty or not, a brother would never be forced to defend himself against blame. He did not provoke quarrels, nor did he wish to hear others argue, as it is written: "If there is strife and jealousy among you, is it not because you are carnal?"[70] and "God's servant must not quarrel, but be kind to everyone."[71]

When someone spoke of the saints' lives, Benedict would always say: "They lived well; let us see how we manage to live our lives, because each of us must carry his own load."[72] Likewise, whatever happened in his monastic life, favorable or unfavorable, it remained for him the heavenly life on earth. When he left Latin territory, he journeyed beyond the mountains to seek God's Kingdom, reciting with the psalmist: "Great are the works of the Lord, sought in all he wills."[73] He left us this proverb of truth as a memorial. On another occasion, John told us: "Although nothing pleases

---

[69] Cf. Ps. 19:10.
[70] 1 Cor. 3:3.
[71] 2 Tim. 2:24.
[72] Cf. Gal. 6:5.
[73] Cf. Ps. 111:2.

the Lord God more than purity, it is certainly not the end of the world if we are distracted in psalmody. But on the other hand, there are the learned who are capable but do not want to understand. To them, this applies: 'Whoever knows what to do but does not do it deserves judgment.'[74]" He also received from Master Romald this brief rule that he carefully tried to observe all his life: *Sit in the cell as in paradise. Cast the memory of the whole world behind you, carefully attentive to your thoughts as a good fisher is to the fish. One way is in the Psalms: this, do not dismiss. If you who have come with the fervor of a novice are not capable of making use of everything, then first in this place and then in that psalmodize in spirit and understand with an attentive mind. And when your mind begins to wander while reading, do not desist, but hasten to correct yourself by applying the understanding. Above all, place yourself in the presence of God with fear and trembling, as one who stands in the sight of the emperor. Completely destroy yourself and sit like a little bird content with the grace of God. For unless its mother gives it something, it neither tastes anything nor has anything to eat.*

Benedict enlisted in God's service with an ardent fervor before his brother John, first as a simple soldier in the monastery, then later as a senior in the hermitage. He made every effort, without envy, to win over his brother. But John was more patient, whatever the circumstances, and had an equanimity facing the changing events of the spiritual life so that, in every way, he lived more the golden mean. Benedict was completely focused on spiritual realities, while John, with his charming tongue, was mild-mannered

---

[74] Cf. James 4:17.

and affable, an agreeable man. Benedict's love of God and neighbor—great charity, on which hangs all of the Law and the Prophets[75]—was more remarkable than in John, who had a kind and constant heart for working amidst the variety of human events and was the more stable of the two in general attitude. Both were good men; the worse of the two was himself excellent enough. Both Benedict and John died martyrs, having lived to the full in a brief period because their souls were pleasing to God.[76] John nurtured patience and holy hope. Benedict, truly blessed, and John, well born, uprightly feared the Lord. Meek and humble of heart, they made a dwelling within themselves for the Holy Spirit, whose words, as though spoken by the mouth of the Lord, are: "On whom shall my spirit rest, if not on the humble and peaceful who tremble at my words?"[77] So, in charity they were inseparable, they walked in humility, they did the truth, they lived well, and they finished their lives even better—having for themselves the "alleluia" while leaving us the "Lord, have mercy." May the living God, who has created every good thing, and Jesus Christ the Son of God, who has redeemed our wickedness with His blood, and the Holy Spirit of God, who has taught us to speak rightly and made us live well, keep us—as it was, is now, and will be, saying "Salve" once and "King of glory, our God" three times—for undying ages of desirable ages. Amen.

---

[75] Cf. Mt. 22:40.

[76] Cf. Wis. 4:13.

[77] Cf. Is. 66:2.

III

The Life of Blessed Romuald

Peter Damian of Fonte Avellana

*Prologue: The author writes about fifteen years
after the saint's death. He intends to commemorate
Romuald's virtues, not dwell on his miracles.*

I must protest against you, O world run amuck
[*inmunde munde*], because you contain an intolerable
group of foolish sages who stand fluent before you, yet
mute before God. You have those who are haughtily proud
of their empty eloquence and inane philosophy. You do
not have anyone who writes down anything edifying for
people today and in the future. You have lawyers willing
to plead any case worth their time before judges of secular
business, but you do not have anyone in Holy Church who
expounds clearly on the saints' virtues and deeds. Your wise
ones know how to do evil, but not good. About fifteen years
have now passed since blessed Romuald left the flesh and
rose to heaven's heights, and none of the wise ones have yet
written a little history about his wonderful life. No one
is very eager to satisfy the devotion of the faithful or has
given anything useful for common reading in Holy Church.
It would seem the most useful thing for me to do would
be to stay in my narrow cell and meditate on my own sins

rather than write the history of someone else's virtue. It would be better for me to weep over my own darkness than to cover the splendors of holiness with unpolished words. Still, a multitude of the faithful goes to his tomb from far-off lands throughout the year, and particularly on his feast day, to see the miracles God works through him. They are eager to hear the story of his life, but there is none and they cannot do so. I am beginning reasonably to fear that, with the passage of time, his fame might quickly fade away from memory among the people.

This fear is not my only reason, for I feel compelled by the requests of so many brethren and bound by fraternal love, so I am putting into script what I have gotten from the disciples of this wonderful man and, with God's help, will try to describe his life from beginning to end. An unskilled man, I am not trying to write a history, but I want to leave a brief testament without worrying about the details of literary rhetoric. I must first advise my reader that I am not interested in writing about the many miracles done through him, but to provide something edifying, for that is the kind of monastic life he lived. The blessed man protected himself from the winds of vanity with the shelter of humility, and whatever might have seemed miraculous to human eyes he hid with the most assiduous care. Had he not even worked miracles, his wonderful life would still be worthy of veneration. For one reads of no miracles done by the Lord's precursor, the Baptist, though Truth Himself testified to his being greater than any other born of woman. There are some who think they honor God by fabricating lies about the saints' virtues. They do not know that God does not want our lies, and that by trying to please Him with falsity, they reject the truth that is God Himself. Jeremiah convicts them by saying, "They have trained themselves to lie, and do so with all their might."[1] How easily they could have related the simple truth they received, instead of fabricating what they did not know. They pretend to be helping God out, but they fight against God with false witness. As the apostle wrote to the Corinthians: "If Christ has not risen, our preaching is empty, and your faith is empty;"[2] then he adds: "We have proven to be false witnesses to God, because we have testified against God that he raised up Christ, whom he did not raise." Because I am forced to write this out of necessity, I have prefaced it with these remarks. But with God's help, and by the prayers of whom I write, I shall begin the narrative.

1. *The noble youth Romuald, long attracted by repentance and solitude, turns his life around after seeing his father kill a relative.*

A native of Ravenna, Romuald originated from a very illustrious ducal family. During his adolescence, he felt drawn to the carnal sins popular in his day, particularly those among the wealthy. Still, he was devoted to God and frequently tried to straighten himself and move toward higher goals. For example, when he was hunting in a pleasant place in the forest, he could feel his soul drawn to solitude and would say: "How pleasant to live like hermits in these forest recesses; how easily one could be quiet, away from all the worldly turmoil!" And so his mind wandered; inspired by God, he

---

[1] Jer. 9:5.
[2] I Cor. 15:14-15.

would prophetically begin to become enamored with what would one day be his life's work.

His father Serge was very intent on the world and involved with all the world had to offer. When Serge feuded once with a relative over the ownership of property, and he saw his son Romuald remaining indifferent to the controversy—though he was profoundly worried about a possible crime of murder—Serge threatened to disinherit Romuald if he persisted in his attitude. But why go on further? In the end, the two sides decided to duel, fought with weapons outside the city, and as they fought, Serge's enemy died by his sword. Romuald wounded no one, but because he was present there, he at once took upon himself the penance for the crime and went to the monastery of St. Apollinaris in Classe to perform the customary penance of forty days for homicides.

2. *Romuald undertakes forty days of penance at*
   Classe in the monastery of St. Apollinaris. After
   the saint appears to him twice, he is enkindled
   by the Spirit and receives the monastic habit.

There Romuald mortified himself with rigorous penance and began to speak daily with a lay brother, who gave him good advice, though he was somewhat limited by his lack of knowledge. He advised Romuald to leave the secular life completely behind him and hasten to follow the monastic life, but without succeeding in convincing him to do so. One day, while they were conversing, he somewhat joked with Romuald, saying, "If I make you see blessed Apollinaris in the flesh, what gift will you give me in return?" Romuald responded, "If you show me the blessed martyr in his bodily form, I solemnly promise to remain no longer in the world."

The lay brother encouraged Romuald to postpone his sleep and stay awake to keep vigil with him in the church. So they remained long in prayer together in the nocturnal silence. After they had done so, toward the first crow of the rooster, blessed Apollinaris visibly began to come out from under the altar dedicated to the Blessed Virgin Mary in the center of the church. He left from the eastern side, by the porphyry slab. The entire church was immediately filled with splendid light, as if the sun had focused all its rays within those walls. The blessed martyr, wondrously clothed in priestly vestments, carried a golden thurible in his hand and incensed all the church's altars. Then he returned whence he had come, and all the splendor soon disappeared.

Like a firm exactor, the lay brother began to insist strongly that Romuald keep his promise. Romuald resisted, insisting that he wanted to see that vision a second time. And on another night, in the same way, he remained in prayer and saw the blessed martyr just as he had the first time. In later years, whenever the question arose, Romuald resolutely insisted that the body of the martyr lay in that church and, during his lifetime, the holy man never stopped testifying about this.

Romuald kept up a habit of coming to this altar in the church and, after the monks retired for the night, would pray to God with much sighing. One day after the vision, he was praying intently, and the Holy Spirit enkindled within him a fire of divine love until he burst into tears and could not stop. He prostrated before the monks with indescribable desire and asked for the monastic habit. But the monks, fearing his father's severity, did not dare open the door for his conversion. Honestus was then archbishop of Ravenna's cathedral, having formerly been Classe's abbot. Romuald lost no time in seeing him and manifesting his heart's desire. He enthusiastically responded to Romuald's holy desire and ordered the brethren to accept him without delay into their community. Reassured by the archbishop's patronage, they received Romuald without fear and gave him the monastic habit. And so he lived almost three years in that monastery.

3. *Romuald reproves his slack confreres, then dodges their plot to hurl him down headlong to death.*

Romuald perceived that some of the monks were living in laxity, walking along the broad way, while he was not allowed to take the narrow path of perfection as his heart was urging him. He began seriously to question what he should do, and many thoughts began to course through his mind. He presumed to criticize harshly their laxity and invoked the *Rule*'s precepts in order to expose them. He insisted on rebuking their vices, but they felt they didn't need to listen to the words of a young novice. Finally, they had had enough and began to agree about eliminating their accuser. Romuald used to rise before the other brethren and, if he found the door to the oratory closed, would pray in the dormitory itself. This was on the upper floor, built as a loft. And so, prompted by the devil, these sons of Cain decided that they would throw Romuald on his head onto the pavement below, the next time he rose before the others. One of those who knew of the conspiracy informed Romuald, so he kept quiet and prayed within the inner sanctuary of his heart to the Father, escaping the incumbent danger. Thus, he avoided death and prevented those brothers from choosing the abyss of iniquity and death for their souls.

4. *After about three years in the cenobium (cf. 2),*
   the saint commences the eremitic life near
   Venice under the rough-and-ready Marino.

Day by day, the love of perfection grew greater in his soul, but his mind found no peace. He heard of a spiritual man by the name of Marino living the eremitical life in the vicinity of Venice. He easily received permission from the abbot and brethren to go to this venerable man, and he placed himself under him as a disciple, remaining in his charge with humble and sincere dedication. In addition to the other virtues, Marino was a man of simplicity and the most sincere purity. He had received no training in the eremitical life but had willingly embraced it under the impulse of good will. So he followed this life regimen: throughout the year, three days each week, he ate a half-loaf of bread and a handful of broad beans, while on the other weekdays, he took a little wine and soup. He sang the entire Psalter each day. However, he was quite uncouth and totally without any formation for the solitary life, as Blessed Romuald was wont to say later, with a smile. Most times when leaving the cell, he would sing the Psalms to his disciple, here and there, around the hermitage— twenty Psalms under one tree, thirty or forty under another. Romuald had left the world illiterate. So when he opened the Psalter, he would try to figure out the verses he came upon, but he would stumble when it was his turn to take up the singing. As he squinted at the page, Marino, sitting in front of him, rapped him on the left side of his head with a stick he held in his right hand. After having received many blows,

Romuald felt the necessity to ask humbly, "Master, please, from now on hit me on the right side because I am losing my hearing on the left." Then Marino, marveling at Romuald's patience, mitigated this indiscreet severity.

5. *The conversion of the doge St. Peter Orséolo. He embarks from Venice for the monastery of St. Michael at Cuixá, accompanied by its abbot Guarinus, Romuald, Marino, and John Gradenigo.*

At that time, Peter Orséolo was ruler of Dalmatia. He had succeeded to this dignity by favoring the murderers of his predecessor, Vitale Candiano. I hope not to get too far off my topic if I briefly touch upon the cause of this murder. Vitale had married the sister of Marquis Hugh the Great and, wishing to emulate him, had hired many armed men from Lombardy and Tuscany with public funds. But the Venetians did not support this and plotted to break in upon the doge's palace and kill him and his family in an armed assault. Doge Vitale had been informed of this plot and, adding guards both day and night, foiled his enemies' plans. Having tried numerous times to effect their plan, they had the idea to set fire to Peter's house attached to the doge's palace, and so bring the doge out into the open while burning down his household. To bring off this plan, they needed the consent of Peter, who had already participated in their conspiracy. He agreed that, in exchange for burning down his house, they would place all of Venice under his rule. Once the hated man had been eliminated, they would place Peter in his place as doge. That is how Peter had obtained supremacy over Dalmatia. But once he had satisfied his ambition, he experienced compunction of heart by divine grace.

Later, the venerable Abbot Guarinus from the

southernmost parts of Gaul had gone on pilgrimage to pray in various places in the world. When he came to meet the doge, Peter suddenly asked his advice on how to rid himself of his guilt for his grave sin. When they had also called together Marino and Romuald, the three together decided that he should leave the world rather than hold on to the duchy he had obtained through a crime and place himself under someone else, since he had wrongly usurped another's authority. But because Peter held too high an office for such an open manifestation of conversion, he felt it more prudent to follow this plan. The titular feast, under the patronage of a holy martyr, of a basilica that he possessed when he was a private citizen was now approaching. On the eve of the feast, he sent his wife ahead with orders to decorate the church and to prepare a sumptuous banquet for those who would accompany him there on the next day, giving the impression he would quickly join her. When his wife had departed, he took as much money as he needed and, together with John Gradenigo, a relative involved in the original conspiracy, and the other three aforementioned holy men, set off in a boat and fled—a great penitent—to the monastery of Abbot Guarinus in Gaul. Peter and John became monks of the cenobium of St. Michael there, while Marino and Romuald established themselves nearby and resumed the solitary life to which they were accustomed. After about a year, the other two brothers joined them and lived their austere solitude together in a cell.

6. *Romuald, recognized as foremost in discernment, excels also in labor and fasting.*

Meanwhile, with ardent desire, Romuald grew wondrously in virtue and surpassed the others on the journey of monastic life. And so, by common agreement among the brethren, they submitted everything to his discernment—matters spiritual and physical. Even Marino began happily to show deference to Romuald, who before had been his disciple. For an entire year Romuald did not eat anything beyond a handful of cooked chickpeas. Then, for three years, he and John Gradenigo lived by the work of their own hands, hoeing and planting grain. And while working as farmers, they doubled the load of their fasting.

7. *The saint's never-ending battle against the wiles and assaults of the devil.*

The devil attacked Romuald with many different temptations, especially toward the beginning of his conversion, and distracted Romuald's mind with many temptations to various vices. Now he made him think of all those things an energetic man like him could have in the world. Then, of all the goods he had left behind in the world for greedy, ingrate relatives. Then he accused him of dedicating himself to petty, worthless activity. And again, he filled him with horror at his hard task and promised him a very long lifetime. How many times he knocked on Romuald's cell as soon as he had fallen asleep, and kept him awake the entire night, making him think it was almost dawn! For almost five years, the devil would sit on Romuald's feet or knees and make it hard for him to turn over in bed. How can we explain the vicious beasts he had to endure? And how many times he had to put the demons to flight with invectives? It actually happened that, if a brother approached his cell at a silent time, the soldier of Christ thought it was the devil and, ready for battle, shouted out in a clear voice:

"Now, what do you want, revolting creature? They have cast you down from heaven; what are you looking for in a hermitage? Go away, filthy dog; clear off, you old snake!" By such words, the brother understood that Romuald was used to fighting evil spirits and confronting the provocations of the enemy with the weapons of faith.

8. Romuald discreetly regulates fasting. Peter Orséolo's foreknowledge in advising his son.

Once, while reading the *Lives of the Fathers*, he happened upon the passage about the brothers who continued their fast throughout the week in solitude, then came together on Saturdays and Sundays for more substantial meals. Romuald immediately embraced that regimen of life and continued on in this austerity for some fifteen years or more. But Doge Peter had been accustomed to a richer fare and found the burden of this fast too much, and his health failed. He humbly prostrated himself before blessed Romuald, who ordered him to stand up. Blushing, he revealed his need: "Father, I have such a big body that, considering my sins, I cannot get along with only a half-loaf of dry bread." With fatherly compassion for his fragility, Romuald added a quarter-loaf to his usual ration. And so, he held out a merciful hand to a brother who was slipping and needed more strength for the way of life he had chosen. Once, Peter's son (by the same name) came to visit him; he was a very experienced man in the ways of the world. The father, whether through the spirit of prophecy or a revelation, predicted the man's future: "I know without any doubt, my son, that they will choose you doge and you shall be successful. But you must carefully safeguard the rights of Christ's Church, and do not treat your subjects unjustly through love or hatred of anyone."

9. *Romuald teaches that a little prayer from the heart is better than much prayer with idle thoughts. A right intention, fixed on God, is of the essence.*

Some time later, Romuald read that St. Sylvester, bishop of Rome, had called for fasting on Saturdays as a way to keep vigil for holy Easter. So Romuald immediately changed the day for breaking the fast from Saturday to Thursday. He came to this decision in deference to the weaker brethren, so that with discretion in fasting, they would be able to do it more often. He established this rule for those living the solitary life: each would be seen as satisfying the eremitical fast if he abstained for three days, and then two more days. On Thursdays and Sundays he could sit and eat some soup and cooked vegetables after saying grace, except for the two Lenten periods each year, when almost all the brethren used to extend the fast throughout the whole week. And it was only fitting that a man always wanting to praise God with choirs and drums would make the ears of boundless Light resound with the most beautiful harmonies of the octave, fifth and fourth musical intervals. Regarding a total fast, without eating anything during the day, Romuald prohibited the others from doing so, although he himself often did so. He said if one wants to grow toward perfection, he should eat what is convenient each day, while still feeling a bit hungry. Adopting this custom, the body will support with lightness what seems heavy to the novices at the beginning of their monastic life. According to Romuald, it is worthless to take on great things temporarily if one cannot persevere with generosity.

He taught them to have temperance and great discretion

in their vigils, because they should not give in to dozing off after the Night Office. The holy man had little indulgence for morning naps, and if one confessed he had started dozing off after the vigils of twelve Psalms, or worse, after dawn, Romuald would not allow him to celebrate holy Mass with solemnity that day. He also said that, if possible, it is better to sing one Psalm from the heart and with compunction than to run through a hundred while daydreaming. But if such a grace had not yet been given one, Romuald exhorted him not to lose hope, but to slow down the rhythm of the bodily exercise, until He who had given the desire in the first place might one day grant the effective possibility. With the mind's intentionality fixed on God, the incense of prayer will be protected, and the breeze of thoughts from the outside will not disturb it. When intentionality is right, any thought coming involuntarily is no cause for alarm.

10. *An oppressor of the poor ignores an appeal from Romuald, to his destruction.*

At one point while still in Gaul, Romuald struck up a friendship with a certain farmer, who at times provided him with tools and other necessities for his cell whenever needed. He was richer in charity than in material goods and joyfully gave whatever was needed. An arrogant and haughty count had his servants grab the farmer's cow with barbaric force. Then he had the meat prepared for his table of gluttony. The farmer hastened to Romuald's cell and, with agonized sobs, told him of his misfortune, lamenting that his only hope, as well as that of his family, had been snatched away. St. Romuald immediately sent a messenger to the count and, with humble pleading, asked him to restore the animal to the poor man. But the stubborn, boastful count rebuffed those prayers and stated that, on that very day, he would taste the flavor of the cow's fat loins. At dinnertime, the meal was prepared and the cow's meat was served. But then the execution of God's justice prevailed. Just as he was beginning to eat, the count choked on a mouthful of tenderloin, and it remained stuck in his throat, despite all attempts to help him, so he could neither swallow it nor spit it out. So, unable to breathe, the count died a horrible death before everyone's eyes. He who had wanted to satisfy his urge against the wish of God's servant lost his life through God's just judgment, and now lies fasting.

11. *The saint counsels Count Oliban to do penance by entering a monastery.*

There was another count in that part of Gaul named Oliban, under whose jurisdiction fell the monastery of Abbot Guarinus. Although he had been raised to a very high earthly status, he was weighed down by his many sins. One day he visited Romuald and ordered the others who were with him to remain outside, while he entered alone to confess all his transgressions. The venerable man listened to all, and then told him that, if he wanted to be saved, he should leave the world and enter a monastery. The count was disturbed by these words and told Romuald that he knew many spiritual men, none of whom had counseled him to do such an unbearable thing. So, he went out to all the bishops and abbots who had accompanied him and asked them if things were really as God's servant had said. Unanimously, all confirmed Romuald's opinion, and they excused themselves for never having said anything to the count by admitting that they had been afraid to do so. Then the count sent everyone away. In total secrecy, he decided with blessed Romuald to go to Montecassino under the guise of a pilgrimage, but once there, to give himself over irrevocably to God's service in St. Benedict's monastery.

12. Romuald entrusts Oliban to others and goes to the aid of his own irresolute father.

About that time, Romuald's father Serge had become a monk. But after a while, prompted by the devil, he reconsidered his conversion and was planning to return to "Egypt". The monks of the cenobium of St. Severus, not far from the city of Ravenna, where Serge lived in the body if not in the heart, found a way to get a messenger to blessed Romuald. He was upset by the news and decided that Abbot Guarinus and John Gradenigo would have to accompany the count on his conversion journey, while he would go help his father, who was falling into perdition. Doge Peter had already died blessedly. And so, Romuald entrusted the count to the other two, especially to John Gradenigo, whom he asked as his superior in religion to remain close to the count, even if Guarinus were to continue on after their destination.

13. The saint escapes death by feigning madness, like David (1 Sam. 21:13-16). He cures his father's backsliding by stiff discipline.

When they heard that Romuald was preparing to leave, the inhabitants of that region were deeply saddened. They debated among themselves the best way of impeding his plans and, in their godless veneration, decided the best way

119

was to send some assassins to kill him. They reasoned that if they could not keep him there alive, at least with his body there, they could have a protector for their territory. But Romuald learned of their plan. So he completely shaved his head and, when the killers approached his cell, he began to stuff his mouth with food even though it was barely dawn. On seeing him, they thought he was crazy and, considering him touched in the head, were unwilling to injure him. In that way, the prudent insanity of that spiritual David defeated the stupid cunning of the wise according to the flesh. He had prevented them from sinning and, not fearing death, had averted the risk of death, increasing thereby his merits. And so, that left him free to act. He left neither by horse nor any conveyance, but on foot with his staff in hand, going from the interior of Gaul to Ravenna. There he found his father intending to return to the world. He placed him in stocks and heavy chains and gave him a good beating until, with God's healing help, Serge's mind returned to a healthy state.

14. God the Holy Spirit appears to Serge. Afire with ecstasy, he falls ill and dies.

Once Serge had regained a healthy perspective, he quickly progressed in the monastic life and corrected in himself all that before was leading him back into the world. Among other things, he now had a habit of frequently stopping before an image of the Savior and, when alone, praying with abundant tears and great compunction of heart. One day he had lingered at prayer with greater attention than usual, when suddenly, something new and unheard of in our days happened. In a flash, the Holy Spirit appeared to him in

I know not what form. Serge asked Him who He was and He responded clearly that He was the Holy Spirit. Seized by ecstasy, burning with the fire of the One he had seen, Serge quickly ran out into the monastery cloister. With intense fervor, he asked the brothers there where the Holy Spirit had gone. They thought him crazy and harshly rebuked him. But Serge claimed, without any doubt, to have seen the Holy Spirit, and that He had to have passed visibly before their eyes. A bit later, he weakened and took to his bed where, in a few days, his life ended. This doubtlessly confirms the words God spoke to Moses: "Man shall not see me and live." And when Daniel claimed to have contemplated not God, but a vision of God, he said: "I was exhausted and felt sick for several days." And so, after Serge had seen eternal life, i.e. God, he had to leave temporal life in short order.

15. *Marino is killed by Saracen pirates. John Gradenigo, repenting his disobedience, lives commendably for thirty years as a hermit at Montecassino.*

Meanwhile, Count Oliban left everything to his son, after loading fifteen mules with valuable goods. Accompanied by Abbot Guarinus and John Gradenigo, he traveled to St. Benedict's monastery. There he bid farewell to all those friends who had traveled with him. They wept profusely with bitter tears because, until that point, they had not suspected he had decided to remain there. After a while, Marino left for Apulia where he lived as a solitary. But before long, Saracen pirates murdered him. After a brief period, Guarinus, used to traveling as a pilgrim to pray, decided to go to Jerusalem, and John wished to follow his religious example. But when

Oliban learned of this, he wept and begged him piteously not to go against his promise, but to remain and help him in God's service, as blessed Romuald had ordered. And he added: "At least you, John, will remember that your master entrusted me in good faith to your care and explicitly said it would be disobedience to abandon me." However, they felt unmoved by this and insisted on their proposal, leaving Oliban and going on pilgrimage. Having descended the mountain and standing before the plain, they stopped to discuss their plans. Guarinus' horse, startled, reared up and, despite all efforts to rein him in, struck John with his hoof and broke his shinbone. John fell to the earth in great pain and remembered, a little late, his master's orders and openly accused himself of disobedience. Through his broken leg, he realized his sin of breaking his promise. Gifted with reasoning, but without watching out for his own safety, he had been disobedient to his master, while an animal deprived of reason had known not to obey his rider! So, he turned back and asked permission to build a cell near the monastery. He stayed there thirty years until the end of his life, living an eremitical life. He was very charitable, admirably humble, and rigorously abstinent, though also discreet enough that no one in the monastery knew what regimen of fasting he followed. Among his other virtues was the antipathy he felt toward the vice of detraction. Every time someone opened his mouth to speak ill of another, he would say that it would immediately return to the sender, as when an arrow bounces off hard stone and ricochets. After John's death, God worked several miracles through his intercession.

16. The demons invade Romuald's cell and beat him up. After invoking Jesus, charity blazes anew in his heart, and he surmounts his injuries.

After correcting his father, Romuald built himself a cell in the swamplands of Classe, in a place called Peter's Bridge. But after a while he transferred to some land belonging to Classe near the church of St. Martin's in the Woods, not because he was afraid of getting sick or was fastidious over the stench of the swamp, but because he didn't want to become weak and unable to maintain his rigorous fast. The place was next to a former cemetery. Once, while he was singing Compline there, his mind wandered to the cemetery, as had often happened. Horrible images began to invade his spirit. While he turned all this over in his mind, some evil spirits broke into his cell and threw him to the ground. They struck and beat his members, exhausted by continuous fasting, with very hard blows. Beneath these blows, Romuald thought of God's grace and exclaimed: "Dear Jesus, beloved Jesus, why have you abandoned me? Have you delivered me forever into my enemies' hands?" At these words, all the evil spirits were put to flight by God's power. Immediately Romuald's breast was inflamed with compunction and so great a divine love that his heart melted like wax into tears, and regardless of all those heavy blows, he felt no pain. Soon after, he rose from the ground healthy and strong and, even though his wounds were still bleeding, he took up again singing the chant at the verse where he had left off. At the moment when the demons had entered, the cell's window had battered him on the forehead. After that, he carried a visible scar there, proof of the wound he had received.

17. Seasoned by spiritual combat, the "soldier of Christ" (2 Tim. 2:3) Romuald goes "from strength to strength" (Ps. 83:8 [84:7]), and the evil spirits back off.

Strengthened by his frequent battles, the soldier of Christ committed himself to proceed ahead each day, going from strength to strength. Bettering himself through continuous struggles, he no longer feared meeting his match in his exhausted enemy. Sometimes when he was in his cell, he could sense the presence of evil spirits constrained to look on from a distance as though they were looking at a corpse. They didn't dare come close and appeared in the form of crows and horrible vultures. Other times, they appeared in human form [*in figuris Ethiopum*] or as various animals. The triumphant victor of Christ mocked them, saying: "Here I am, ready and willing. Come on! Show me your power if you have any! Are you already worn out? Have you been beaten? Have you no more weaponry to fight against this poor servant of God?" Shaming the evil spirits with words such as these, like sharpened javelins, he put them to flight. Seeing that he could not prevail directly against the servant of God, the devil tried out more devious methods. Wherever the saint went, the devil would stir up the hearts of his disciples against him. If he could not dampen the ardent force of his fervor, he would try to curb his concern for others' salvation. And if it was not possible to make Romuald surrender to the enemy, at least his influence over others might be impeded.

18. Romuald, driven out by the monks of St. Michael's, masters a fleeting temptation against forbearance. The avaricious monks pay a heavy price.

One time Romuald moved near the place called Bagno in the territory of Sarsina. He remained there a while and built a monastery dedicated to Michael the Archangel, while fixing his own abode in a cell not far away. Marquis Hugh sent him seven pounds of coinage to cover necessities, which he accepted so he could give it away generously and mercifully. And indeed, when he learned that the monastery of Palazzolo had been destroyed by fire, he sent those brethren sixty coins, keeping the remainder for similar purposes. But when the monks of St. Michael learned of this, they were as furious as bulls with him, both because he showed himself contrary to many things to which they were accustomed, and because he spent part of the donated money on others instead of giving it all to them. Conspiring together, they broke into his cell with clubs and sticks, beat him, took all his money, and sent him away, after heaping insults on him. Banished so, he fell into an intense sadness as he went away and resolved within himself that in the future he would concern himself with his own salvation, while completely letting go of the care of others. But after thinking so, a great fear seized him; he feared dying condemned by God's judgment, if he would obstinately keep this resolution. Meanwhile, the monks sent to perform this long-desired vendetta, as if they were unloading a dead weight, were proud of what they had done to the servant of God and, seduced by this joy, began to joke and laugh at Romuald's expense. To celebrate with the greatest gaiety, they wanted to buy some luxurious food and have an abundant banquet. It was winter, and the weather's temperature reflected their own coldness. The one who had been the cruelest to the blessed soldier of Christ thought he would go buy the honey to prepare the honeyed wine. While crossing the Savio River, he tripped and fell off the bridge and was swallowed up into the abyss of flowing waters. God's justice was satisfied by this death in turbid waters of one who had wanted to celebrate sumptuously with honey's sweetness an action over which he should have wept. That night, all the other monks were sleeping, as usual. A heavy snowstorm brought down their building, fracturing a skull, arms, legs, and other members. One of them lost an eye, and there is justice behind such a deprivation of bodily light, because by separating himself from his neighbor, he had lost one of the two lights of love, though he had preserved the other.[3]

19. Romuald obeys St. Apollinaris and returns to Classe.

One time the saint was living not far from Mount Catria. When he had been there a while, blessed Apollinaris appeared to him and, with great authority, ordered him to return to his monastery.[4] The saint decided to obey this injunction and, without delay, abandoned the place where he was living and hastened to where he had been sent.

20. Reclusion in a swamp changes Romuald's appearance.

For some time the venerable man lived as a recluse in a swamp in Comacchio called Origarium. A little later, because

---

[3]   Cf. Mt. 22:37-40.
[4]   St. Apollinaris in Classe

of the excessive stench of the swamp slime and unhealthy air, he swelled up and lost his hair, so that he no longer resembled the one who had withdrawn to that place. His complexion had become green, like a lizard's.

21. "Through faith... [they] quenched the power of fire...." (Heb. 11:33-34).

At another point, he lived on the island of Peréo, about twelve miles from Ravenna. While he was chatting with a venerable man, William his disciple, flames broke out in the walls of the little cell, rose up, and began to spread uncontrollably onto the roof. The saint had quick recourse to his usual defense. Rather than tossing furniture outside or uncovering the roof, as would be the normal recourse, or throwing a lot of water on it, or worrying about trying to put out the fire in various ways, he simply recited a prayer. And immediately God's power extinguished the growing whirlwind of fire.

22. At the emperor's insistence, the saint accepts the abbacy of Classe. The monks resist his reform.

At the same time, Emperor Otto the young,[5] hoping to reform the abbey of Classe, gave the monks permission to elect whom they wished. And at once, they unanimously chose Romuald. But the emperor doubted that the blessed one would come to court if invited by a mere messenger. So he decided to go to him personally and arrived at his cell toward dusk. Finding himself with such an illustrious guest at his little hermitage, Romuald offered him his bed for the night. But the

---

[5] Otto III

king would not accept his blanket, considering it too bristly.
The next morning, the king brought him to the palace and
began to ask him insistently to accept the abbacy. Romuald was
reluctant and resolutely refused to consent to the king's request.
So the king threatened to have him excommunicated by all the
bishops and archbishops and the entire synodal council. Faced
with the inevitable, Romuald accepted the governance of souls.
But he added that none of this was news to him, because God
had revealed it to him five years earlier. And so he governed
his monks according to the strict discipline of the *Rule* and
permitted no one any leeway. Even the highborn and learned
did not dare to deviate either to the right or left so as to remove
himself from the straight path of the common life. In other
words, the saint turned the eyes of his heart toward heaven,
hoping to obey God in everything, even while displeasing the
brethren. These brothers whom he had consented to govern
realized all of this too late. First, they blamed one another for
his election. Later, they turned against him with defamatory
murmuring and tormented him sharply with scandals.

23. *After throwing down his abbatial staff,*
Romuald makes peace at Tivoli.

When he had realized that his perfection was diminishing
somewhat and his monks' actions were becoming worse,
Romuald presented himself without delay before the
king and, notwithstanding the objections of the king and
Romuald's archbishop, threw his abbatial staff to the ground
before their eyes and left the monastery. The king later
laid siege to the city of Tivoli. Its citizens had killed their
illustrious duke Mazzolino and, taking up arms, barred the
city gates to the king. God's providential care doubtlessly sent

Romuald there at this time, for he mediated peace and staved off a danger threatening so many souls. The pact insisted that the citizens of Tivoli demolish part of their city walls as a sign of respect for the king and give the king hostages until the duke's murderer would be delivered in chains to the duke's mother. Romuald's prayer to God moved her to pardon the murderer's crime. Although his torture had already begun, she let him return to his home.

24. Romuald exhorts the hermit Venerius to obedience and teaches him about the spiritual combat. The holy life and death of Venerius.

While at Tivoli, the venerable man produced another good fruit that I should not pass over in silence. A holy man named Venerius had lived for a while in a monastery. His humility and simplicity were so great that all the brethren derided him disdainfully and considered him insane. One of them began to pummel him at one point, another threw dirty dishwater on him, and yet another exasperated him by yelling at him about every little thing. Thinking he could not maintain his tranquility in the midst of all those hardships, he left their company and fled to a solitary place. He lived there for six years, abstaining from wine and cooked food in a regimen of extreme austerity. Romuald asked him under whose authority he lived this way, and to whom he was obedient in his state of life. He answered that he was free of all authority, and that he did what seemed best. Romuald told him: "If you are carrying the cross of Christ, you cannot forget the obedience of Christ. Go, then, and get your abbot's permission. Then come back and live humbly in obedience to him. Thus the building of your holy work, constructed with good will, will be built on humility and raised by the virtue of obedience." He gave him this and other admonitions, taught him to resist his own thoughts and how to defend himself against evil spirits. He left him confirmed, instructed, and very eager.

Joyfully receiving the saint's counsels, Venerius went at once to his abbot, received his permission, and returned quickly to his beloved solitude. But wanting to live on his monastery's land, he found an inaccessible spot on a cliff, far from everyone. There he lived alone for four years, deprived of every human comfort, except three small loaves of bread he had carried from his monastery. He ate no bread, drank no wine, and took no cooked food. He lived exclusively on fruit and roots. There was a cavity in the cliff where water collected during the winter season that served the saint for the entire summer. But when it came to be known that a servant of God lived there, many people began to flock to him, carrying him food and bringing him what seemed necessities. But he did not need any of it, so he gave it all away to shepherds and other needy people. Exhorted by the bishop of the place, he allowed them to build and consecrate a basilica there. He died inside it a little while later. Some people looking for him found him bent over in front of the altar, as if he had prayed on his elbows and knees. There the Lord deigned to work some miracles. And so, the good earth that received from Romuald's mouth the seed of the Word so that it could be multiplied, bore much fruit.

25. *The conversion of Tammo and of Emperor Otto III.*

In the vicinity of the aforementioned city, the blessed man converted Tammo, a German who, they say, was so dear and well known to the king that they wore each other's clothing and shared food from the same plate. The Roman senator Crescentius had angered the king and fled to Mount St. Angelo. Because this is an impenetrable fortress, he confidently prepared himself to resist the king's assault. Then Tammo went to him, promising him safety at the king's order, but Crescentius was captured and, with the consent of the pope, who was his enemy, received capital punishment from the king. His wife was then taken and became the king's concubine. Because Tammo had been an accomplice and was guilty of perjury, blessed Romuald ordered him to leave the world.[6] When Tammo asked the king's permission, he easily received it from the very happy king.

This emperor was quite well-disposed toward the monastic order and cultivated a fond devotion toward servants of God. When he had confessed his crime to the blessed man, for penance he had to walk barefoot from the city of Rome to the church of St. Michael on Mount Gargano. He also spent an entire Lenten season at the monastery of St. Apollinaris in Classe with few attendants. There he dedicated himself as well as he could to fasting and psalmody. He wore a hair shirt beneath his royal purple and, instead of availing himself of a bed prepared with splendid blankets, he mortified his delicate body on a paper-reed mat. He also promised blessed Romuald that he would abdicate his role as emperor and take on the monastic habit. He who enjoyed power over so many mortals submitted himself to Christ the poor one, to whom he owed his life.

26. To Montecassino, then Peréo. The humility and austerity of Romuald and his disciples.

Together with Tammo, the most famous Boniface[7] whom

---

6 That is, become a monk.
7 Bruno-Boniface of Querfurt

the Russian Church now venerates as its own most blessed martyr, and some other German converts, Romuald went from Tivoli to St. Benedict's monastery at Montecassino. There he became gravely ill, but recovered quickly through God's mercy. He possessed a fine horse given him by the son of Poland's King Boleslas whom Romuald had mentored into a monastic vocation. In humility, he exchanged the horse for a mule in a good deal, for he was a sharp businessman. In his desire to be like our Redeemer who was seated on an ass, the venerable man voluntarily preferred to ride this animal. With all the above-mentioned people, Romuald returned to Peréo, where he had previously lived. Many other brethren joined him there, and he assigned each a cell. So fervent were they all in the rigorous observance of the eremitical life that news of their life spread everywhere and was considered admirable. And who would not be amazed and have acclaimed it a change wrought by the right hand of God when they saw men formerly clad in silk and wearing gold, surrounded by crowds of servants, and used to abundant delights of every kind, now content to wear rough capes, live alone, barefoot, unkempt, and gaunt from rigorous fasting? They all worked hard in manual labor: some carved spoons, others wove, and still others braided nets.

27. Archbishop Bruno-Boniface evangelizes the Prussians. Tried by fire, he attracts a multitude to baptism. His beheading, and the conversion of those who martyred him.

Blessed Boniface's life surpassed most all the others. He was related to the king, who was quite fond of him and called him "my soul". He had enjoyed a good education in the liberal arts, but particularly in musical studies. When he was the royal chaplain, he saw a church dedicated to the martyr Boniface and suddenly felt the desire to become a martyr in imitation of his patron saint. He said: "My name is also Boniface. Why should I not also be a martyr for Christ?" Later, when he became a monk, his abstinence was so frugal that he would often eat food only on Sundays and Thursdays. Sometimes, when passing nettles or thorn bushes, he would throw himself into them and roll around. A brother once reproved him for doing this, saying: "You hypocrite, why are you doing this in front of everyone to draw attention to yourself?" He answered: "Confessors for you, but martyrs for me!" After a long period of eremitical life, he began preparation to preach. First, he went to Rome, where the apostolic see ordained him archbishop. An old monk who had accompanied him there from Ravenna told me that, for the entire journey, that venerable man proceeded on foot, continually chanting psalmody with his companions. He was always barefoot, ahead of the others on the road. Only because the traveling was tiring did he eat every day, but only half a loaf of bread and water, while on feast days—still abstaining from soup—he would add a little fruit or roots to his daily portion.

After he had been ordained archbishop, he celebrated the Hours daily by adding the canonical Office to the monastic one. He traveled on horseback whenever in mountainous territory. But they say that the venerable pontiff always went barelegged and barefoot, suffering in frigid areas so that, when he came to dismount, his feet could not separate from the stirrups without the help of hot water. Having once arrived in pagan territory, he began to preach with such fervor that no doubt remained that he desired martyrdom. After the martyrdom of Blessed Adalbert, many Slavs had converted through his splendid miracles. Others feared a repetition with Boniface, so they long refrained with deliberate malice from accommodating the blessed man. Not wanting to kill him was actually cruel, since he had such a vibrant desire to die. The venerable man went into the presence of the king of the Russians [sic] and preached with firmness and ardor. Seeing Boniface poorly clad and barefoot, the king expected the saint to speak not for religious motivations so much as for financial ones. He promised to relieve his poverty with riches if he would refrain from his ravings. So Boniface returned to his dwelling, simply put on his most precious pontifical clothing, and presented himself again at the king's palace. Seeing him in such splendid garb, the king said: "Now we know that you dedicate yourself to such ravings not out of poverty, but out of ignorance of the truth. However, if you want me to believe what you say, pass between two high stacks of wood on fire close to one another, after the two flames have become one. If you come out burned anywhere, we will throw you back into that fire. But if you pass through unharmed, incredible though that seems, we will all unhesitatingly believe in your God." Boniface and the pagans liked this deal. So Boniface vested himself for Mass, turned to the fire with holy water and incense, then entered the flames and came through unharmed. Not one hair on his head was singed. Then the king and the other onlookers threw themselves at this feet and begged forgiveness, asking him insistently for baptism.

Crowds seeking baptism began to gather and were so numerous that the saint had to move to a large lake with abundant water to baptize them. The king decided to leave his kingdom to his only son and not to separate himself from Boniface for the rest of his life. One of his brothers who lived with him was put to death by the king, during Boniface's absence, because he refused to become a believer. Another brother, who was already living on his own, apart from the king, had not wished to listen to the venerable man from the moment of his arrival. When his brother converted, he felt great anger against Boniface. Wishing the saint eliminated, he had him beheaded before his eyes in the presence of a large crowd. But he immediately became blind, and such a stupor befell all those attending that they could not speak or hear or perform any human activity. Everyone stood rigid and immobilized like stones. When the king heard of this, he fell into a great sadness and decided that he had to kill not only his brother, but also all the others who had championed this crime. He went at once to the site and saw the martyr's body lying in their midst and, all around, everyone standing insensible and immobilized. He and his men first decided to pray for all those people that God, in His mercy, might restore them to their senses. Afterward, if they were to become believers, they would pardon them; if not, the sword would kill them all. When the king and the other Christians had prayed for a long time, not only were their senses restored, but they also began to ask for true salvation. They burst into tears and asked to be punished for their crime, receiving the sacrament of baptism with great eagerness and building a church over the body of the blessed martyr. If I were to refer to all the gifts of virtues that this admirable man had, truly my tongue would give out before I would run out of material. But because the virtuous life of Boniface still awaits its writing separately, we want at least to record it here, as well as the virtues of Romuald's other disciples, showing—by praising them—how great was their glorious master. And so, until his sublimity resounds in the ears of the faithful, one can know by his students how sublime their instructor must have been.

28. An account of the martyrdom of SS. Benedict, John, and their Polish companions.

During the time Romuald lived at Peréo, King Boleslas happened to ask the emperor to send him some spiritual men who could call the people of his reign to the faith. The emperor immediately turned to Romuald and asked him to place some of his monks at his disposition for this mission. But Romuald did not want to impose this on anyone in his role as superior. He let each monk choose if he would remain or leave. On a matter so risky, he did not know what was God's will. So he preferred to leave it up to each monk's personal decision. The king humbly prayed and consulted with each one, but he could find only two who would spontaneously volunteer to leave—John and Benedict. These two arrived at Boleslas' realm where, supported by the king, they lived in a hermitage and applied themselves to learning Slavic, so they could preach to them. Six years later, when they knew the language well enough, they sent one of their monks to Rome to ask the pope for permission to preach. They also asked him to bring back from Romuald other well-established hermits who would live with them in Slavic territory.

Boleslas wanted to receive a king's crown from Rome. He requested it with insistent supplications. He asked the venerable men to take many gifts along and bring back a crown from the Apostolic See. But they absolutely refused to honor the king's request. They said: "We are in holy orders and are not permitted to be involved in any way with secular affairs." So they left the king and returned to their cells. Some people knew of the king's project but did not know the saints' response. They thought that they had taken a huge amount of the king's gold to their cells to take to the pope. So they got together and conspired to enter the hermitage at night, kill the monks, and seize the gold. When the blessed men heard them trying to break into the hermitage, they realized at once what were their intentions. They confessed to one another and began to seek refuge under the sign of the cross. There were two servants with them, sent from the court to be at their disposition. With all their strength, they resisted and tried to defend the saints against the thieves. But the thieves succeeded in breaking in and killed everyone with swords. They thoroughly searched for the treasure, throwing everything into disorder, but found nothing. Then, wanting to hide their evil deed and have others believe they died accidentally and not by weaponry, they tried to set the cell afire and burn the martyrs' bodies. But the fire lost its natural qualities. No matter how hard they tried, nothing would burn. The surface of the walls would not burn, as if they were constructed of stone rather than wood. Thwarted, the thieves tried to flee, but divine providence would not permit it. Throughout the night, despite their every effort, they could not find the path through the woods, but wandered through brush, deep gorges, and thick undergrowth. They could not even put away their daggers, for their arms seemed paralyzed. Over the place where the bodies of the saints lay, an intense light shone continuously until dawn, and the sweetest songs of angels could be heard.

At dawn, the king heard what had happened. He went to the hermitage at once with many attendants and surrounded the woods with his troops, so the thieves could not escape. They were found and recognized as the culprits because, through divine justice, they could not loosen their grip on their weapons. The king examined the situation and reflected on their punishment, deciding not to kill them, as they deserved, but decreed that they be chained to the martyrs' tomb. They were to stay there miserably until their death, except that the martyrs decided differently and wanted them free of this misery. When the king's order was about to be executed, the thieves were led to the saints' tomb. Suddenly, through the ineffable power of God, the chains were broken and they were set free. So they built a basilica over the saints' bodies, where God worked—and continues to work—innumerable miracles.

29. St. Barnaby freed from captivity by an angel.

Meanwhile, Emperor Henry knew about Boleslas' project and had set up surveillance on the various roads, so he could capture Boleslas' messengers to Rome. So the monk sent just before the saints' martyrdom was taken and immediately imprisoned. But during the night, an angel of the Lord came and visited him in prison, informed him that his senders had achieved their end, and opened the prison for him by divine power, while letting him know that a boat would be ready for him next to the river he had to cross. The monk hurried there and discovered that the angel's promise was true.

30. The monastery at Peréo.
The death of Emperor Otto.

While Romuald was living at Peréo, at his suggestion Emperor Otto built a monastery there in honor of St.

Adalbert. He assigned to it some lands belonging to the cenobium of Classe, which, in turn, received other royal lands in the territory of Fermo. A disciple of Romuald was named abbot and a number of brethren attached themselves to it. Romuald kept watch over it and taught them to live according to the discipline of the *Rule*. He asked the abbot to retire to a hermitage and live there during the week, while joining the brethren at the monastery on Sundays. But the abbot, disdaining the saint's command, set himself up to live like the seculars and, having taken this wrong turn, distanced himself increasingly from the road to righteousness. Seeing that he could no longer work there according to the ardor of his will, Romuald presented himself before the king. Reminding him of his promise, he energetically insisted that the king become a monk. The king assured him that he would do so, but first he would go to Rome where a rebellion was in progress and, after squelching the rebellion, he would return to Ravenna. Romuald told him, "If you go to Rome, you will never see Ravenna again." In this way, he foretold openly the king's imminent death. He did not succeed in persuading him, and since he had no doubt about what would happen, Romuald sailed by boat to the city of Parenzo, while the king traveled to Rome. As the blessed one had foretold, the king became sick during his return from Rome and died suddenly near Paterno.

31. *Romuald is graced with prophecy, the understanding of Sacred Scripture, and tearful compunction. He lives as a roving recluse.*

Romuald lived in the region of Parenzo for three years— one of which he dedicated to the construction of a monastery and the other two to the life of reclusion. It happened here that God's grace brought him to the heights of perfection so that, under the inspiration of the Holy Spirit, he predicted some future events and penetrated with the rays of his intelligence many hidden mysteries of the Old and New Testaments. While at Parenzo, he felt anguished with a desire to shed tears, but regardless of his efforts, he could not arrive at the compunction of a contrite heart. One day, while praying the Psalms in his cell, he came across this verse: "I will instruct and teach you the way to go; I will counsel you with my eyes upon you."[8] Suddenly, a great outpouring of tears overcame him, and his mind was so illuminated with a comprehension of Sacred Scripture that, from that day forward, he could shed tears anytime he wanted to do so, and the spiritual sense of the Scriptures was always open to him. Often he remained so enraptured in the contemplation of God that he melted in tears completely and burned with an unquenchable fire of divine love, crying out like this: "Dear Jesus, dearest! My sweet honey, inexpressible desire, sweetness of the saints, the angels' delight!" These were words that, under the dictation of the Holy Spirit, were transformed into songs of joy that the human mind cannot fully understand. As the Apostle says, "We do not know how to pray as we should, but the Spirit himself intercedes for us with inexpressible groans."[9] If Romuald did not wish to celebrate Mass in the presence of many people, it was because he shed so many tears that he could not hold back. For the same reason, once this had become habitual, thinking in his simplicity of heart that God had granted a similar grace to everyone, Romuald often repeated to

---

[8] Ps. 31:8.
[9] Rm. 8:26.

his disciples, "Be attentive not to shed too many tears, because they can ruin your eyesight and damage your brain." Afterward, wherever the saint happened to live, he would first build a chapel with an altar in his cell, so he could enclose himself and prevent access to others.

32. *The saint perceives at a distance the arrival of monks from Biforco. He instructs them on virtuous living and fighting the devil.*

The brethren who lived in solitude at a place called Biforco sent word to him one time, asking his advice on how to conduct the eremitical life and how to resist diabolical assaults. When those sent had arrived at the monastery, the venerable man knew they had arrived, although Romuald's cell was a good distance away, and he told Abbot Anso, who was nearby: "Go and prepare a dish for the brethren who have arrived from afar." Anso thought he was joking and told him he was, doubtless, a false prophet. In the end, he was more or less constrained to go to the monastery and, in the church, found the men of whom the saint had spoken gathered in prayer. Romuald shared with them the salt of his saving doctrine and armed them with many virtues against the snares of the ancient enemy. Having ministered to them in every way, he sent them back to their hermitage cheerfully encouraged.

33. *Voyage to Biforco. Like a latter-day St. Paul (Acts 27:10,24), Romuald foreknows peril and averts a shipwreck through his prayers.*

Later on, these same brethren sent messengers to him a second time to consult with him in increasing anxiety about these same matters. The venerable man told them, "I am presently writing a little book on fighting against demons. When you return, I will give it to you. And perhaps I myself will go with you." Hearing this, they fell prostrate before him and earnestly begged him to go with them. The next day, he assured them he would go with them and ordered them to find a ship. At this bit of news, the bishop of Parenzo was very upset. When he happened to meet the monks while they were still arranging their trip, he scolded and insulted them. Then he sent out a decree to all the port's inhabitants, forbidding reentry to Parenzo to anyone who dared to furnish a ship to Romuald, leaving with him on a journey without return. Quickly, they sent a messenger to the bishop of Pola, because he would not hesitate to send them a boat. This bishop had often exhorted him not to remain a recluse forever in that obscure nook, but to come instead to Pola, where he would have the opportunity to win many souls. Instead of burning for himself like a coal, he could spread his rays on all those standing in God's house, like a lamp when placed upon a lampstand.

Meanwhile, after waiting for the messenger's return, Romuald said to the brethren with him: "Doubtless, that brother will arrive too late and we will already have disembarked on another ship before his return." The following Sunday at the break of dawn, he said to Ingelbert—a brother who was standing nearby and who would later become a missionary archbishop—"Look out to sea. You will see two ships still far off, coming toward us at the same speed. One of those will take us." Ingelbert curiously scrutinized the horizon in every direction, but he could see no sign of shipping. Then, as the day progressed, he could just see the two ships on the horizon coming from afar, but they were so far off they seemed like two birds. When they entered port, he asked the sailors if they were willing to take on board Romuald and his companions. They were immediately filled with unexpected joy and placed themselves completely at his disposal, saying they were happy to have in their charge so precious a pearl. They did not want to depart that day, however, because a storm was threatening. Romuald exhorted them to trust in divine grace and begin the voyage, guaranteeing that they would encounter no risk. But they remained in port the whole day and only set sail at nightfall.

Toward dawn, the wind suddenly broke out, a storm began, and the sea became very agitated. The stormy waves began to engulf the sailors on all sides, toss the ship about, and break apart all the ship's timbers. Some of the men were stripping and throwing themselves into the water; others were attaching themselves to the rudder; still others were holding on to their oars or other pieces of wood so they could remain afloat. The danger was so grave that imminent shipwreck seemed certain. But Romuald had recourse to his usual line of defense and began to pray. He pulled up the hood of his cowl a bit, put his head on his lap, and silently prayed to God. Then he turned to Abbot Anso who was standing before him and said: "Tell the sailors not to be afraid. We are surely out of danger and everyone will come out of this, healthy and whole." A few minutes later, in spite of everyone's expectations and without any human intervention, the ship righted itself and quickly entered the port of Caorle. Everyone rendered thanks to God their liberator, and they openly testified that they had been saved from death by Romuald's prayers.

34. Romuald's exhortations to reform spurned at Biforco. He periodically withdraws from Vigils to weep.

When Romuald came to Biforco, he looked at all the cells of the brethren and, because they seemed sumptuous in their superfluity, he would only stay in the cell of his venerable disciple Peter who, truly admirable in his abstinence and his great simplicity, imitated St. Hilarion and only allowed cells to be built less than four cubits square. This venerable man later said that Blessed Romuald, during the time they lived together and alternately sang verses of the Psalms, would excuse himself three or more times during the night to answer the call of nature, while in reality he could not contain his sobbing and abundance of tears. Romuald stayed at Biforco for some time. He admonished the brethren not only about the spiritual combat, but also about placing themselves under an abbot and maintaining all things in common. But they did not much welcome Romuald's teaching, because each of them had someone to provide for him and each followed his own will.

35. In the Vale of Castro, the seraphic Romuald sets many on fire for penitence, almsgiving, and even total self-renunciation. He also forcefully combats the prevalent vice of simony.

Unwilling to live in sterility [*sterilitatis impatiens*] and anxious to do good, Romuald left in search of earth apt for bearing the fruit of souls. He sent messengers to the counts of Camerino who, hearing mention of Romuald's name, were filled with joy and offered him possessions from their property: woods, mountains, and even cultivated lands, if he wished. In the end, he found among their possessions a particular place suitable for conducting the hermit life. It was surrounded by mountains and woods; in the middle was a vast plain, well watered by numerous springs and suitable for growing grain. From antiquity, this place was called Val di Castro. There was already a chapel, near which a women's convent had existed for a time. No sooner had the counts ceded the place to him than the venerable man built cells there and began to live there with his disciples. How can one describe with ink or voice how much fruit of souls the Lord gained there through him? People from all over began to flow to him to perform penance, or to mercifully donate their goods to the poor, or to abandon the world altogether and fervently profess the monastic life. And the blessed man was like one of the seraphim: divine fire beyond any comparison burned within him, and wherever he went, he lit the torches of others through his holy preaching. Often, when he preached, compunction so moved him to tears that he would have to suddenly interrupt his discourse and run out of church like a madman. And when he traveled on horseback with the brethren, he would draw behind, psalmodizing and weeping continuously. He did likewise in his cell.

He would reprimand especially the secular priests who had purchased their ordination. He affirmed that unless they would spontaneously resign their state, they would surely be damned as heretics. When they heard news of Romuald, some of them plotted to kill him. Up to Romuald's day, one could buy church offices, and the heresy of simony was hardly considered sinful because it was so commonplace. And he told them, "Bring me your canon law books so you can see with your own eyes on those pages that what I say is true." And after a thorough look, they recognized their error and wept. Then the saint organized various groups of canons and taught the secular clerics to obey their superiors and live in community. He also counseled some bishops to do penance because they had obtained their episcopal sees through simony. They came to the venerable man, promised to quit their episcopacies and enter the monastic life. But it is doubtful that the saint during his entire lifetime could really convert a bishop. That poisonous heresy, particularly when it touches the episcopal order, is so obdurately set against conversion that those who promise such keep putting it off from one day to the next. So it is easier to convert a Jew to the faith than to move one of those heretical usurpers to complete his penance.

In the same region, the saint also established a monastery for women.

36. A burglar is caught red-handed at Romuald's warning. He is treated kindly by the saint and let go.

One feast day, the venerable man was sitting in the chapter room with the brethren and nourishing them with the doctrine of salvation. He suddenly interrupted his discourse with great anxiety and exclaimed: "Quick, quick, run; someone is breaking into Brother Gregory's cell." This Gregory was later consecrated a missionary archbishop. They quickly ran to the cell, where they found a thief trying to knock down the walls. They took him and dragged him before their master and asked what they should do to someone guilty of so great a sacrilege. The saint spoke cheerfully: "Brothers, I do not know what we should do to so evil a man.

Pluck out his eyes? But then he could not see. Cut off a hand? But then he could not work, and might die. Cut off a foot? But then he could not walk. Bring him inside and, to begin with, give him something to eat, while we discuss what action to take." Then the saint rejoiced in the Lord. After feeding the thief, he corrected him moderately and admonished him gently, allowing him to return home in peace.

37. To Orvieto. "He seemed to want to convert the whole world into a hermitage."

He finally left some of his disciples at Val di Castro and went to the region of Orvieto. Here he built a monastery on the property of Count Farolfo, who contributed the major portion, though there were also other contributors. The burning fire for bearing fruit was so intense in the saint's heart that he never felt content with anything he did. And while still involved with one task, he was already getting ready for the next. One might suppose he intended to convert the whole world into a hermitage and to make all people share in the monastic order. He also drew from this area many men whom he distributed in various holy places.

38. The good death of a boy disciple of Romuald and his subsequent miracles.

Some sons of nobility also left their parents and took refuge with the blessed man. One of these was the son of Count Guy, who joined the monastery while still a boy. Not long after, the moment of his death arrived. He saw two evil spirits, like black vultures, that looked at him with terrifying eyes. The boy told this to Blessed Romuald, who was assisting him, and then added: "And now, master, there are very many demons in human form, entering and filling my entire room." Romuald exhorted him to confess anything remaining unconfessed. A fortunate sinner, he confessed with great apprehension his only fault: The prior had ordered him to submit himself to some blows of the rod, but he had not yet done so. Romuald pardoned him his peccadillo and he died in peace. The next day, a blind man who lived as a beneficiary of the boy's father came to his tomb and shouted in a loud voice, "Ah, my master, if you are with God, as I believe, ask him to restore the light of my eyes." As soon as he spoke these words, he saw light. Many other sick people came to his tomb and obtained healing. His tomb even breathed forth perfume, as though filled with many spices. In this way, he who through his great love had despised in life the inheritance of his earthly parents received great honor from God after his death.

39. *The saint and twenty-four companions set out for Hungary in the hope of martyrdom, but nobody attains it.*

Meanwhile, Romuald heard that Blessed Boniface had been martyred. He felt a tremendous desire to shed his own blood for Christ and quickly decided to go to Hungary. While remaining strong in this intention, however, he founded three monasteries in a brief period of time. One was that of Val di Castro, where the body of the saint actually lies in repose,[10] another near the Esino River, and the third in the vicinity of Ascoli. Later, once he had obtained permission from the Holy See and two of his disciples had been

---

[10] Romuald's body was subsequently moved to Fabriano.

consecrated archbishops, Romuald began his voyage with twenty-four of the brethren. In all of them, the zeal to die for Christ was so strong that the holy man could hardly have set out with just a few companions. They had almost reached the territory of Pannonia, when Romuald suddenly became so ill he could not proceed. He had been sick a long time, but when he decided to turn back, he was suddenly healed. Again, he tried to continue the original voyage, but his face began to swell and his stomach would not hold down food. So, he called together the brethren and told them: "I understand that it is not God's will for me to continue the voyage. But I do not want to ignore your desires and do not want to force anyone to turn back. Surely, many others before us have tried with every effort to reach the summits of martyrdom, but divine Providence judged differently, and they were forced to remain in their state. Now, though I do not foresee any of you undergoing martyrdom, I am leaving each one to decide to continue or to turn back with me." Fifteen of them went to Hungary, and two others had already gone off to another destination, so only seven disciples remained with their master. Some of those who went were beaten, or sold into slavery, or subjected to the local nobility. But as the saint predicted, not one of them attained martyrdom.

Romuald converted a number of Germans, among whom the most noble was a relative of Duke Adelbehrn, who became a monk and persevered in that holy life until death. Then Romuald returned to the monastery he had built in the area of Orvieto. It is worth noting that the holy man had not been vainly mistaken in his plan through fickleness. In his intention, he had already undergone martyrdom, while by God's counsel he had been sent to save those he converted. In the aforementioned monastery he had to suffer through many scandals and persecutions. He had wanted the abbot to be a true monk, detached from secular affairs, and not to spend the monastery's goods through vanity, but provide for all the monks' needs. When he turned a deaf ear to all of Romuald's desires, Romuald and his disciples abandoned that place and went to live near Preggio, on land belonging to Ranier, the future marquis of Tuscany.

40. *Worldly potentates stand in awe of Romuald.*

To please his relatives, Ranier had repudiated his wife and united himself with the wife of a kinsman whom Ranier himself had killed involuntarily, it would seem, while he was being pursued. For this reason, Romuald did not want to become an accomplice and did not wish to live free-of-charge on his property, so he paid him a piece of gold for water rights and another for firewood. Ranier had wanted to refuse him outright, because he had preferred to give to the saint rather than receive something from him. But in the end he agreed, so that Romuald would not go away. Once he had received the marquisate of Tuscany, Ranier said: "Neither the emperor nor any other mortal can frighten me equal to the terror that Romuald's gaze gives me. Before him I do not know what to say and can offer no excuses to defend myself." And so, by divine gift, the saint possessed the grace to make any sinner who found himself in his presence—especially the world's powerful—tremble with fear, as though before the majesty of God Himself. And surely the Holy Spirit, who dwelt in his heart, divinely causes this kind of terror among the wicked.

Also at that time, the venerable man built a monastery not far from the castle of Massiliano.

41. *The corrupt abbot of Classe attempts to throttle the saint.*

Hearing that a certain Venetian had become abbot of Classe through simony by purchasing his office and was also sinning wickedly, the soldier of Christ wanted to go there immediately without losing any time. He tried in various ways to purge the monastery of that person. But the reprobate, fearful of losing his abbatial office, was unafraid of perpetrating homicide to keep it. On a stormy night, while Romuald was securely sleeping in his bed, he sneaked upon him and tried to strangle him with his own hands, making him suffer cruelly. Not yet deprived of all breath, the saint cried out noisily with what little breath he could still muster. Awakened by the wheezing sounds of his master, Ingelbert quickly took a firebrand from the embers and drove away that minister of the devil from committing the crime he had undertaken.

42. *Romuald recalled to Italy by the Holy See.*

After that, Romuald once again embarked for Parenzo. But the pope and Roman citizens sent a delegation to force him to return. They promised to follow all his prescriptions if he would return. If not, they would pass a sentence of excommunication. By such an expedient, his disciple Italy gained back Master Romuald.

43. *A house guaranteed secure by Romuald is protected from a thief.*

At that time, Romuald remained for a certain period among the mountain valleys of Cagli and then moved to Mount Petrano, not far from the monastery of St. Vincent near the Candigliano

River. Wherever the saint went, he would always bear more fruit, always winning over an increasing number of souls and drawing men away from their worldly way of life. As though completely transformed into fire, he enkindled in men's souls a desire for heaven. Now he wanted to find a suitable place in which to build a hermitage. He asked a priest who was returning home for some food for himself and his companions. Then he began to search thoroughly the mountains, and finally he came across a monk living next to a little church. He asked him to accompany him and show him where he might find water. The monk answered that he could not leave the house unguarded, for fear of thieves. Romuald promised him that, in such an eventuality, he would reimburse him for everything. And so, having insurance against loss, the monk could then conduct him to the place. While they were in search of it, the priest came bringing food, as he had been asked. He came upon a thief breaking into the house, captured him, and held him under surveillance until Romuald's return. When Romuald found that man, he first scolded him with paternal severity, then gently admonished him, and finally allowed him to return home, safe and sound. Evidently, divine Providence wanted what had been entrusted to Romuald kept intact, even in his absence.

44. Distant thieves are foiled at Romuald's command.

On another occasion, the venerable man was intent on building some cells in the same area, and the brethren had placed their things beneath a rock at some distance. All at once, Romuald dispatched one of the brothers there, ordering him to act in haste. He surprised some thieves there trying to steal, but he saw that nothing had yet been taken from what had been deposited there. This just goes to show how the blessed one had sent the brother there with such dispatch through the impulse of divine revelation, at exactly the moment in which the thieves had approached their unguarded things.

45. *The abbot at the Vale of Castro resists and repels the saint's preaching of reform.*

Romuald next returned to the monastery of Val di Castro. There he immediately exhorted the abbot to govern the others without forgetting to watch himself. Besides, he wanted him to stop abandoning his solitary cell with the excuse of taking care of duties, but rather to live spiritually in solitude, limiting his fraternal visitations of the brethren to feast days in order to minister to them. The way we see abbots living today was so odious to the blessed one that getting rid of this kind of abbacy gave him the same joy as influencing any of the powerful secular leaders to enter the monastic life. But as Solomon said: "Songs to a perverse heart are like vinegar on lye."[11] With the venerable man's preaching, that abbot became even worse. He quickly presented himself before the Countess who owned the place and persuaded her with shrewd sacrilege to have the wood set aside for the building of Romuald's cell chopped to pieces. Thus was this tall cedar of paradise hounded from the woods of earthly men.

46. *"We give Thee thanks, O God almighty, for deigning to illumine our region with the splendor of such a star."*

Leaving there, he established his abode in a place called Aquabella near Mount Apennine. While certain lay helpers

---

[11] Cf. Prv. 25:20.

were building their dwelling along with his disciples, Romuald was now too old for such work, so he alone stayed in charge of the guesthouse. Due to a severe toothache, one priest involuntarily left this work with the permission of the brethren and turned toward home in terrible pain. As he was departing, he passed by Romuald, who asked him why he was suffering and where he was going. Holding open his mouth, Romuald touched him with his finger at the spot causing the pain and said: "Place a glowing coal on a twig so you will not burn your lip, and touch it here. The pain will go away." The priest had hardly gone a further two-thirds of an acre when the pain suddenly ceased. He returned, safe and sound, to the work he had abandoned, shouting in a loud voice: "We thank you, almighty God, because you have deigned to visit our area with the splendor of so great a star. Surely, an angel of God has appeared in our land, a holy prophet, a great light hidden from the world." He proclaimed this and other praises to God, to the point that the blessed one's disciples tried to quiet him down. For indeed, if words of that kind ever reached Romuald's ears on any occasion, his heart was smitten by indignation.

47. A felled tree falls clear of the saint's cell.

On another occasion, he had ordered that a large beech tree near his cell be cut down. This beech was leaning over the cell so that, if it fell, one could see that it would surely destroy the entire building. In executing the order, the workers were worried about the tree's falling. When the axe blows had chipped around the trunk, it seemed certain that it threatened to fall on the blessed one. They began to beseech him and shout out forcefully to get out of his cell, to let the cell go while saving himself. Ignoring their shouts, he told them to finish the work they had begun. The beech fell with a loud roar but, by divine power, ended up in another direction. To the wonder of all, the cell remained completely intact. Amazed by such a great miracle, all raised their joyful voices to heaven and gave boundless thanks to God.

48. *Another felled tree rolls over a farmer without harming him.*

Why speak about how God protected that venerable man, when we know how many others were often saved from grave danger through his presence? It should be enough now to mention one of these occasions, and the reader can deduce what all the others must have been like. One time, he was with his workers on Mount Petrano cutting down an enormous oak tree. The tree, hanging over a precipice, began bending toward the bottom, but a little below it was a farmer. Once it was cut, the tree fell down heavily, rolled over the precipice and down the slope, struck the farmer, and dragged him down. All began to shout out in grief. They thought the man was dead and that his body had been completely torn to pieces. But the divine power was amazing. The man came out at once, safe and sound, as if an oak leaf had fallen instead of a tree. One can see from this how the saint's merits must have carried great weight with God: in his presence, the enormous mass of the tree lost all its weight.

49. *Romuald is calumniated by the depraved monk Romanus, who comes to a bad end.*

After some time, Romuald left the Apennines and went to live on Mount Sitria. Hearing about all of these moves of the saint, one should be careful not to attribute this to the vice of fickleness, but to how seriously he took his religious activities. Surely his movements were motivated by the fact that, wherever the venerable man stopped, a mob of almost innumerable people surrounded him. His good sense dictated that, once the place was filled, he would name a prior and then be off to fill up another place.

We would be unable to expose all the injustices and scandals he had to endure from his disciples at Sitria. We will cite one, passing over the others in the interest of brevity. There was a disciple by the name of Romanus, of noble birth but utterly degenerate in his actions. The saint reproved him by word for his carnal impurity and often with serious corporal punishment. Then that diabolical man accused Romuald of the same fault. Impudently, he barked out sacrilege with his mouth against that temple of the Holy Spirit and said that the saint had committed the same sin with him. All of his disciples immediately turned against Romuald with anger and hostility. Some said they should hang the old villain; others wanted to burn him in his cell. What amazes one particularly is that spiritual men could believe that a decrepit old man over a hundred[12] years old could commit such a wicked crime. Even if he had wanted to do so, nature and the frigid sterility of his body would have rendered it impossible. But we should believe without a doubt that it was from heaven and for the increase of the saint's merits that he came to be scourged by so grave a misfortune. In fact, he had asserted at the hermitage where he had last stayed that this was going to happen and that he would be ready to undergo this dishonor. As far as that reprobate is

---

[12] Romuald's age is inflated in Peter Damian's *Life*.

concerned, a sarabaite[13] who had accused the saint of such a sin, he later acquired the episcopacy of Nocera through the heresy of simony and held it for two years. During the first, his dwelling burned down, as he deserved, along with his books, the bells, and sacred vestments; in the second year, the divine sentence was carried out in full, and he lost both his dignity and his life.

50. *The saint endures six months of penance due to calumny. Then he is told by revelation to celebrate Mass again and to compose a commentary on the Psalms.*

As though he had committed that sin, the disciples imposed a penance upon the holy man and took completely away his faculty to celebrate the sacred mysteries. He willingly embraced their prejudicial action, accepted the penance as though he had really been guilty, and did not presume to approach the sacred altar for some six months. But finally, as he himself would later tell his disciples, he felt told by God to give up completely his indiscreet simplicity and to celebrate faithfully the sacred mysteries of the Mass, if he did not want to lose God's grace. So he began to celebrate the next day. When he reached the Eucharistic prayer, he became rapt in ecstasy and remained that way a long time, to the amazement of everyone present. They asked him afterward why he made those unusual pauses during the offering of the sacrifice. He answered: "I was swept up into heaven and presented before God. And immediately a divine voice commanded me to explain the Psalms according to the intelligence God had

---

[13] A monk who follows his own self-will

given me and to write down my exposition methodically, according to my comprehension. I felt myself seized by an enormous, inexplicable terror and could only say: 'So be it, so be it.' " Hence, the saint later composed a splendid commentary on the entire Psalter and some of the prophetic canticles, and though his grammar contained certain inaccuracies, he always kept to the right meaning.

51. Romuald's rapture (cf. 2 Cor. 12:2-4).

One time, his disciples asked him, "Master, what age has the soul? And under what form will it appear at the Last Judgment?" He said: "I know a man in Christ whose soul was presented before God resplendent as snow, in human form and of full grown stature." They asked him who the person was, and he, indignant and reproving them, wished to say no more. But speaking among themselves, the disciples attributed the thing to him, as was really the case, and understood with certainty that he was that man by that explanation.

52. Seven years of reclusion, in great austerity, at Sitria.

At Sitria, Romuald remained a recluse for almost seven years, observing perpetual silence without exceptions. Still, with a silent tongue and preaching with his life [*tacente lingua et predicante vita*], he was able to do more than ever, whether it was drawing people who wanted to convert or dealing with those who came to him in penitence. He lived in great austerity, despite his advanced years, when even perfect men allow themselves to live with a certain liberty and ease the rigor of their resolutions. During an entire Lenten season, he took no food or drink other than broth made with flour and some herbs, in imitation of Hilarion. For five weeks, he limited himself to a little chickpea soup and took nothing else. And with many other practices of living, Romuald put to the proof his capacity for virtuous conduct, first trying one thing, then another. Discreetly, this soldier of Christ kept himself always ready for yet some new battle. But whenever he was at the point of no longer holding out, he would make use of mercy, so that his shaky body might be lifted up. He wore two and sometimes three hair shirts to check the insolence of the body. He would not let anyone wash them; he would just leave them in the rain and change every thirty days. He never let a razor shave his head, but whenever his hair and beard grew too long, he would cut them himself with scissors. At times, when the vice of gluttony tempted him toward some tasty morsel, he would quickly have it cooked carefully. He would draw it close to his mouth and nose, allowing himself only to smell the aroma. Then he would say: "Glutton, glutton! How sweet and pleasant this food would be! But, too bad for you! You will never taste it." And he would send it back untouched to the steward.

53. The saint cures Brother Gregory's headache by breathing on him (cf. Jn. 20:22).

Regardless of how much the saint made use of such austerity, he always showed a happy face and a serene bearing. One time, a brother by the name of Gregory was experiencing a very bad headache. With loud cries, he arrived at the blessed one's cell, where other brothers were present. The venerable man saw him and attributed the pain, calmly, not to a disequilibrium of the humors but to a ploy of the ancient enemy. Suddenly, as though playing a joke on him with his usual cheerfulness, he leaned through his window and breathed on his forehead, asking all the others present to do likewise. When they had done so, Gregory was healed to the point that he never again experienced the slightest trace of a headache. I am certain that, if the saint wanted to perform this gesture, it was because he believed that the wicked enemy and perpetrator of the pain had to be driven out by the Holy Spirit, who reigned in his heart. Not to bring praise upon himself, he made a game of it and looked for collaborators. For we read that our Savior breathed when He gave the Holy Spirit to the apostles.

54. *"A holy kiss" (cf. Rom. 16:16) brings sanity.*

A man suffered from madness and had lost his reason to the point that he never knew what he was doing or saying. Romuald did not do anything to him except give him a kiss that brought him back to his former health. Offering peace to that restless man restored him to peace of mind. Later, the man who had been cured said: "In the same moment the saint's lips touched me, I felt a driving wind from his mouth on my face and whole head that extinguished suddenly the flame that had burned in my brain."

55. *Diseased flesh restored by cold-water washing (cf. 2K 5:14).*

On another occasion, the aforementioned Gregory was suffering from scabies on his legs. They were so virulent and putrid that one would assume a swelling of that gravity would be caused by elephantiasis. Romuald prescribed for him the original therapy of washing his legs in cold water for three days. He promised him that he would recover his health this way. He did what he was told, more out of dutiful obedience than out of faith in the treatment's healing power. And behold, a wonder attributable only to God's power: the legs' swelling stopped, the putrefaction went away, and the brother was completely healed of every discomfort. One can reasonably believe that Romuald commanded his disciple to wash the swollen legs three times in water by the same spirit by which Elisha commanded Naaman the leper to wash seven times in the Jordan.

56. A recluse loses his vocation because of a rash oath against Romuald.

Some carnal men did not hesitate to rebuke Romuald maliciously and to attribute his words and actions to the vice of fickleness. Once one of his disciples, living in another hermitage, was needed by his relatives and agreed unwillingly to go to Rome on their account during Lent. The saint at once knew in his spirit about this and wrote indignantly to a brother near him, asking why he had had the presumption to go to Rome for that sort of business. The other was amazed that the Master was informed about this matter, because no one from outside could have told him about it. He investigated accurately and discovered that things were as the venerable man had said. He went to Ingelbert, another disciple who was a recluse, and told him that the Master had said those things and doubtless possessed the spirit of prophecy. But the other reproved the brother, disapproving and denying the whole affair. To show he considered it all a trick, he bound himself by oath: "If he has spoken through a spirit of prophecy rather than by the devil's work, may almighty God no longer permit me to persevere in reclusion." No sooner said than done! A few days later, Ingelbert ended his reclusion and went away without the Master's permission. They say that he had no further opportunity to see him in this life.

57. The fault of Gaudentius, who evades obedience for the sake of fasting, is pardoned after death.

Another brother named Gaudentius, who is the father of the abbot of this monastery of St. Vincent, was converted with great fervor and lived afterward with an even more ardent spirit for God's service. At one time, he had asked Blessed Romuald permission to deny himself all cooked dishes and restrict himself to water, fruit, and raw vegetables. Obtaining permission, he followed that course without growing tired of it. Another brother, Tedaldus, indiscreetly feeling compassion for Gaudentius' fragility, went to the saint and suggested he put an end to this obstinacy, because that brother was ill suited to so heavy a burden. Romuald, a man of simple heart, took to heart Tedaldus' words and retracted Gaudentius' permission to live that way. Gaudentius felt very offended and could no longer continue living with Tedaldus in the hermitage Romuald had assigned to them. He placed himself under obedience to Ingelbert, who had separated from Romuald, and obtained his permission to live in the aforementioned manner. Gaudentius died not long afterward and was buried in St. Vincent's cemetery, next to Berard, a venerable man who had also been Romuald's disciple. But because he had died in the state of disobedience, Romuald forbade any prayers for him. Sometime afterward, while celebrating the morning Office with some other brothers, a monk of the same cenobium suddenly experienced a toothache so violent he could no longer remain in choir or sing the

Psalms. He left immediately and, moaning, threw himself on the graves of Berard and Gaudentius. After remaining there in prayer a long time, he fell asleep for a bit. At once, he saw Berard dressed splendidly in priestly vestments, holding a book written with gold letters in his hand, standing in front of an altar, and intent on celebrating the sacred mysteries of the Mass. Then he saw Gaudentius behind, saddened and humiliated. He assisted at a distance and did not dare come forward to the sacred mysteries, like an excommunicant. He said: "Brother, do you see the book splendidly written in gold that Berard has? I would also have a similar one if the monk Tedaldus, alas, had not taken it away from me." Suddenly that brother woke up and rose, sound and unhurt, without any pain. He later joyfully recounted his vision to the brethren. When Romuald heard it, he ordered the brethren at once to treat Gaudentius with fraternal charity and pray intensely for him. And it is reasonable to suppose that he who had lost the deserved book by disassociating himself from Romuald would now have reattained that book, having been readmitted into Romuald's favor and sustained by his prayers. Through Romuald's hand, Tedaldus had taken away what Romuald now restored to him, praying for him with all the brethren.

58. When Romuald is absent, only those who have asked permission repose safely in his bed.

One time, the venerable man was going on a journey, so he entrusted his cell to one of the disciples and ordered him to live there until his return. But that inconsiderate one did not have the respect he should have had for the Master and did not hesitate to lie down on Romuald's straw bed. But that same night, evil spirits fell upon him, beat him with severe blows, threw him out of the bed, and left him half dead. He had sinned through lack of humility before such a great man and deserved to have proud spirits wreak vengeance on him for that offense. He had not shown respect for his holy master, so he had to suffer punishment from hard, ungodly hands. On another occasion, the venerable man similarly left another disciple in his cell before leaving on a journey. The disciple told him: "Master, I do not intend to lie down on your bed, because I am afraid what happened to the other brother might also happen to me." And he answered: "My son, lie down and sleep peacefully. The other one fell into the enemy's hands when he went to bed because he had not asked my permission, even if I am not important. But with my consent, hope in God and sleep without fear." According to the order received, he lay down and suffered no harm.

59. A morsel of bread blessed by the saint quells the frenzy of the wife of a would-be monk.

A layman named Arduinus placed himself under Romuald to receive the monastic habit, then returned home to settle all his affairs. His wife saw him coming, became furious, and shouted at him: "So, my good man, you have been with that heretic, that old seducer; and now, will you leave me wretched and deprived of every human comfort?" With these words, she went crazy. She began to rave and become agitated, as though openly tormented by a demon. The saint had the habit of giving the brethren going on a journey some bread or fruit, or something else, as a blessing. The disciples knew with certainty from much experience that giving a piece of bread blessed by the Master to the sick made them recover their health completely. Other sick people had been healed with the water in which he had washed his hands. But this had to be done with the greatest caution, so as not to provoke deep sadness in the saint, if he were to perceive it. Because that woman was so miserably tormented, some of the brethren gave her a little piece of bread blessed by the Master. When she had eaten it, her mind at once calmed down, and she found herself completely free of any fury. She immediately gave thanks to Almighty God, and His servant Romuald, for healing her, and she gave her husband permission to become a monk.

60. *Exorcism by a morsel of blessed bread.*

On another occasion, a boy possessed by a demon was brought to the blessed one. He did nothing but give him a little piece of blessed bread. No sooner had the boy eaten than he was immediately free of the demon. Obviously, the blessing of Romuald entered the possessed boy's body, and scorched by it, the evil spirit had to leave.

61. *The invocation of Christ puts the ancient foe to flight.*

The devil could never feel secure from the saint's attacks. His hidden deceits were worth nothing against Romuald, so he would not stop showing the poison of his evil quite openly. Once, while the venerable man was in his cell, the evil spirit showed himself with all his ugliness—shaggy and horrible—and began to terrorize the saint. Assailing him with fury, he threatened to kill him. Unflinching, Romuald sought help from heaven and shouted out in faith for Christ to help him. The ancient enemy immediately ran away, battering against the cell's walls with such rage that he cracked a heavy wooden table over a cubit wide. So the devil showed openly in the dwelling how burning was his cruelty against its inhabitant, by leaving on the wall a sign of what lay hidden in his heart, as if he had written it out.

62. *The evil spirit, appearing as a dog, spooks Romuald's horse.*

One time, the venerable man was traveling on horseback with his disciples. Suddenly the evil spirit, under the appearance of a red dog, ran at him heatedly and frightened his horse, so that the saint almost fell off. He asked the disciples if they had seen anything. They said they saw a terrified horse, but nothing else. Then he told them: "How miserable must that spirit be, who, we know, was once a splendid angel and now is not ashamed to show himself under the guise of a filthy dog."

63. *The devil loudly celebrates disagreement among the brethren, and then violently bemoans their concord.*

At another point, the saint had decided to build a monastery for women servants of God at Valbona. But there was at once a quarrel among his disciples. Some were against it, while others ardently insisted on its establishment. When the two sides set themselves up to argue in front of the venerable man and give their reasons, the devil began to make a loud noise in front of the cell's door, as though with a mallet. One could hear the thundering of those thumping, frequent blows throughout the woods. But when all were agreed about building the monastery, the evil spirit started howling in tears and lamentations heard by all. Finally, when the brethren were returning to their own cells, the ancient enemy accompanied them with a storm so turbulent that it seemed it might uproot the entire woods, unleashing every wind possible. One of the brothers reprimanded the devil with these words: "Filthy spirit, I order you in the name of the Holy Trinity not to follow us any further." And so, he was put to flight. It would seem the author of discord had let them hear his pleasure when the quarrel began but had not held back his wailing once peace returned. If he had first tried to pull out the hoop of an empty barrel and scatter the pieces composing it, he retired in gloom once the bonds of peace and the solidarity of charity had reunited the disciples.

64. A golden age was that age of Romuald.

In Sitria, they led a lifestyle that seemed like a second Nitria[14] by a resemblance of works as well as of name. Everyone went barefoot; all were unkempt, pale, and happy in their extreme poverty. Some had bolted their doors in order to be recluses and so seemed dead to the world, like those truly dead. No one drank wine, not even when gravely ill. Not only the monks, but also their servants and shepherds, fasted, observed silence, took the discipline among themselves, and sought penance for every idle word. O golden age of Romuald, that did not lack its voluntary martyrdom, though there were no persecutors' tortures! A golden age, I say, in which so many citizens of the heavenly Jerusalem lived in the midst of the forest animals of the mountains and woods. When the brethren became so numerous that all could no longer live there, Romuald built a monastery there and appointed

---

[14] Nitria was one of the main general monastic settlements in early Christian Egyptian desert monasticism.

an abbot and, keeping an inviolate silence, returned to live at Biforco. However even there, when he wanted the abbot to live spiritually and keep to the straight path, he had to leave to escape more unjust persecutions.

65. Romuald pays a requested visit to the Emperor (St.) Henry II. He admonishes him on just governance and is conceded a monastery.

During that time, Emperor Henry descended from the Alps into Italy and sent one from his delegation to the blessed one to ask him if he might be worthy to have him visit him. He promised to fulfill whatever he might command, as long as he would not refuse this meeting. The venerable man was at first reluctant to break his silence. Then all of his disciples came together to ask him unanimously: "Master, you see that we who follow you are too numerous here to live as we ought. So please go and ask the emperor for a large monastery, and gather there the multitude of your followers." I do not know whether it was by an earlier revelation or a spontaneous inspiration of God, but the saint faithfully wrote: "Know that you will have the monastery of Mount Amiata as a gift from the king. You must only decide whom to choose as abbot." He then went to the king without violating his silence. The king at once rose to his feet and exclaimed with great, heartfelt emotion: "If only my soul were in your body!" He implored him to speak, but he was to hear nothing throughout the day.

The next day, when Romuald came to the palace, an entire multitude of Germans came to meet him. They humbly bowed their heads as a sign of greeting, but they greedily plucked at the hair of his garments and carefully set them aside to take home as sacred relics. The venerable man was so grieved by this that he wanted to return at once to his cell and would have done so, had it not been for the desire of his disciples. Approaching the king, he had much to say to him about restoring the Church's rights, the violence of the powerful, and the oppression of the poor. After touching upon several of these topics, he asked for a monastery for his disciples. The king consigned to him the monastery of Mount Amiata and expelled the abbot, a man implicated in many offenses. What adversity the saint had to endure, not only on the part of the deposed abbot, but also from the new one he had chosen from among his disciples. He knew how to suffer adversity with the greatest patience, but we do not have the words to describe what he had to endure. Let it suffice to give one example how God was his help in every situation, and this might reasonably give you some idea of what usually occurred.

66. Romuald saves the life of a monk who had intended to kill him.

Furious with Romuald, a certain monk had a sharpened knife hidden away and was waiting for an opportunity to kill the blessed one. During the night, while he was sleeping, he saw an evil spirit who attacked him ferociously, wrapped a noose around his neck, and tried to strangle his throat so fiercely that he could scarcely breathe. Then the monk, on his last breath, begged Romuald to come to his help. It seemed to the monk that Romuald flew to him and snatched him out of the hands of the ancient enemy. He awoke at once and went and prostrated himself at the feet of the venerable man, asking him to look at the bruises on his neck, but still too ashamed to confess his own perverse plan. He thanked him for saving his life and received a penance for his serious sin. So he who had planned to take Romuald's life was able to preserve his own, thanks to that saintly man. He escaped death with the help of the man he himself had wanted to die.

67. Romuald foretells to his disciples that God will send them bread in the wilderness.

When governing a monastery, the saint usually ate every day with the brethren, unless he was fasting. He would eat one cooked dish and then, paying attention to the reading or watching the others, he would eat no more. He remained in his cell uninterruptedly during Lent, unless forced by some unavoidable necessity. During the period in which the blessed one ruled the aforementioned cenobium, as Lent was approaching, he and his disciples went looking for a place to build a hermitage among the mountainous surroundings. The search went on and, at a certain point, they found themselves surrounded on all sides by flooding torrents, so they could no longer turn back or get help from the monastery. They lived on a few chestnuts they had brought along. Sunday arrived, and unable to count on another meal, the brethren had begun to peel the last chestnuts. They felt a certain fear that they were preparing their last meal. But Romuald, cheerful as ever, told them confidently that he would eat nothing that day unless God would send someone with bread for them. The disciples were amazed that he could hold out for such a hope. However, certain that their master could not make predictions without a reason, they began to wait confidently for a meal, as though on a feast day. And a little before the sixth hour, three men came bearing bread, wine, and other food. They spoke of coming from a land far away, after much toil. All blessed God joyfully and ate together, knowing that the blessed one had known it all through a heavenly revelation.

68. *After prayer, a monk pulls a big fish for Romuald's table out of a depleted brook.*

Once, when the venerable man arrived at Sitria, he was fasting, and the brethren in those steep mountains had no fish to give him to eat. They felt mortified and worriedly asked themselves what they might obtain for such a venerable guest. Then a brother—inspired by God, I believe—ran down to the almost dried up stream that flowed nearby. But the water was very dark, and no one had ever seen a fish there. The brother prayed devoutly to God that, as He had given the People of Israel water from a rock, so He might show him a fish in that dried up stream. At once, he thrust a hand in that bit of water and found a fish more than sufficient to feed the blessed one. God evidently provided nourishment for His servant and so, on a rocky, dry mountain, a fish was found, as though in a valley abounding with fish. I have only narrated a few of the events in the life of the blessed one. But we believe they are sufficient, and now we come to his passing.

69. *The blessed transit of Romuald.*

The saint lived in many places and underwent many wrongs, particularly at the hands of his own disciples. He also performed many miracles, but we prefer to avoid prolonging this narrative. At the end of all his various sojourns, when he perceived his imminent end, he returned to the monastery he had built at Val di Castro. While he awaited, without any preoccupation, the event of his passing, he had them build a cell with an oratory in which he could enclose himself and observe silence until death. Twenty years before, he had openly predicted to his disciples that he would die in that monastery, would breathe his last without anyone present, and would need no funeral. When the cell was built and his mind was set upon enclosing himself quickly, his body began to suffer increasingly and decline, not so much from illness as from old age. During the last six months, he spit up mucus and other humors from his diseased lungs; a cough tormented him, rendering his breathing difficult. For all that, the saint had still not agreed to go to bed and, as much as he could, continued his fasting. One day, bit by bit, he began to lose his strength and feel more seriously the effects of his illness. Toward dusk, he ordered the brothers helping him to leave him, close the cell door behind them, and return at dawn to celebrate the morning Office with him. Concerned about his passing, they left reluctantly. Instead of leaving at once to sleep, worried that the Master might die, they positioned themselves near the cell as though hiding to watch over that talent of precious treasure. After remaining there for some time, they listened with a more attentive ear and, not hearing any movement of body or voice, guessed what had happened. They pushed open the door and quickly went in. Lighting a light, they found the holy corpse lying supine where the blessed soul had been snatched up into heaven. The heavenly pearl lay there as though abandoned, soon to be put back with honor into the treasury of the highest King. Having died in the manner he predicted, he certainly passed over to where he had hoped. The blessed one had lived one hundred and twenty years: twenty years in the world, three years in a monastery, and ninety-seven years in the eremitical life. Now he shines in an inexpressible way among the living stones of the Heavenly Jerusalem, exults with the flaming ranks of blessed spirits, is clothed with the whitest stole of immortality, and is crowned with a radiant diadem by the King of kings.

70. *A piece of the saint's hair shirt exorcises a demoniac.*

Regarding the miraculous signs God worked through that venerable man after his holy death, who would feel the need to read an account, when it is frequently possible to see them happening anew? Because the miracles taking place at his tomb have been so frequent, it seems better to omit them all than to write too little. It suffices here to mention only two performed elsewhere by the blessed confessor. A brother who had been the saint's disciple had given a small oratory to the monastery for suffrages for his own soul. He had also sent to that oratory a piece of the blessed one's hair shirt and ordered that it be placed with honor on the altar. But the man who had brought it was not careful to put it on the altar, as he had been ordered. He had carelessly placed it in a crack in the wall and left it there. Later, a possessed man was brought into that church. Standing in the center, he turned his head back and forth, and scrutinized everything around him. Finally, he began to fix his eyes with terror on the wall and, turning to the place in which the piece of the saint's hair shirt was placed, began to shout repeatedly: "He is casting me out; he is casting me out!" And while he was shouting like this, it was expelled from that man. From this we can ask how he could fail to obtain anything before the divine clemency, if the demon could not even resist a small fragment of his clothing.

If he is capable of such things in his absence, what will he not do when he is bodily present?

71. *The robbery of a poor woman's cow is foiled.*

In another situation, a landowner arrogantly seized a poor woman's cow, despite her cries and many supplications. Then she suddenly ran, took two chickens to the church mentioned above, and threw them in front of the altar. Prostrating herself, she wept and cried: "St. Romuald, hear this poor woman; do not look away from this desolate woman. Give me back my sustenance that has been unjustly stolen from me." And a surprising thing happened! The landowner with his stolen goods was no further away than bowshot from that woman's house, when he suddenly fell ill. He left the cow there, went home, and died immediately.

72. *Exhumed after five years, the saint's body is found incorrupt.*

Five years after the saint's death, the Apostolic See granted permission for the monks to build an altar over his venerable body. A certain brother named Azo went into the woods because he wanted to prepare a little casket that would contain only the bones and ashes of the holy confessor. That night, an old man appeared to a sleeping brother and asked him: "Where is the prior of this monastery?" The other answered that he did not know. So the old man added: "He has gone to the trouble of going into the woods to fashion a box, but he will be unable to place the blessed one's body in such a small casket." The next day, the prior returned with the finished box. The brother who had had the vision asked him why he had gone to the woods. With the excuse of being tired, the other did not answer him. So the brother himself told the prior why he had gone, and told him in detail about his vision, hiding nothing. When they opened the tomb, they found the saint's body completely intact and incorrupt, as when they had buried him. They simply noted some light down of mildew formed on some spots. So they set aside the little casket already prepared and immediately prepared a sarcophagus to fit the blessed one's body. They placed the holy relics inside and solemnly consecrated an altar above it. The blessed man died on June 19[15] in the reign of our Lord Jesus Christ who, with the Father and the Holy Spirit, lives and is glorified for infinite ages upon ages. Amen.

---

[15] .IIIX. kalendarum Iuliarum [1027]

IV

Letter 28 *Dominus Vobiscum* (The Lord Be With You)[1]

Peter Damian of Fonte Avellana

Address: To one shut up for love of supernal freedom.

(1) To Lord Leo,[2] hermit-recluse out of love for heavenly freedom, from Peter the monk-sinner, his servant and son:

(2) Your holy wisdom, dearest father, knows that I look upon you not as a comrade or friend, but as a father, teacher, master, and lord, dearer to me than most. I trust that, with your earnest prayer, I can obtain a hearing in God's mercy. And what else can I say? Because I have considered you my guardian angel, I have always unquestioningly taken your advice when in doubt or hesitating, as though it were an angelic voice from heaven. And so, whenever questions arise, before coming to consult with you, I first pray that God will mercifully use you as an instrument of His will, that I might discern by your counsel what course of action to take when in doubt. Following my customary way once again, I am asking you to tell me what I should say to the many seekers who have sought

---

[1] This is the title commonly assigned to Letter 28.
[2] Leo of Sitria

an answer from me. In fact, several of the brethren who follow an eremitical path often ask me if it is all right for them, when alone in their cells, to say "The Lord be with you," and "Pray, Lord, a blessing," and whether, because they are alone, they should respond in the customary ecclesiastical fashion. Some, as though arguing with themselves, say: "Maybe we should ask the stones or wood of the cell for a blessing? Or should we say that the Lord be with them?" Still others, however, fear that if they omit the customary ritual of Church tradition, they would be sinning by not fully performing the Lord's service. And when asked for some solution to this, not knowing the answer, I likewise feel obliged to search elsewhere. Besieged by doubts, I turn as usual to my guardian angel and follow the well-worn path to the source, not of Ciceronian eloquence, but of divine wisdom.

1. Holy simplicity is preferable to worldly philosophies.

(3) I want nothing to do with Plato, who delved into the secrets of hidden nature, nor with Pythagoras, who determined the planetary orbits, measured the movements of the stars, and divided with his rule all the climates of the spherical world. I also reject Nicomachus who wore out his fingers on his astronomical books, and Euclid, hunchbacked from studying complicated geometrical figures. I avoid without distinction all the rhetoricians with their excuses and arguments. I consider all the dialecticians with their syllogisms and sophistries unworthy of this question. Let the gymnasts shiver in their nakedness for love of wisdom and the Peripatetics search for truth at the bottom of a well. But I seek the greatest truth from you: truth that rose from the earth and does not now lie hidden in a well, but is manifest

to the whole world and reigns eternally in majesty in heaven. How can poets' fictions serve me with their madness, or the grandiose struggles of the tragedians? Let the comedians stop the poisoned stream of silliness from their mouths, and let the crowd of satirists stop burdening their tables with bitter banquets of wicked slander. The oratorical followers of Cicero will not seduce me with their elegant smooth talk, nor will the rhetorical followers of Demosthenes convince me with clever arguments. Let all those who glory in their worldly wisdom slip back into the shadows of the night with their rubbish. I take nothing from those blinded by the sulfurous splendor of obscure doctrine. Let the simplicity of Christ enlighten me and the authenticity of true wisdom break the bonds of my doubts. "For," as Paul says, "since the world did not know God in its wisdom, God wanted to save believers through our preaching."[3]

(4) Away, then, with the letter that kills. Let the life-giving spirit come to help us. As the same apostle says: "The wisdom of the flesh is deadly, while spiritual wisdom brings life and peace, because the wisdom of the flesh is God's enemy, since it does not and cannot submit to God's law."[4] Because it cannot submit to God's law, how can eyes tearing up from pride's smoke even pretend to penetrate it? Come then, father, and quickly undo the knot of this question asked of me, and do not let the grandiloquent schools of puffed-up philosophers coil around the disciple of the humble Christ. Let my guardian angel tell me what the crowd of unskilled dialecticians does not know; let wise ignorance tell me what

---

[3]   1 Cor. 1:21.
[4]   Rm. 8:6-7.

foolish wisdom does not understand. And so, dearest father, prudently expound on what has been asked, so that after divine wisdom is arrived at, no one will have further need to waste breath over this matter.

2. *Why we say: "Jube, Domne, benedicere."* [*Command, my Lord, a blessing.*]

(5) But maybe you will have me give my own solution to this question before you give your opinion, like the teachers do in schools when they ask boys what they think about a difficult problem before them, and thus apprehend from their answer their disposition for learning. So, I will not hesitate to express what I think about it, naturally within the bounds of the faith, so you may correct me authoritatively where I state it poorly, or approve what is right. Besides, it is relevant to show first why these customs came into vogue in the churches before expressing my opinion on this question, with God's grace. A lector will ask a blessing with the grace of humility, not from a priest but from one designated by the priest, saying: "Pray, Lord, a blessing." And the priest, responding similarly in humility, does not delegate this task of blessing to any of his ministers, nor does he presume to give the blessing himself, but asks God who is above all to grant a blessing.

3. *The origin of "The Lord be with you."*

(6) The expression "The Lord be with you" is the way the priest greets the people. For he prays that the Lord might be with them, as the Lord deigned to say through the prophet: "I will live in their midst."[5] And the Savior said to his disciples

---

[5] 1 Cor. 6:16.

and all the faithful: "Behold, I am with you."[6] This formula of greeting is not an arbitrary, modern, human invention, but it is obviously taken from ancient sacred literature. It can be found by diligence to be appropriate for both singular and plural usage: singular, when the angel says to the blessed mother of God, "Hail, full of grace, the Lord is with you,"[7] and likewise, when an angel says to Gideon, "The Lord is with you, strongest of men;"[8] plural, when Boaz greets his harvesters in the Book of Ruth, "The Lord be with you,"[9] and in Chronicles, when the prophet sent by God greets King Asa of Judah and his victorious army returning from battle, "The Lord be with you, for you were with the Lord."[10] When the Church receives the priest's greeting, she prays in returning the greeting that, as he had asked the Lord to be with them, so He might also be with him, saying "And with your spirit," meaning: May almighty God be with your soul that you may worthily pray God for our salvation. Note that she does not say "with you" but "with your spirit", reminding us that all ecclesial matters should be done in a spiritual way. And surely God prefers to be with a person's spirit, because in mind and spirit rational humanity is created in the image and likeness of God and so can receive divine grace and illumination.

(7) Similarly, the bishop's greeting for the people, "Peace be with you,"[11] is not the product of human invention,

---

6   Mt. 28:20.
7   Lk. 1:28.
8   Jdg. 6:12.
9   Ruth 2:4.
10   2 Chron. 15:2.
11   Lk. 24:36; Jn. 20:9, 21.

but it flows forth from the authority of Sacred Scripture. In the Old Testament, we find an angel saying to Daniel: "Fear not, man of desires, peace be with you, take courage and be strong."[12] In the New Testament, we read that the Lord almost always greeted His disciples by saying: "Peace be with you." And He recommended the same greeting to those same disciples: "When you first enter a house, greet it, saying: Peace be to this house."[13] So it is proper for the successors of the apostles—the heads of the churches—to use this form of greeting in the house of God, where all should be children of peace, that the greeting of peace resting upon them may be fruitful for both those greeting and those greeted.

4. *This phrase, just like the rest of Holy Scripture, must not be changed.*

(8) From the aforementioned it is clear that, just as God made known to us in the prophetical writings the modulation of the Psalms and the grace of the Gospels, so also the phrase "The Lord be with you" derives not from human invention, but from the authority of the Old and New Testaments. And so, just as nothing can be subtracted from or added to the authority of divine scriptures according to various circumstances, but all is according to Church tradition, so also this sacerdotal greeting does not change—sometimes used, sometimes omitted according to circumstances. Even if only one person is present, we do not change Church tradition.

---

[12] Dn. 10:19.
[13] Lk. 10:5; Mt. 10:12.

5. *Holy Church is one in many and whole in each.*

(9) The Church of Christ is united in all her parts by the bond of love, so that she is both one in many members and mystically whole in each member. And so we see that the entire universal Church is correctly called the one and only bride of Christ, while each chosen soul, by virtue of the sacramental mysteries, is considered fully the Church. Indeed, the whole Church was present to the prophetic nose of Isaac when he said to one of his sons: "See, how my son's odor is like the smell of a flowering field."[14] And that woman in debt who, at Elisha's order, poured out what oil she had like seed that reaped a good harvest overflowing her jars, surely prefigured the Church.

(10) If we diligently search the fields of Sacred Scripture, we find that a single man or woman frequently represents the Church. Although the Church seems multitudinous because of so many people, it is still one and simple in the mystery of the one faith and divine rebirth. Regardless that seven women took one husband, only one virgin was considered espoused to the celestial bridegroom.[15] The apostle said of her: "I betrothed you to one husband, so as to present you as a chaste virgin to Christ."[16]

(11) From all the aforementioned it is clear that, because the whole Church can be found in one individual person and the Church itself is called a virgin, Holy Church is both one in all its members and complete in each of them. It is truly simple among many through the unity of faith and multiple

---

[14] Gen. 27:27.
[15] Cf. Is. 4:1.
[16] 2 Cor. 11:2.

in each individual through the bond of love and various charismatic gifts, because all are from one and all are one.

6. *The implications of the unity of the Church.*

(12) Indeed, Holy Church is divided by the multiplicity of persons but fused into one by the flame of the Holy Spirit. So, even though she seems divided into parts through her physical state, the mystery of her intimate unity can in no way be disrupted vis-à-vis its integrity. "For God's love has been poured into our hearts by the Holy Spirit given us."[17] This Spirit, who indeed is undoubtedly one and multiple— one in the essence of His majesty and multiple in the variety of charisms—gives gifts to Holy Church, which He fills, so that she is both one in her entirety and whole in all her parts. Truth Himself pointed out the secret of this indivisible unity when He spoke of His disciples to His Father: "I pray not only for these, but also for those who will believe in me through their words, that they may all be one, Father, as you are in me and I in you, that they also be one in us, so the world may believe that you sent me. And I gave them the glory you gave me, that they may be one as we are one."[18]

(13) If those who believe in Christ are one, then wherever an individual member is present, the whole body is also there through the mystery of the sacrament. And whatever suffices for the whole somehow seems sufficient for each part, so it is not absurd for a single individual to say what the gathered Church says together, just as what one rightly utters can also be said by the many without fault. For when we are assembled

---

[17] Rm. 5:5.
[18] Jn. 17:20-22.

together, we rightly say: "Listen to me and answer me, Lord, for I am poor and needy; guard my soul, for I am holy."[19] Likewise, we do not improperly chant when alone: "Shout to God our helper; acclaim Jacob's God."[20] Nor are we wrong for many to say together: "I shall bless the Lord at all times, his praise always in my mouth."[21] And alone, we often say in the plural: "Magnify the Lord with me, and let us together exalt his name,"[22] and many other such sayings. Because it is clear that being solitary does not preclude plural usage, so also a multitude of the faithful does not cause discord by using the singular, because by virtue of the Holy Spirit who dwells in each person and fills all, both our solitude is plural and our multitude, singular.

7. If "The Lord be with you" cannot be said when alone, then many other phrases must also be left out.

(14) Now, therefore, let those who say: "Are we to ask a blessing of the stones or boards of the cell, or ask that the Lord be with them?" answer me why solitaries in their cells say: "Come, let us sing to the Lord?"[23] Tell me, brethren, please tell me (if I may ask, with your permission), when you are alone, whom do you exhort? Whom do you invite to the Night Office of divine praise when you say: "Come, let us sing to the Lord," or "Come, let us adore the Lord, King of the martyrs?" Such phrases are called invitatories, doubtless because, with them, one invites the faithful to

---

God's praises. However, if no one hears you at all, whom are you encouraging to sing to the Lord with your exhortations?

(15) Come, brethren, tell me whether you are not considering the mystery of the Church's unity, rather than the number of those physically present, when you say: "Let us all rise in the night and keep vigil," or, "Let us rise quickly after sleep's refreshment." Why do you not either silently omit, or do violence to, by singularizing them, all the hymns and prayers Church doctors composed in the plural form?

(16) When you come to the readings, moreover, if you think it wrong to ask a blessing when no one is present, why do you read the homilies of the fathers and the sermons of preachers in which, by reading them aloud, you seem to be speaking to the people and speaking all your words in the second person, as if to a crowd? And looking at the exact words of the homilies, to whom, please, do you say, "Listen, dearest brethren," and all the rest, although no brethren are there present? If you want to do violence to the style by changing them to suit your singular state, it is impossible. You would have to omit them and compose new ones. Besides, why would you say, "Let us pray," when you come to prayer, and no one is there with you? Whom do you invite to prayer's communion, when you see no one is there? And at the end of Divine Office, why do you add the customary "Let us bless the Lord," when no one is there to bless the Lord with you?

(17) You should think, therefore, about these things, as well as many others too numerous to count, and whether alone or with others, you should always observe the rule of Church tradition. For if the doctors of the Church had thought it useful, they would have given us one sequence for celebrating the Offices of the Church when alone and another

when with others. But they were content to compose only one, without distinction, and taught us to maintain that one method always the same. They saw in advance that whatever a single member of the Church might reverently offer in the divine services is also universally supported by the faith and devotion of all. For the spirit of the Church, by which it enlivens the body, is one, presided over by Christ as its head. The entire Church is composed of different members, but is doubtless one body founded on the firmness of one faith and permeated by the one strength of a life-giving Spirit. And so, the apostle says: "There is one body and one Spirit, just as you were called in the one hope of your vocation."[24] Therefore, it is fitting that whatever one of the faithful individually does in the holy Offices, the Church herself seems to do unanimously through the unity of faith and love of charity.

8. *The sacrifice of the altar is offered by both men and women.*

(18) For this reason, when we say at the celebration of Mass: "Remember, Lord, your servants and handmaids," we immediately add, "for whom we offer or who offer you this sacrifice of praise." In such expressions, we clearly mean that the sacrifice of praise is offered by all the faithful, not only men but also women, even if it seems offered in a special way only by the priest. Actually, what he does with his hands in offering to the Lord, the multitude of the faithful offers with its earnest devotion. That is clearly expressed when he says: "And so we beg you, Lord, please accept this offering of our service and that of your whole family." These words make it

---

[24] Eph. 4:4.

even clearer that the whole family of God offers in a general sense the sacrifice placed upon the altar by the priest. This unity of the Church is clearly affirmed by the apostle when he says: "Because there is one bread, we who are many are one body."[25] So strong is the unity of the Church in Christ, that throughout the whole world, there is the one bread of Christ's body and one chalice of His blood. For as the divinity of God's Word is one and fills the whole world, so too there is only one body of Christ, even though that body is consecrated in many places at different times. As the bread and blood[26] really change into the body of Christ, so also do all who worthily receive it in church undoubtedly become the one Body of Christ, as He Himself declares: "Whoever eats my flesh and drinks my blood remains in me, and I in him."[27]

(19) Now if we are all the one Body of Christ, even though we seem disjoined according to bodily appearances, yet we who remain in Him cannot be separated from one another spiritually. I do not see any harm in observing the common practice of the Church when we are alone, because by the mystery of our undivided unity we never withdraw from her. When I pronounce alone the customary words of the Church, I am showing I am one with her and, through the presence of the Spirit, truly abide in her. And if I am truly a member of the Church, I am properly fulfilling my role of universality.

---

[25] 1 Cor. 10:17.
[26] Wine—*vinum*—is meant instead of blood—*sanguis*.
[27] Jn. 6:57.

9. The proper function of the individual member is common to the whole body.

(20) Surely in the human body the eyes, tongue, feet, and hands each have their natural function. But the hands do not touch for their own sake, the feet do not walk, the tongue does not speak, and the eyes do not see for their own sake. Whatever an individual part does is done for the common good of all. And whatever by nature is assigned to each member can be considered as done by the whole body, so it is not wrong to say that the whole acts for its parts, and the part for the whole. This is why Paul's tongue could say: "I labor and am in chains for Christ's gospel,"[28] even if his tongue was not chained. He continues: "The Word of God is not bound."[29] And Peter ran to Christ's tomb with John, with only his feet doing the running. Stephen saw the heavens opened, with only his eyes doing the seeing. Isaac touched and felt his son Jacob, with only his hands doing the touching and feeling. So we see that whatever any member does is correctly said to be done by the body itself, and whatever the body does is accomplished by the consent and cooperation of all its parts.

10. The priest, who is a part of the body of the Church, speaks for the Church.

(21) Why wonder, then, if a priest, who is certainly part of the ecclesial body, should fulfill the role of both giving the greeting "The Lord be with you" and responding to the greeting "And with your spirit," and again, both ask

---

[28] 2 Tim. 2:9.
[29] Ibid.

and give a blessing when he is alone? For by the mystery of intimate unity, the whole Church is spiritually present where one person is, sharing in the same faith and fraternal love. Surely where there is the unity of faith, neither is solitude in one accepted nor is the schism of diversity among the many allowed. What harm is there in the same mouth pronouncing what normally different voices would alternate, as long as one faith animates them? The whole Church, as I have already said, is certainly one body, as the apostle testifies: "Just as a body comprising many parts remains one body, so it is with Christ. For we are all baptized into one Body in the one Spirit."[30] And again: "Christ's Body, that is, the Church."[31]

(22) If the whole Church, then, is the one Body of Christ, and we are members of the Church, what impedes any of us from using the words of the Church, our body, if we are really one with her? So if though many, we are all one in Christ, each of us possesses our wholeness in Him; and even though we seem distanced from the Church by our solitude, we are always very present through the inviolable mystery of unity. In this way, what belongs to all belongs to each. And what is singularly unique to each, in the common integrity of love and faith, is there for all. As the people correctly exclaim: "Have mercy on me, God, have mercy,"[32] and, "O God, come to my assistance; O Lord, hasten to help me."[33] Similarly, a single person can say: "May God show mercy and bless us."[34] Our holy fathers decreed that this bond and communion of

---

[30] Col. 1:24.

[31] 1 Cor. 12:12-13.

[32] Ps. 56:2.

[33] Ps. 69:2.

[34] Ps. 66:2.

Christ's faithful were so necessary that they inserted it in the symbol of catholic profession and instructed us to repeat it among the elementary articles of Christian faith. When we say, "I believe in the Holy Spirit and in Holy Church," we quickly add, "in the communion of saints," so when we witness our faith to God, we profess also the communion of the Church that is one with Him. This communion of saints in the unity of faith is such that, believing in the one God, believers are reborn in the one baptism, confirmed by the one Holy Spirit, and by the grace of adoption are admitted into the one eternal life.

(23) Just as in Greek man is called a "microcosm", i.e., a little world, because in essential physicality the human being consists in the four elements of which the whole world is made, so also each one of the faithful is a little Church, as it were, because, without violating the mystery of her inner unity, each person also receives all the sacraments of human redemption that God has given the universal Church. And so, if each person doubtlessly receives the sacraments common to the whole Church, why would one be prevented—when alone—from pronouncing the words common to the Church, since the sacraments are certainly more important than words?

11. The people of Israel built an immense altar in witness to their communion.

(24) Yet, if there is still some petty critic of my argumentation who says, "Whatever has been established as applying to the common assembly of the faithful should not be usurped by individuals," and requires reasons besides my words, we will give an example from the authoritative sacred writings.

For we know, from the Book of Joshua, that the Reubenites, Gadites, and half of the tribe of Manasseh left the Israelites at Shiloh so they could go to Gilead, their own territory, and built a huge altar in the land of Canaan. The people of Israel became quite agitated and took up weapons against them, because they had presumed to construct an altar other than the altar of the Lord. They responded that they had done so as security for the future, not to deviate from the Lord. They said: "In case your children might one day say to our children, 'Who is the Lord God of Israel to you? The Lord placed the Jordan River as a boundary between us and, therefore, you have no part in the Lord.' And for that reason your children might stop our children from fearing the Lord."[35]

(25) Should there be anyone who has not understood why I have recalled this historical point, I will explain briefly. Some of my simpler brethren, when in solitude, might be tempted to consider themselves in some way cut off from the fellowship of the faithful if they did not dare to use the customary words of the Church in their prayers. So they use the customary words of the Church to indicate they are still in the Church communion, and these same words that witness to the spiritual presence of the faithful serve to satisfy their wavering minds. Those tribes built the altar not to offer libations but to witness their union with the people of Israel, when they said, as though on behalf of their children: "Behold the altar of the Lord that our elders made, not for holocausts or other sacrifices, but as a witness between us and you."[36] They acted so to witness to their fellowship with

---

[35] Josh. 22:24-25.
[36] Josh. 22:28.

Israel, and we use these words as a sign of the real unity of the Church. They acted to avoid the scorn of their brothers, while we act to escape our nagging thoughts. They erected the likeness of an earthly altar, while we show the reality of a spiritual harmony. They did it as a witness for their children, and we to maintain the inviolable mystery of our new birth and fraternal communion.

12. Why the twice-married are barred from the priesthood, but not repentant fornicators.

(26) Some things that happen in the Church seem unnecessary to human reasoning, but if we look to the mystery of their inner power, we see they are divine. For does one not wonder why the canons proclaim that no one who has married twice can be promoted to the priesthood, while even a priest who has lapsed into fornication can be restored to his former office after performing penance? The apostolic teaching about fornication is clear: "Neither fornicators nor idolaters nor adulterers will inherit the Kingdom of God."[37] About those who remarry he continues: "A wife is bound by the law while her husband lives, but if he dies, she is free to marry whom she wishes, but in the Lord."[38] From both of these references, it is clear that those who remarry do not transgress God's law, while fornicators are condemned to be cut off from God's Kingdom by their carnal excess.

(27) So why are those who do not sin deprived of hope for the priesthood, while others whose sin excludes them from the Kingdom of God do not lose the Church's trust,

---

[37] 1 Cor. 6:9-10.
[38] 1 Cor. 7:39.

provided they do proper penance? Perhaps it is because second marriages, though not sinful, somehow affect the Church's mystery. For just as Christ who is the "high priest of all future good,"[39] and a true "priest according to the order of Melchisedech"[40]—that is, who has offered to God the Father the lamb of His own body on the Cross for the world's salvation—is husband only to one bride, the whole Church, surely a virgin because she preserves inviolate the faith's integrity, so also He demands that every priest be married only to one wife, so that he will reflect the image of the supreme bridegroom.

(28) Accordingly, regarding second marriages, there is no question of determining the degree of sin, rather one is concerned with the nature of the sacrament. So there is no punishment of sin in their rejection, but the Church safeguards the mystical nature of the true priesthood. For how could we consider a crime what apostolic teaching has allowed? The sacred canons themselves number those who condemn second marriages among the Novatian heretics. For us, however, to show we always preserve the mystery of the Church's unity, our liturgical usage is blameless, despite any unnecessary prolongation of words.

13. If "The Lord be with you" may be used between two, it may also be used when alone.

(29) And now, in all charity, I would ask my brethren: If two brothers are together, could one say, "The Lord be with you," to the other? If so, how can one speak to the other in the

---

[39] Heb. 9:11.
[40] Ps. 109:4.

plural form,[41] following Church custom but not the rules of literary discipline? According to grammatical art, one should address "The Lord be with you" to the other in the singular form. If it is not allowed to use the plural when speaking to one person, one should say, "The Lord be with you," in the singular form. But everyone familiar with the rule of order in the institutional Church knows how differently it works in reality. Certainly, neither the most blessed high priest of the Apostolic See when celebrating Mass privately, nor any prelate or Catholic priest anywhere, uses the singular form when addressing these words to another.

(30) If, then, it is the custom of the venerable priests to say "The Lord be with you" to one another in the plural, where it is neither inconsistent nor forbidden by Church order, why should one who is alone be impeded from doing so? As far as grammatical norms are concerned, such usage for one person is no less compatible than for two. Church custom has such authority that every rhetorical rule must humbly make way for it. In the Church we must be more concerned with the meaning than with the words themselves, and if the rule is set aside when there are only two persons, it should also be set aside when there is only one. If Church authority permits "The Lord be with you" to be said in the plural between two, it is not contrary to the same authority if one person alone does likewise.

(31) Finally, we can reflect similarly about the response, "And with your spirit," as well as about a lector asking and receiving a blessing when he is alone. For we are rightly concerned here not with the number of persons, but with the

---

[41] The phrase "the Lord be with you" employs a plural pronoun in Latin.

mystery of the Church's unity. In this matter unity does not exclude multiplicity and multiplicity does not violate unity, because one body is divided among many members, and out of various members one body is filled out. In the plurality of members, the body does not lose its integrity, nor is the multitude of members lost in the body's unity.

14. The people of Israel kept the rule of Church unity.

(32) No wonder we refer to Holy Church as multiple in unity and one in multiplicity, when we remember that the earthly Israel, related by birth, seems to have maintained this regulated unity among them! For it sent messengers to the king of Edom to say: "Thus says Israel your brother."[42] And again, when King Arad of the Canaanites was fighting Israel and defeated them, taking spoils, Scripture says Israel vowed to the Lord: "If you deliver this people into my hand, I will destroy their cities."[43] Again, it is clearly set out in the Book of Kings where, on David's return to his kingdom, the people of Israel said to the people of Judah: "I have ten shares in the king, I am firstborn and have more in David than you do. Why have you injured me? Why was I not told first, so I could return the king?"[44]

(33) This people originating from one stock, or rather conserving the worship of one God, could speak in the singular as though one person and so bear witness that, though many, they were one. Is it then any wonder that Holy Church—sanctified and guided by the one Spirit of God, filled with the mystery of one faith and one baptism,

---

[42] Num. 20:14.

[43] Num. 21:2.

[44] 2 Sam. 19:43.

and called to claim the same inheritance through the grace of adoption—should have such a communion among its members that one may use the words of all, and all may use the words of each? And so it often happens that, in celebrating the Divine Office, we sing in honor of one saint words belonging to the whole Church. This is clear if we diligently examine the hymns of the Blessed Mother of God and the other saints.

15. Some feasts are not celebrated on their proper day.

(34) The Church of Christ is an immovable pillar that received the keys to the Kingdom of Heaven and is not a slave to case and number, but ties together all modes of speech within her laws. She is not out to catch words, but souls. So she is not concerned with the presence of bodies or moments of time, but rather with devotion and the unity pertaining to souls. "For she judges all, but is judged by no one."[45] That is why we say on the most holy solemnity of Easter, "O God, who on this day overcame death and opened for us the entrance to eternity through your only-begotten Son," while we know full well, according to common calculations, that the Jewish Passover when the Lord died and rose occurred first, and we celebrate the paschal feast on the following Sunday. Similarly, we use "today" on the feast of the Lord's Ascension and on Pentecost, when these feasts are consequently reckoned by the date of Easter. The beheading of St. John the Baptist is also celebrated during August, when there is little doubt that Herod killed him during the time of the Lord's Passion.

(35) We can say the same for the feasts of St. James and

---

[45] 1 Cor. 2:15.

St. Peter's Chains. For it is written by the apostle in Acts: "When Herod beheaded James the brother of John and saw that it pleased the Jews, he also decided to arrest Peter."[46] Then he goes on, "This was the time of Unleavened Bread," and immediately adds, "He arrested and imprisoned him, placing four squads of four soldiers each to guard him, intending to produce him for the people after Passover."[47] It is patently clear that this all happened during one time of the year, while the feast commemorating the event was assigned another. As we know, these feasts are celebrated at the end of July and, no matter how thoroughly we search the entire Old Testament, we cannot find the Hebrews celebrating either Passover or Unleavened Bread at this time. Since those venerated ones could not be solemnly celebrated during Eastertide, the Church provided another time for their liturgical celebration.

(36) I have given this compendium of these sacred solemnities so it will be clear that holy Church is not constrained by laws of time, but controls the vicissitudes of time at her own pleasure. The Church does not serve the elements, but these elements instead subject themselves to her and obey her. So the teacher of the Gentiles says: "Everything is yours: Paul, Apollo, Cephas, the world, life, death, the present, and the future. All is yours, but you belong to Christ and Christ belongs to God."[48] And to show how much authority the Church has, he again writes to the Corinthians: "Do you not know that the saints will judge this world? And if this world is to be judged by you, how can you be unworthy to judge even

---

[46] Acts 12:2-3.
[47] Acts 12:4.
[48] 1 Cor. 3:22-23.

the smallest things? Do you not know that since we will judge angels, all the more should we judge everyday matters?"[49]

16. In the Church, one can supply the words of another.

(37) And so, to return to what we were saying above, why wonder if Holy Church, to whom God granted such power, changes at will the words so that either individuals may speak as many, or many speak as individuals? Who can object if what specifically applies to some is pronounced by others? Certainly we know that, when children are catechized, the priest asks: "What do you seek?" We know that it is not the child but another who replies, "Faith," etc.—all of which correctly apply to the child, while another replies instead of the child. Therefore, if one can speak for another in the very mystery of our rebirth, on which the origin of the salvation of all humanity is based, what impedes us when alone from using the ecclesiastical greetings or asking for blessings? That one can respond for another in the Church is not due to some modern recklessness, but comes down to us from apostolic authority. For Paul writes to the Corinthians: "If you bless by the spirit, who will make your meaning clear to the uninstructed?"[50]

(38) It can be added here that if somebody is afraid to say, "The Lord be with you," or to respond in the absence of other people, he must also be afraid to say, "Let us pray," and perhaps will say instead "Let me pray", so that he may not appear to be inviting the absent to pray. And if anyone thinks it a sacrilege to request or give a blessing when no one else is

---

[49] 1 Cor. 6:2-3.
[50] I Cor. 14:16.

there, he should also stop saying, "But you, Lord, have mercy on us," at the end of a reading and replace it with "Have mercy on me." But if this seems altogether silly and absurd, then one should not be afraid to utter the words of the Church when alone, since he considers himself not separated from her in mind and spirit. If he professes to be her spiritual member, he should not assert in words that he is physically divided from her. If he is truly one with the Church of Christ, he should confidently fulfill the office of her universality and work harder at preserving the strength of the Church's mystery than at attending to propriety of conversational usage.

17. Almost all liturgical usages have some mystical significance.

(39) As I said above, there is much in Church observance that seems frivolous and trivial when seen superficially, but that, considered more attentively, proves to be based on very important truth. To limit ourselves to just a few examples: Who would believe that there is anything admirable about the priest's vestments, unless he knows the symbolism involved? Yet, if gifted with spiritual knowledge, he will see why clerical sandals completely cover the soles of the feet, but only partially the tops of the feet. He will consider why the alb reaches to the ankles and why the amice is always made of linen. He will also consider the significance of the stole and cincture. He will understand why the dalmatic is cruciform, the chasuble is worn over the other vestments, and the maniple worn on the left side to clean away spiritual rather than physical moisture from the eyes and nose.

(40) He will also notice that the deacon, without a dalmatic, wears a chasuble when he reads, and that the

dalmatic is fringed on the left side. He will also not consider it an empty gesture to wear the pallium over the pontifical vestments, nor that in ancient times the high priest wore on his forehead, for ornamentation and glory, a golden strip inscribed with the Lord's name as a tetragrammaton: "Holy to the Lord." Though composed of just a few letters, it contained within itself the strength of great meaning. But why go on and on, when we see that whatever was performed during the divine services of both the Old and New Testaments was done almost entirely in mystical symbols and allegories? For what meaning have the entire composition of the tabernacle, the number of Levites, the priestly ceremonies, or the modern rites of Holy Church, unless one finds the virtue of their spiritual significance? Or again, mystery is concealed in the ministry because the hidden mystery of allegorical knowledge is contained in the exterior forms of worship.

18. A brief recapitulation.

(41) Let us briefly set forth again what I set out to explain here, so that all may be clear and understood, leaving aside what can better be obtained from erudite commentators. The vice of arrogance is familiar to some readers, particularly in one who is eloquent and whose unstoppable tongue runs through the open fields of Scripture, allowing the spirit of pride to enter the heart given over to public adulation. And so, while pointing others in the right direction, he goes astray into erroneous confusion. This is why we customarily tell readers in the refectory: "May God keep you from a spirit of pride." But so that humility might counteract any pride, the lector rightly asks for a blessing at the beginning of the reading, not from the priest, but from whomever the priest may command.

(42) The priest must give the liturgical greeting in the church to indicate he is at peace with all the faithful. For in the Gospel the Lord commands: "When you stand to pray, let go of whatever you have against anyone, so your Father in heaven can let go of your sins."[51] And again: "If you bring your gift to the altar and there remember that your brother has something against you, leave your gift at the altar and be reconciled with your brother, then return to your offering."[52] And so the priest, who shows in mutual greeting that he not only takes the Lord's precept to heart but also manifests it in external ritual, shows that he is one in fraternal charity with the assembly before he offers his sacrifice of prayer to God. Whether they are present or absent, with his spiritual eyes he looks upon all for whom he intends to pray as present, because he believes in their spiritual fellowship. He does not consider any with whom he joins himself in prayer to be absent. With the eyes of faith, he directs his greeting and receives a greeting from those whom he considers spiritually present. So, let no brother who lives alone in his cell fear using the common parlance of the Church. Even if he is physically separated from the assembly of the faithful, the unity of faith binds him with all in charity. Though others are not physically present, they are with him through the mystery of the Church's unity.

19. In praise of the eremitic life.

(43) But while I am on this topic, I want to say a few things about the merits of the solitary life, stating what I

---

[51] Mk. 11:25.
[52] Mt. 5:23-24.

think about the heights of this virtuous life by way of praise rather than debate. The solitary life[53] is a school of heavenly doctrine and the practice of the divine arts. God is present there, where one learns to what end life is moving, and attains knowledge of the highest truth. Indeed, the hermitage is a paradise of delights where the beauty of glowing colors or aromatic flowers emit the fragrant scents of virtues. There the roses are enflamed with the red fire of charity; there the lilies shine in snowy white chastity; there the violets of humility are content with lowly places and are never disturbed by the winds; there exudes the myrrh of perfect penance and the incense of incessant prayer arises.

(44) But why speak of each one separately, since all the blossoms of holy virtue glisten there in various colors. Because it is always green there, they bloom incomparably well. O hermitage, delight of holy souls and inexhaustible sweetness! You are the furnace of Babylon where, by their prayers, holy youths check the raging fires and extinguish the dense mass of flames around them with their burning faith, and their bonds are burned while their members do not feel the heat, because sins dissolve and the soul is moved to sing a hymn of divine praise, saying: "You have broken my chains, O Lord, and I will offer you a sacrifice of thanksgiving."[54] You are the kiln where the vessels of the supreme King are formed and gain a perpetual gloss with the hammer of penance and the file of salvific correction, whereby the rust of a neglected soul is consumed and the rough slag of sins falls away. "The kiln

---

[53] This final section of the letter is found separately in some manuscripts. Scholars find influences of Eucherius of Lyons' *In Praise of Solitude* and Jerome's letters in this paean of eremitism.

[54] Ps. 115:16-17.

tests the vessels of the potter, as the temptation of trial tests just men."[55]

(45) O cell, the storehouse of heavenly merchants, where the best of those goods can be found that gain us the land of the living! O happy transaction, where earthly goods are exchanged for heavenly ones. Happy the marketplace where passing things are exchanged for eternal ones, at which price even the little we have is enough, where a brief affliction of the flesh can buy a heavenly banquet, tears give way to eternal laughter, earthly possessions are stripped off, and we enter into our eternal inheritance. O cell, wonderful workshop of spiritual exercises where the human soul is surely restored to the image of its creator and returned to its original purity; where the unleavened sincerity of our defective nature is recovered. You grant that what now seems pallid from fasting will be fattened by God's grace. You allow the man of pure heart to see God, whereas before, wrapped in darkness, he did not even know himself. You bring man back to his origin and recall him from an exile of dejection into the heights of his former dignity. You help man to see from the heights of the mind that earthly things pass away, and that he himself is crossing over the stream of perishable things.

(46) O cell, tent of the holy army, battlefield of the triumphant host, God's camp, "tower of David built as a fortress with a thousand bucklers hanging—each the shield of the brave."[56] You are God's battlefield, the arena of spiritual combat, a sight for angels, and a wrestling match of strong combatants where spirit meets flesh and the strong is

---

[55] Cf. Sir. 27:5.
[56] Cant. 4:4.

overcome by weakness. You are a rampart for those running into the fray, a fortification for the strong, and a defense for fighters who do not know how to give up. Let the barbarity of the surrounding enemies rage. Let them come with their siege machine and hurl their missile weapons. Let the clash of swords thicken like a forest, dance beneath the victorious protection of their leader, and triumph already in the certain defeat of their enemies. To them it was said: "The Lord will fight for you, and you will be quiet."[57] And to each one: "Do not be afraid, for there are more with you than with them."[58] O hermitage, you are the death of the vices and surely the kindling and life of the virtues! The Law exalts you; the Prophets wonder at you; those who have attained the heights of perfection know your worth. Moreover, Moses was twice in debt to you for receiving the Decalogue; through you, Elias recognized the Lord's passage; and through you, Elisha received a double share of his master's spirit.

(47) What else should I say? See how the world's savior made His own herald a desert dweller at the beginning of humanity's salvation, so that in the dawn of the new age the morning star might break forth from you, and then would come the full sun to enlighten a darkened world with its bright splendor. You are that Jacob's ladder leading men to heaven, while bringing angels down to help humanity. You are the golden road leading men back to their homeland. You are the racecourse leading runners to the prize. O eremitical life, you are the bath of souls and the death of sin and the purgatory of filth.

---

[57] Ex. 14:14.
[58] 2 Kings 6:16.

You purify the secrets of the heart, wash away sinful squalor, and join souls to the brightness of angelic purity. In fact, the cell is the meeting-place between God and man, a place where the enfleshed meet heavenly spirits. For there the citizens of heaven join in human converse, where they speak not with bodily tongues but open up the secrets of their minds without noisy talk. The cell is an accomplice to the secret counsels that God holds with men.

(48) How beautiful it is to see a brother in his cell, chanting the night psalmody as though a guard before God's encampment. He contemplates the course of the stars in heaven while the Psalms course through his mouth. And as the stars rise and set before the day arrives with its vicissitudes, so also the Psalms rise on his lips as though in the East, and flow with the stars until they set. He performs his ministry as the stars perform their function: he reaches out in spirit toward the inaccessible light with his chanting, while each star, following upon another, restores light to his physical eyes. And while either moves toward its goal on its own path, the natural elements seem somehow subservient, in harmony with the servant of God. The cell is a witness to how much a heart burns with the love of God and seeks God's face with perfect devotion. The cell knows when the human mind is showered with the dew of heavenly grace and watered by the tears of compunction. Even if tears do not flow there from bodily eyes, heartfelt sorrow is not far from gaining the fruit of tears, because what is not gathered from the branch that is exteriorly shown is always present at the heart's center, vigorous with moisture. It is enough for the mind to be sorrowful, even if it cannot always weep. The cell is the workshop where precious stones are polished so they

might afterward be placed in the structure of the temple without any damage from hammer blows.

(49) O cell, you are like the Lord's tomb, as you welcome the dead in sin and revive them through the breath of God's Holy Spirit. You are the tomb separated from the turbid torments of this life, while you open the entrance to heavenly life. Those who escape the shipwreck of worldly life find in you a port of tranquility. The battle-wounded, escaping enemy hands consider you a space of powerful medicine. As soon as one enters under your shade with a perfect heart, every bruise of the wounded soul and, certainly, every wound of the inner man is cured. Jeremiah spoke of you when he said: "It is good to wait in silence for the Lord to save. It is good to carry the yoke from one's youth; he will sit in solitude and silence because he has raised himself above himself."[59] For one who lives in you lifts himself above himself, because the soul that hungers for God lifts itself above earthly matters and sustains itself in divine contemplation—separating itself from earthly cares and soaring into heavenly heights on the wings of desire. When gazing upon Him who is above all, man transcends himself, as well as the rest of this abject earthly valley.

(50) O cell, completely spiritual dwelling, you humble the proud, sober the gluttons, make the cruel kind, and make the hateful fervent in fraternal charity. You curb the idle tongue and bind lustful loins with a cincture of shining chastity. You move the light-minded to sobriety, jokers to cease their silliness, and chatterers to restrain themselves under a discipline of silence. You are the promoter of fasts and vigils, the guardian of patience, the teacher of the purest simplicity,

---

[59] Lam. 3:26-28.

ignorant of all fraud and duplicity. You help the restless bind themselves to Christ and the morally loose to restrain their depravity. You lift men to the heights of perfection and escort them to the summit of perfect holiness. You help a man to be smooth and well rounded, not lacking in manners. You also make a man a squared stone, ready to help build the walls of the heavenly Jerusalem—never unstable in habitual levity, but always persistently focused on the seriousness of holy religion. You help men pull back from themselves, and make vessels of vices blossom with virtues. "You are black but beautiful, like the tents of Kedar and the bedding of Solomon."[60] You are like the bath of shorn sheep, and the pools of Heshbon. "Your eyes are like the eyes of doves by streams of water, that are bathed in milk and rest near abundant waters."[61]

(51) You are the mirror of souls where the human spirit—reflecting itself perfectly—can acquire what it lacks, free itself from the superfluous, straighten what is crooked, and restructure what is misshapen. You are the bridal room where the dowry of the Holy Spirit is handed over, and the happy soul unites with its heavenly Spouse. The upright love you, and those who flee you are deprived of the light of truth and do not know where to step. "May my tongue cleave to the roof of my mouth, if I remember you not, if I do not count you the source of my joy."[62] Joining the same prophet, we can sing of you: "This is my rest forever; here will I live because I have chosen her."[63] "How beautiful you are, how pleasant, dearest

---

[60] Cant. 1:4.
[61] Cant. 5:12.
[62] Ps. 136:6.
[63] Ps. 131:14.

one, my delight."[64] Beneath the figure of Rachel, beauty
adorned your face, and Mary chose the better part that will
never be taken from her. You are a seedbed of spices, a garden
fountain, and a pomegranate. Though your skin tastes bitter
to those who do not know you, your great delight lies hidden
within for those who reach the center of your sweetness. O
hermitage, escape from the world's persecution, you are quiet
for those who labor, consolation for the sorrowful, respite
from the world's heat, renunciation of sin, and the freedom
of souls. David sought you when he suffered the world's evil
and endured the burden of a dark and fearful heart: "Look, I
have fled away and lived in the desert."[65]

(52) Why must I mention others? From the moment our
Savior deigned to visit you, He sanctified you by dwelling
in you at the beginning of His public life. For after bathing
in the baptismal waters in which He washed, the Spirit
immediately drove Him into the desert, as the evangelist
testifies: "He stayed in the desert forty days and forty nights,
tempted by Satan, and he was with wild beasts."[66] Let the
world recognize its debt to you, since it well knows whence it
received the Lord when He preached and performed miracles.
O hermitage, frightening dwelling-place of evil spirits, where
monks' cells rise like tents in a field, like the towers of Zion,
like the ramparts of Jerusalem against the face of Damascus
and the Assyrians. When various tasks are accomplished with
one spirit in these cells—one is singing Psalms, one is praying,
one is writing, and various labors are undertaken in other
cells—who cannot see how appropriate to the hermitage are

[64] Cant. 7:6.
[65] Cf. Ps. 55:7-8.
[66] Mk. 1:13.

God's words: "How beautiful are your tents, Jacob, and your camps, Israel, like valleys in the shade, like gardens near rivers, like tents the Lord pitched, and cedars beside the waters?"[67] What more can I say, O eremitical life, holy life, angelic life, blessed life, souls' garden, hall of celestial gems, and court of spiritual senators? Your fragrance surpasses all others; your taste is sweeter than honey to the enlightened heart. What can be further said is unequal to what you deserve because no earthly tongue can sufficiently express what the spirit senses invisibly in you, nor can any voice explain how tasty you are to the interior taste at the center of our being. Those who love you know you; those who delightfully recline in the arms of your love, sing your praises.

(53) For the rest, those who do not know themselves cannot know you. I myself am unable to fully sing your praise. But one thing I know for sure, O blessed life: I know for certain and say beyond all doubt that whoever perseveres in loving you dwells in you, and God dwells in him. The devil with all his temptations is subject to him and groans to see him on the way to that place whence he himself was ejected. The victor over devils becomes the companion of angels. The exile from earth becomes the inheritor of heaven. Whoever denies himself is Christ's follower. Because he now walks in His footsteps, he will surely be raised to the glory of His presence when his journey is done. And I confidently say it again: Whoever lives the solitary life unto death for the love of God, leaving his earthly dwelling, will come to the eternal dwelling in heaven, not made by hands.

---

[67] Num. 24:5-6.

20. *The disputation concludes by addressing the hermit Leo.*

(54) So, now, dearest father, carefully examine with the brethren all I have proposed to you, as I have told you what I think. I do not wish to usurp the role of the doctor teaching others, but have clearly set forth what I, in my ignorance, hold to be true. What I have put forth is for your study, not to assert my opinion. I do not offer it as a definitive statement, but as a debate, airing my reasons.

(55) Therefore, dear father, after you have read attentively all I have written down, obliterate with a sharp knife whatever falsity I have presumed to be true, but if any things are consonant with sound doctrine, confirm them strongly with your authority. I could have been briefer in what I have written, but it pleased me to prolong this occasion of speaking with your sweetness. For we gladly prolong the pounding of spices, especially when he whom we serve has a sweet fragrance.

(56) May almighty God instruct His servant Leo with a secret inspiration to shed three tears, or breathe three sighs, each day for poor me. Blessed be the Lord's name!

V

CONSTITUTIONS

Rudolf of Camaldoli

1. Address.

In the name of the holy and undivided Trinity. I, Rudolf, unworthy monk and priest, prior of the Hermitage of Camaldoli not through my own merits but through the grace of Him who created me, with the counsel of my religious whose names can be read at the end of this document, have briefly drafted this notification.

Always act with counsel, and you will not be sorry. We want all to know—not only the readers but also those who hear this text read—how the venerable Hermitage of Camaldoli was built, and to make known those rules that our holy fathers established here, observed perfectly, and transmitted to us who, though inferior to them, have kept them with God's help. With the unanimous consent of all the brethren, we promulgate them today, so that no one dare to change them over the passage of time, through physical weakness or any other motivation.

2. The origin of Camaldoli.

We announce to you then, dearest brethren, that the Hermitage of Camaldoli was built by our Holy Father Romuald the hermit, through the inspiration of the Holy Spirit and at the request of the Most Reverend Theodald, Bishop of Arezzo, along with a church consecrated by the same bishop under the patronage of the Holy Savior, in the year of His Incarnation 1027. He built five cells there, where the saint then established five confreres, that is, Peter, another Peter, Benedict, Giso and Teuzo. He chose Peter Dagnino, a prudent, devout man, and placed him over the other four brothers, and he gave them a rule of fasting, keeping silent, and staying in the cell. After that, he found a place further down called Fonte Buono, where he built a residence and established a monk with three lay brothers to welcome guests, receive them gently, and refresh them lovingly. So the Hermitage remained set apart and far from the world's noise, like an armed soldier on the battlefield who raises his shield against the enemy's arrows, or like the tabernacle and the altar covered with cloth to meet various needs. Then the saint ordered the same Peter whom he had established as prior to build a church at the hospice of Fonte Buono—a church that Peter later built with God's help and had consecrated by the bishop. What else? Blessed Romuald finally exhorted all with care, kissed them tearfully, and left for Val di Castro. There he again built another monastery and rendered his soul to the Lord. The Lord manifested various miracles through him both during this fragile life and after his death, not only in those places but also in many others, like those written in his *Life* by Peter Damian, bishop and cardinal of the Holy Roman Church.

3. The growth of Camaldoli, and its observances.

But let us return to the beginning. God, the source of all good, granted those five brothers and the lay brothers such humility, patience, fortitude, and constancy, that their reputation spread to many places. Hearing their names through many, numerous people began to come to them, not only from nearby but also from a distance, to enjoy their conversations that were sweet as honey. Some of them, coming not only from poor but also noble families, received the monastic habit from Prior Peter—touched by the breath of the Holy Spirit and disdaining within their hearts the desires of the world—and enriched the Hermitage with their inheritances as they began to live a penitential life. Others, flying on wings of contemplation for the love of their heavenly homeland—fixing their inner eyes on the divine light, and tasting in some measure the ineffable sweetness— enclosed themselves in solitary cells and decided to remain there until death, battling against the ancient enemy under the protection of God's grace. Others remained in their cells in silence, living more austerely, during both Lents. Still others did so for a hundred consecutive days, or for a year, struggling with various thoughts and shining always like the other brethren in charity, obedience, and the holy virtues, while strictly following the life and teaching of Venerable Romuald, and simultaneously respecting fervently the customs and traditions of the Hermitage. They always kept in mind the words of John the Evangelist, "cold or hot, but never lukewarm,"[1] and that other passage that reads: "To enter the hermitage is the summit of perfection, but not to live rightly in the hermitage is the summit of damnation." Indeed, we know well, brother, what harm you will suffer if you are called a hermit but do not live the life. If you really

---

[1] Cf Rev. 3:15.

want to be one, and not only to be called such, now is the time to fight, to resist, to triumph. Is it not so? Of course it is. But what shall we say to all that, dearest brethren? Shall we be complacent? Never. Instead, we must resist these and other harmful thoughts with a vigilant heart, as Solomon says: "Son, when entering God's service, stand firm in justice and fear, and prepare your soul for temptation."[2] And Blessed James says: "Blessed is the man who endures temptation, because after the trial he will receive the crown of eternal life."[3] And Blessed Paul adds: "The sufferings of this world are not comparable to the future glory that will be revealed in us."[4] Therefore, dearest ones, let us not be frightened over temporary fears, nor proud about fleeting honors, but doing good, let us flee the eternal torments of Hell and aspire to the eternal joys of Paradise. Let us raise our thoughts and turn our inner eye to these joys proceeding from the vision of God and angelic contemplation. As the prophet says, "let us raise our hearts and hands" and always confess from the depths of our souls with full heart and voice that we are sinners and penitents. Let us not be proud for any reason, even when we seem to have performed a virtuous action. Let us rather weep over our sins and those of others, because for this reason we left the world and have come to this place. With these and other similar thoughts, many secular men in our day have left the world behind and found refuge in this Hermitage, as though in a very secure port. Renouncing their own will, they have received the monastic habit and begun at once to climb toward the summit of the eremitical life. But as the

---

[2] Sir. 2:1.
[3] Jas. 1:12.
[4] Rm. 8:18.

saying goes, flying for the summit before assuring that the tree strikes root, some of them fell back quickly and gave up the ascent in dejection and pain.

For this reason, we gathered together and discussed among ourselves various proposals, until we decided what would seem useful for those brethren who wish to embrace our kind of life. In the hospice of Fonte Buono, some brothers perfectly trained in these instruments will observe the regular life according to the order of Blessed Benedict. Thus those who flee the world will be instructed by these masters in the life, order, and regular discipline—observing the fasts and other ascetical practices customary there even more rigidly than in the monasteries. Once instructed, they can then enter the Hermitage, with the Prior's permission, and live the life of the Hermitage. When they or other brothers at the Hermitage become sick or very weak, as often happens, they can be moved to the hospice of Fonte Buono and receive there with attentiveness the care necessary for their health. Cured of their sickness, they can return to the Hermitage. But if they die in the hospice, their bodies should be taken back to the Hermitage and be joyfully buried there where they served God with such fervor. The recluses, however, whether well or sick, should remain always in their cells and receive there everything necessary for physical health, as though they were Christ.

4. *The supremacy of the hermitage is essential for the Camaldolese.*

When the brethren who had meditated upon these ideas in their hearts had proposed them to all, the others approved them by common agreement, and we all confirmed them.

Then, lest the envier of every good—the ancient serpent who never tires of persecuting God's sheepfold—take the opportunity to sow discord among us, we decided with this document to reveal to your holiness how the Hermitage from its very onset was established by our fathers as lord and master over the hospice. All the brethren, monks and lay brothers of the hospice—past, present, and future—should obey its will and governance, and always obey all the Hermitage brethren. So all of us, in common accord and desire, in the name of Almighty God and all the saints, establish and inviolably confirm that this venerable and renowned Hermitage of Camaldoli, under the Holy Spirit's protection, shall remain always stable, unchangeable and free, as prescribed and established by the apostolic, regal, and episcopal privileges in our possession; and that it remain, as it has been, and is, the origin and head, lord and master of the hospice of Fonte Buono. All the monks and lay brothers who live there or will live there should be subject in body and heart, and always obey the brethren living at the Hermitage, so that those brethren, or rather fathers, may live serenely in peace, without any reason for murmuring, and observe with virile heart the usages and customs of the Hermitage, as we do today through God's grace. We need to avoid any situation where, due to the brethren living the rule at the hospice, or the order itself, or religion, or any monk or layman living there, the brethren at the Hermitage might suffer any lack or need regarding the food, clothing, and other material goods they are accustomed to have. They should not be annoyed, nor should they ever have to relax their practices and customs. So that the usages and practices of this Hermitage always remain unchangeable, with Christ's help, let us mention some of them here.

5. *The observance of Lent, and other customs concerning the liturgy and food.*

During the two Lents, it is customary for all the brethren living at the Hermitage to remain in their cells without interruption, except the two or four living near the church where they celebrate the Divine Office before quickly returning to their cells. All must abstain from cheese and eggs during the Lents, nor do they eat fish or drink wine, except on the feasts of St. Andrew, St. Benedict, St. Mary, Palm Sunday—should the Lord in any way provide such things on those days—and at the Lord's Supper. It is customary that on the day of the Lord's Supper, those who can do so leave their cells and gather together in the church to celebrate Matins and the Hours of the day and to wash the feet of as many poor men as there are monks, with each monk giving a poor man some money, a loaf of bread, and some wine. Those who do not leave the cell do likewise for the poor in their cells. It is also customary for the prior to wash the feet and offer the same service to as many poor men as there are deceased brethren at the Hermitage dating from the time he was elected by the brethren. This is done for the salvation of those deceased. The monks and lay brothers of the hospice do likewise. The prior also washes the feet of three poor men and gives them the aforementioned gifts as suffrages for each deceased bishop of this diocese.

But let us return to the point from which we have digressed a bit. During the two Lents, it is customary to fast on bread, water, and salt five days a week, while allowing a main course and water to those who wish it on Thursdays and Sundays. Some of the brethren take only bread and

water on these days as well, and some fast in this way during
Lent and Pentecost. During the rest of the year, outside
the two Lents, it is customary to stay in the cell, fasting
on bread, water, and salt, and keeping silence, on Monday,
Wednesday, Friday, and Saturday, except during the octaves
of Christmas, Easter, and Pentecost. If a feast with twelve
lessons falls on these days, as often happens, it is customary
to do this: if it falls on Monday, postpone it until Tuesday;
if on Wednesday, postpone it until Thursday; if on Friday,
postpone it until Saturday, while allowing a main course
and wine. We do this to respect the fast on Mondays,
Wednesdays, and Fridays. Otherwise, if the feast falls on
a Wednesday, and a main course and wine are served on
that day, fasting on bread and water is then performed on
the preceding Monday and Tuesday, until the vigil of the
feast. If the feast should fall on Friday, fasting on bread
and water occurs on Wednesday and Thursday. But if one
follows upon another, they are celebrated on those days.
The following feasts are never transferred: Holy Savior, the
four feasts of His Mother, St. Martin, all the Apostles, the
finding and exaltation of the Cross, St. John the Baptist,
St. Donatus, St. Lawrence, St. Michael, and All Saints—as
well as those falling during the two Lents, and during the
octaves of Christmas, Easter, and Pentecost. No octaves are
celebrated outside these three. During these three octaves
and on all Sundays outside the two Lents, as on feast days
with twelve lessons, all monks except the recluses must
gather in church for Matins and the Hours of the day—
chanting the Psalms in a clear voice to the end, diligently,
seriously, slowly, attentively, not in a hurried fashion, but
keeping them in mind and meditating, following the tones

and pauses, as the prophet says, "Sing artfully,"[5] and again, "I will sing with the spirit, I will sing with the mind."[6] No one is allowed to sing with a high voice or with sibilance—this is strictly forbidden—but a soft and moderate tone. For this reason, our fathers and we have had to send away some of the more obstinate and contentious brothers. Indeed, we are more suited to mourning than to singing. It is not customary for us to process on Sundays and feast days, or to bless the candle. In this Hermitage, it is customary to gather in chapter on Christmas, Easter, Ascension, Pentecost, and on three days following these solemnities—but for the Ascension, only on the day of the feast itself. There is chapter also on Sundays outside the two Lents and on the feasts of All Saints, St. Martin, St. Mary, Epiphany, the Purification of Our Lady, St. John the Baptist, the Apostles Peter and Paul, the Assumption of Mary, St. Michael, and Holy Savior. On these feasts, on every Tuesday and Thursday outside Lent, except when feasts are transferred as explained above, and every time a feast is celebrated with twelve lessons, we eat in common. After the common meal, we observe silence during the rest period and return at once to our cells, unless we are detained by obedience. On those ferial days when we are allowed to leave the cells and take two meals, it is customary to remain in the cell until the third hour, when we gather in church for Terce and celebrate Mass, and then return to the cell after dinner. When we have a common meal at None, we remain in the cell until then, leave for None and celebrate Mass, and then eat—unless we must go

---

[5] Ps. 46:8.
[6] 1 Cor. 14:15.

out for obedience's sake. It is not permitted to give or receive anything, or to speak with outsiders without the prior's permission. There are many other observances, too lengthy to list. It is customary in this Hermitage to cook two dishes of any vegetables and legumes, or also of fish and other foods permitted the monks. We never use lard, unless someone from the outside offers us something flavored with lard, but all of our dishes are flavored with oil year round. Bread and all the food necessary for meals are prepared with care at the hospice of Fonte Buono, and then brought here. Each brother has in his cell a scale with which he measures the three loaves of bread he receives every Sunday and Thursday, eggs, and other necessary items, as the *Eremitical Rule* clearly indicates to every prudent reader. But we need to note that one should not overlook the norms we have briefly recorded in this work, as when it is prescribed to eat in common on Saturday—something we never do here—or other norms that appear contrary to the customs of this Hermitage. As one can well see, our norms are particular, and more austere, and were observed in this Hermitage by holy men before that *Rule* was written. For the rest, whatever is in accordance with the observances of this Hermitage should be observed with Christ's help, without ever abandoning the holy customs of St. Romuald and our other fathers: how it teaches us how to abide in the cell and outside the cell, how to resist the vices and to acquire the virtues, and to maintain discretion in every situation.

6. *Although the customs of Camaldoli are past telling, they are sketched here as a safeguard.*

We call upon God present here as witness, dearest

brethren, that we write these customs for you not out of vainglory, but only for your instruction. Who could ever adequately describe all the holy works performed by the brethren of this Hermitage at all times, the disciplines, the many tears, the innumerable prostrations, the heartfelt sighs, the uninterrupted chanting of Psalms, the constant prayer, the vigils, the struggles with the devil, and the other virtuous deeds known only to God? Therefore, you must all take care that the holy customs not be corrupted by anyone, and those from the hospice should not keep back whatever is necessary. And so, we firmly prescribe and confirm that all the brethren resident at the hospice, monks and laymen, will obey your orders and furnish all your necessities as is customary, without changing anything in the customs of this Hermitage insofar as it depends upon them, so you here can continue to observe these holy traditions while they can remember to live according to the *Rule's* discipline. And you, brother, whoever you are, who find yourself down there for this reason, always take care not to find pleasure only in the common life and in the high-sounding chant or other pleasant exercises, so that you forget the eremitical life—the real reason you came here—and slowly come to despise the Hermitage. You must be there out of respect for the obedience placed on you by the prior.

7. *The hermitage must never become a cenobitical monastery or come under cenobitical governance.*

So that the customs and practices of this Hermitage and the Hermitage as such may endure, under the protection of the Holy Spirit, following the apostolic, regal, and episcopal privileges in our possession, in the name of the Almighty

God and Savior of the world to whom this Hermitage is consecrated, His Mother Mary ever virgin, St. Michael, St. Benedict, SS. Peter and Paul, and all the holy angels, archangels, apostles, martyrs, confessors, and virgins, and in our own name, we forbid that this holy place and venerable Hermitage ever be transformed into a monastery of cenobites. Likewise, we forbid all the brethren who will live here in God's service to change the practices, customs, and lifestyle of this Hermitage to anything other than the eremitical and solitary life lived now. We forbid that an abbot instead of a prior be placed as head of this Hermitage—something prohibited by episcopal privilege. In the same way, we forbid that an abbot or prior be appointed to the hospice and it be transformed into a monastery of cenobites. It should always remain the hospice of this Hermitage, at its service, as is inscribed on its altar's epigraph. No one may ever remove it from the service and governance of this Hermitage. Whoever is prior of this Hermitage will also be the prior of the hospice of Fonte Buono, as well as lord of all the monasteries, cells, hermitages, canonical churches, dependencies, and secular and spiritual properties belonging to this Hermitage, and any it might acquire or have received in the past. The prior will establish and place in these dependencies abbots, priors, and confreres according to the need, always preserving his lordship and authority.

8. *Those who might ever corrupt or destroy the hermitage are anathematized.*

If a prior of this Hermitage, or someone else of a diabolical nature, murderous and sacrilegious, should dare to transform this glorious Hermitage into a monastery of cenobites and uproot the customs of this place, its lifestyle and holy practices; or to establish here or in the hospice another abbot or prior different from the prior of this Hermitage and hospice; or to establish deans over the other brethren of the hospice, even on condition that he and all of them keep to what we have commanded above; or should he dare to destroy this holy Hermitage: in the name of Almighty God, who will disown him, the Blessed Virgin Mary, St. Michael, all the heavenly powers, Angels, Archangels, Virtues, Principalities, Powers, Dominations, Thrones, Cherubim, and Seraphim, patriarchs, prophets, apostles, martyrs, confessors, virgins, and all God's servants, and in our own name, we curse, excommunicate, and anathematize him forever with many lit candles. Amen.

These are the names of those with whose counsel we have established the aforementioned: Bishop Ranier of Florence, Bishop Maurice, Fr. Martin, another Fr. Martin, Fr. John, another Fr. John, and many other monks and laymen.

VI

BOOK OF THE EREMITICAL RULE

Rudolf of Camaldoli

Here begins the *Book of the Eremitical Rule*, published by Rudolf, the eminent doctor.

Prologue

Among the many forms of religious life by which we serve the one God, fight for the one King, and seek the one life, as the prophet says, "Only one thing have I asked of the Lord, only one thing do I seek: to live in the Lord's house all the days of my life,"[1] the solitary life holds the primacy. For this is the life that conquers the world, represses the flesh, vanquishes demons, cancels sins, holds vices in check, and exhausts the carnal desires that fight against the soul. This is the life that purifies the mind, illuminates the conscience, cleanses the intellect, gives birth to knowledge, refines the intelligence, follows God, speaks with angels, yearns for heavenly goods, meditates on eternal things—accumulating treasures in heaven where rust and moths cannot touch them, where thieves cannot break in and steal. This is the

---

[1] Ps. 26:4.

heavenly woman who, being sober, just, and devout in this world, sits as queen at the right hand of God. Clothed in gold, wrapped in a multicolored garment, robed with the sun of justice, she treads down the moon of worldly glory and savors the things above rather than those of earth. She suffers the pangs of birth because the fruit of holiness does not come to light without the labor of battle. And without the torment of temptation, the fruit of justice (that is, charity, joy, peace, patience, and other similar virtues) cannot come to birth. The dragon stands before the woman, hoping to devour the fruit of her womb, but the woman flees into the desert, where she is nourished for a time, and times, and half a time, until the end of the battle.[2] From this it appears most evident that there is no more secure refuge against the ambushes of the ancient serpent, and there is no more valid protection, after God and through God, than the defense of the solitary life. So many authoritative examples of this holiest life of battle exist that their number cannot be counted. We will choose some of these, advising the prudent reader to search out on his own the many we omit.

1. The Example of Moses

Moses first prefigured this life and realized it in practice. For when he had led the sheep into the inner desert, he saw the wonderful marvel of the burning bush that was not consumed. And you, whoever you are, who seek solitude and live a solitary life, when you have led the sheep of your simple thoughts and humble feelings into the intimacy of your devout purpose, you will see the bush of your humanity, that

---

[2]   Cf. Rev. 12:1-17.

previously only bore thorns and briars, become illumined by divine light, while you will be glorifying and bearing God in your heart and body. Indeed, this is the divine fire that does not burn but enlightens, does not consume but radiates, and bestows upon its faithful ones charismatic gifts. For, besides the allegorical meaning regarding the Immaculate Virgin, the unconsumed burning bush is human nature enkindled by the flame of divine love, intact and incorrupt. Afterwards, that same Moses set down the fundamentals for this life, having left the crowd in the plain and scaled the mountain where he lived alone, without any human assistance, and fasted forty days to deserve to receive God's law and to be glorified by His presence. With his example, he showed that whoever desires to attain the celestial vision and comply with the heavenly discipline must withdraw from human company and companionship, and mortify his earthly members with hard abstinence.

2. *The Example of David and Elijah*

When David, king and prophet, was fleeing Saul into the desert of Edom, he found a very secure refuge, of which he said: "Behold, I fled away and stayed in the desert, waiting for him who saved me from discouragement and the storm."[3] Elijah also found safety from wicked Queen Jezebel's persecution by hiding in the desert, where he was comforted by the food and words of angels. Strengthened by that food, he journeyed forty days and forty nights, until he reached Horeb, God's mountain, where he earned the respite of a vision of God. And you, too, if you want to escape the

---

[3] Cf. Ps. 55:7ff.

power of Saul or Jezebel, and not be dominated by any kind of injustice or governed by insolence, avarice, or pride, you must not only flee but also distance yourself from the world's seductions. You flee in action but distance yourself with the soul, flee with the body but distance yourself in desire. It costs more to remove yourself from the world with the heart than to separate from it in the body. To withdraw both belongs to the perfect. A soul that is delicate and inconstant in virtue must be distanced from the crowd, so that bad company and conversations will not corrupt good habits. For you will be holy with the holy, you will be innocent with the innocent, and you will be perverse with the perverse. You must flee to Horeb, God's mountain, that is, to the heights of sobriety, the peaks of abstinence, the mountain of drought: for such is Horeb's meaning. When the humors of pleasure have dried up in you, the enemy who lives in swamps can no longer stay inside you, as the Lord's prophet says: "You have dried up the rivers of Ethan,"[4] that is, you have forsaken the vices of pleasure. He seeks rest in arid and waterless places, but he will not find it. No adversity can touch you if you are not dominated by iniquity; no temptation of the devil can conquer you, if you are not subject to the pleasures of the flesh.

3. *The Example of the Prophet Elisha*

Elisha and the sons of the prophets were also eminent ancestors of this form of life. They were content with a few barley loaves and herbs, and one reads that they ate poisonous, bitter plants [*colloquintidas*] and drank the barren waters of

---

4   Cf. Ps. 74:15.

Jericho. To treat briefly the sacred meaning of this episode, we need to gather some salutary herbs from the garden of spiritual doctrine and to take up the examples of the saints in the discipline of the solitary life. We know we must avoid bitter plants and barren waters. There is no doubt that Solomon's polygamy, David's fall with Bathsheba, Samson's sin with Delilah, Judah's sin with Tamar, and other similar episodes in the Scriptures—understood literally—are very bitter plants and barren waters. No one gathers these examples or literally imitates these leaders, because they are barren and infertile, bitter and poisonous—to be kept at a distance from every form of Christian life, not only the eremitical life. Detraction, insults, reproaches, and quarreling are also bitter plants and barren waters that leave a bitter taste like wild gourds in the mouth of whoever tastes them. These and the preceding examples must be carefully avoided and rejected with full will. The virtues of the saints should be imitated, not their errors, and the ruin of those who precede should serve as a warning to whoever follows, because the error of another should warn you, not spur you on to imitation. But if it sometimes happens that we gather similar herbs and follow such example, their bitter taste should make us raise our voices to the heavenly Elisha who was a prophet powerful in word and deed before God and all the people, so he might treat the most bitter foods and barren waters in the pot of the eremitical life with the flour of His grace and the flavor of His wisdom. Also, the prior of the Hermitage, or another experienced one holding the place of Elisha, must heal the waters and sweeten the food by correcting excesses, adding salt or flour, that is, infusing correction and doctrine into the pot of the eremitical life—where one is meant to attain life, not find death. The Rechabites, recommended by Jeremiah as an admirable example for absolutely refusing wine and strong drink, also gave a glorious incentive to the eremitical life. We read that these, who had the desert for their homeland, suffered from the first effects of the Chaldean captivity, when they were forced to enter the city and endure the human throngs. For them, the city really was a prison, the desert a paradise, and abstinence the greatest delight. We have touched fleetingly upon these examples because we must hasten to turn to others. Now we have to touch briefly upon the notable examples in the New Testament.

4. *The Example of John the Baptist*

John the Baptist, exceptional martyr and lover of the desert [*heremique cultor*], wonderfully laid down the foundation for the solitary life in the New Testament. Already, at a tender age, he fled the company of city dwellers, sought out the desert, and lived as a solitary—preferring wild food, camel's hair and the rustic life to his father's wealth and worldly pleasures. Through these ways, he deserved to be preferred over others by the Lord.

5. *The Example of the Savior*

After him, or rather before him—later in time, but prior to him in importance—the Savior consecrated this form of life with His example. Indeed, led into the desert by the Spirit, He fasted for forty days, endured hunger, and underwent the temptations of the devil. He did this so that He might conquer the devil in the same manner in which the first Adam had been overcome by him. The manner of our salvation demanded that art should conquer art and wisdom overcome malice, not by virtue of power but by rational argument. Later, often ascending a mountain, sometimes alone and at other times together with a few disciples in prayer, He gave us a model of this form of life for imitation.

6. The Example of the Ancient Fathers

Who could adequately commend the ancient fathers who lived in the deserts of Egypt, the Thebaid, and Nitria, the Pauls, Antonies, Macariuses, Arseniuses, and so many others who lived the solitary life, shining like the luminous Pleiades and most brilliant stars? The more they withdrew from the world's allurements, the more they glowed with God's glory. These are they who went around covered in sheepskins and goatskins, poor, distressed, and afflicted. The world was not worthy of them. They wandered through the deserts, on the mountains, in caves, and in grottoes. They crucified their flesh with its vices and concupiscences.

7. The Example of the Philosophers

If we may look at an alien encampment, the sages of this world and secular philosophers should not be disdained, for they also embraced a life of retirement with great passion and cultivated it with wondrous constancy. For their philosophizing, they chose places like Elea, the Academy, and other villages desolated by plague, struck by lightning storms, bereft of human comfort, and very roughly situated. There, with less concern about the flesh and living constantly with the dread of death and in the midst of physical deprivation, they could better meditate on the hidden mysteries of wisdom. They saw the first step of philosophy in the consideration of death or the renunciation of pleasure, and the second step in constancy in suffering or the perfection of virtue. They despised allurements, trampled on riches, and fled the world to such a point that one of them threw all his gold into a well, saying: "Begone, despicable riches! Better that I drown you before you drown me." For they said that it was difficult to possess at the same time both money and wisdom. We read that one of them plucked out his eyes, so he would not see anything his soul might covet. O the sad state of today's monks and the wretched tepidity of the hermits in our own day! We are less fervent in seeking an eternal reward than those were who were on fire for nothing more than the integrity of this age and were bored with the world. Not yet instructed by doctrine, nor encouraged by examples, nor attracted by promises, they led so wonderful a life. But we, informed by innumerable testimonies, illuminated by the holy Gospel, and assured of heavenly reward, are more tepid than they. At the moment of our entrance into the Order, we are told about the hard and harsh [*dura et aspera*] requirements of the *Rule*, and we make profession, embracing everything voluntarily. But afterwards, as soon as something a bit harsh comes our way, we immediately refuse to obey, and soon we are seeking out places where there is an abundance of food, prepared fish, and clothing. For shame! We are not embarrassed to be more tepid than worldly people and infidels. It is no wonder that the children of this age are more prudent than the children of light toward their own kind, but that they are also more fervent amazes and deeply saddens us. From where, if I may ask, does this abuse arise? Do we really search for a homeland in exile and a sumptuous table in the desert? Do we learn concupiscence in the school of penance, or seek joys and pleasures in a dreadful and desolate solitude?

Shame on them, I dare to say, shame on the solitaries as well as on the cenobites and on all those bound by religious profession who are less aglow for the heavenly Kingdom than are secular people for an earthly one and worldly glory. Having digressed a bit about these matters, let us return to the principal object of our discourse.

8. *The Example of St. Benedict*

Blessed Benedict, the kind father of monks, also founded his religious institution on the eremitical life. Having a mature mind from the time of his early youth, he undertook the road of perfection not merely from his adolescence, but even from his infancy, after hearing the words: "It is good for a man to bear the yoke from his adolescence. He will sit as a solitary and remain in silence because he has raised himself above himself."[5] For he has raised up the summit of his mind above his bodily nature, and he has done more by being intent through devout zeal than he could have accomplished in virtue of his humanity. And although he had afterward marvelously established the cenobitical order, he continued to preserve warmly a place for his beloved solitude, to further form it, and to adorn it with virtues and signs.

9. *The Example of St. Romuald*

Blessed Romuald put behind him the pomp of worldly nobility, moved on to monastic discipline, then to pastoral teaching, and finally passed on to single combat and the hermit life. He built many places for the eremitical life, among which is the Hermitage of Camaldoli, constructed in a wonderful way.

---

[5]   Cf. Lam. 3:27-28.

10. How the Hermitage of Camaldoli Was Built

Having arrived in the territory of Arezzo and wanting to find a suitable place for his purpose, he met a man named Maldulus, who told him that he possessed a nicely positioned field in the Alps. While sleeping one time, he had dreamed like the prophet Jacob of a very high ladder reaching to heaven, on which were climbing a band dressed in shining white. When he heard this, as though illumined by a divine revelation, the man of God immediately went to the field, saw the place, built cells there, and, turning to the bishop of Arezzo, asked for and received his help for this work. Miracles occurred in that place too numerous to list, and our purpose here is not to recount miracles, but to assemble the rules of the solitary life.

11. Lenten Observance in This Place

It is time to relate the customs and norms of life for this place. From the beginning of the greater Lent until the feast of Easter, we observe an abstinence in this Hermitage of three days and of two days. Abstinence here means bread and water, with a bit of salt if desired, and nothing else, except the rare merciful concession of a bit of onion and fruit for the weaker and more delicate. Every Sunday and Thursday, the usual food is administered, with fruit and other products of the earth added. Wine is only allowed here during Lent on the first Sunday, the feast of *Laetare Ierusalem* Sunday, Palm Sunday, Holy Thursday, and the feasts of St. Mary, St. Benedict, and St. Gregory. Abstinence must be observed on Holy Saturday, the day of baptism, but the brethren may be allowed some biscuits and a moderate portion of wine to offset the fatigue from the ceremonies of Easter.

12. *The Observance of Paschaltide*

Not only is the abstinence relaxed during Easter week, but fasting is as well. Afterwards, until Pentecost, abstinence is observed three days a week, with a simple fast on Saturdays. On Rogation days, some observe the three-day abstinence, but common custom only requires a simple fast on Tuesday. The simple fast is also observed on the feast of St. Mark, due to the Gregorian litanies. On the Vigil of Pentecost, we do as already described for Holy Saturday. The same norms prescribed for the Easter feast must be observed for Pentecost, except that the fasts of the four times must be celebrated during this week with a simple fast, according to ecclesiastical ritual, while abstinence on Friday remains firm.

13. *Observance after Pentecost*

Afterwards, until the feast of St. John, abstinence is observed four days a week, with a simple fast on Tuesdays, and two (served) meals on Thursdays. From then until September fourteenth, we continue to observe abstinence on the same four days, while serving two meals on Tuesdays and Thursdays. On the feasts occurring from Easter until this time, both abstinence and fasting are relaxed. After September fourteenth, until the feast of St. Martin, we regularly observe a continual fast with abstinence four days a week. On feasts falling between the Christmas Octave and Lent, abstinence is dispensed, while the fast is observed.

14. *The Lent after the Feast of St. Martin*

From the feast of St. Martin until Christmas, we have a Lenten observance, as has already been outlined for the greater Lent. We serve wine moderately on the second Sunday, at the beginning of Advent, and on the feasts of St. Andrew, St. Nicholas, and St. Thomas. The same prescriptions for Holy Saturday must be observed on the Vigil of Christmas.

15. *The Observance of Christmas*

The fast is also relaxed on Christmas Day, but it remains unbroken during the Octave, while abstinence is relaxed. Afterward, until the Octave of Epiphany, a continuous fast and the abstinence of three days a week are observed, along with a simple fast on Saturday. From then until the beginning of Lent, we must observe four days of abstinence per week.

16. *Discretion in Abstinence on Saturday*

Abstinence on Saturday is observed with discretion, so it can be relaxed during the Octaves of saints celebrated here, during the three weeks each year when we practice bloodletting, for the arrival of an important guest, and when we work outside. On the Saturdays preceding the two Lents, abstinence is relaxed, while we remain enclosed in our cells.

17. *The Vigils of the Saints*

On the Vigils of the saints established by the Church, of Epiphany, and of SS. Philip and James, abstinence is observed in this Hermitage—though not in secular usage.

18. *Customs of the Divine Office*

Day or night, at the sound of the bell, all the brethren except the recluses and the infirm must gather quickly with great reverence for the Divine Office, to perform the work of God. In this Hermitage, we celebrate the solemnity of

Mass toward the third hour [9:00 a.m.], and rarely at other times.

19. The Custom of Chapter and Good Friday (Parasceve)

During the two Lents, the hermits usually do not gather in chapter except on Holy Thursday, which they observe according to the cenobitical custom, not only participating in chapter, but also in the Divine Office, a meal in common, and the washing of the feet. In the same way, they imitate the canonical or monastic order of the Divine Office on the next two days. On Holy Saturday and the Vigil of Christmas, solemn chapter is held. During other periods of the year, they gather in chapter every Sunday, beginning with an exhortation to the brethren before accusing one another in charity. Then after the communal confession, they receive blows of the rod on their bare flesh, not so much to torment the body—since they inflict more severe things upon themselves in the privacy of their cells—but to imitate the passion and humility of Christ, and to confuse him who is king over all the sons of pride. One time in the region of Etruria, a possessed man, who was tormented only on Sundays, was asked where he hid himself on the other days. He answered, "I live at the Hermitage of Camaldoli all week, but on Sunday the hermits drive me away with the disciplines that they spontaneously offer, intent on humility." Surely he is thrown down to the earth by that virtue that he himself disdained to observe in heaven. On the feasts of saints celebrated with greater solemnity, they gather in chapter on the preceding vigil, if falling on Sunday.

20. The Custom of Meals in Common

The brethren gather at table on all days with two meals or a simple fast, to nourish themselves both physically and spiritually, except during the two Lents. During these periods and on all days of abstinence, they eat their food in their cells—seated barefoot on the floor and reading some holy book—in order to receive food for the mind with their eyes, while savoring with their palate the refreshment of their body.

21. Silence

Silence must be observed here without exception during the two Lents and on all days of abstinence. On other days, the rule of silence is kept unbroken from Vespers until the end of Mass on the next day. It is also forbidden to speak when leaving from or returning to the cell. The rule of silence is kept inviolate at all times in the oratory and refectory.

22. Services Rendered by Those at Fonte Buono

After this brief preamble, let us turn to the services and acts of respect rendered to the hermits by those residing at Fonte Buono. Each week the brethren should receive from that place six loaves of unleavened bread each—three on Sunday and three on Thursday—according to the ancient custom regarding quality and quantity. If someone wishes leavened bread, this should never be denied him. The servers responsible must provide loaves that are not unbaked, or burnt, or too small. If this should happen, it is right that those responsible be reprimanded for their laziness or negligence, whether it is the cellarer or another.

23. The Use of Wine

We know that wine does not befit hermits, but due to the defects of our times and the weakness of human nature, they receive it rarely and moderately, so that those who cannot be abstemious and frugal, like John, may at least make a sober and moderate use of it, like Timothy. Because we know from experience that wine drunk rarely is harmful and detrimental if it is not pure and healthy, we firmly establish, as it was in ancient times, that only healthy wine of the best quality should be served. Let the responsible servers at vintage time reserve wine that is pure and not watered down in very clean vats for this purpose, to bring to the hermits on the prescribed days. Indeed, as on days of abstinence when they serve only pure water, so also they use only pure wine on days with common meals. If the wine is spoiled, sour, or musty, perhaps it can be given to others, while a better wine is found for the hermits.

24. The Use of Prepared Dishes

On days with meals, they should serve the brethren two good courses and, depending on the occasion, add a little fruit, onions, or chestnuts. The first course should consist of vegetables, while on Sundays and some solemn feast days, grain paste, locally called "grains" [*granellorum*], is used for the second course. On major feast days, namely the two days of Christmas and Easter, they have the custom of serving a course of spelt brought up from Fonte Buono. On the Thursdays of those two weeks, tarts or chestnut cakes should be brought to the Hermitage for supper; on other days with two meals or a simple fast, servings of chickpeas or broad beans should be offered to the brethren.

From May first until the feast of St. Martin, we have the custom of adding a course of curdled milk called "curds and whey" [*iuncata*] every Sunday, Thursday, and major solemnity. From the Easter Octave until the feast of St. Martin, they prepare the chestnut cakes and tarts at Fonte Buono every Sunday and serve them to the brethren at the Hermitage on alternating suppers. Every Thursday from the feast of St. John the Baptist until September fifteenth, the same supper of chestnut cakes is prepared.

25. Supper on Solemnities during Lent

On solemnities during either Lent, they bring fritters or pancakes to the Hermitage in place of those other courses. But after Epiphany, the cellarer of Fonte Buono brings to the cellarer of the Hermitage different kinds of cheese, so that a quarter cheese may be given to each brother every Tuesday and Thursday until Quinquagesima Sunday.

26. How They Sustain Themselves on Bloodletting Days

During times of bloodletting, that occur three times a year for all, we nourish ourselves on the three days reserved for bloodletting in this way: on the first day, a serving of spelt; on the second day, grains; on the third day, fritters— all in the morning. For supper: on the first day, soup; on the second day, vegetables; on the third day, a tart with pancakes and a half-loaf of bread for each brother. Regarding the regulation of the meals of those who do not undergo bloodletting, we do not establish anything, but leave each decision to the judgment of the administrator [*provisor*] of the Hermitage.

27. *The Distribution of Gifts and Offerings*

Before the solemnities of Easter and Christmas, they customarily purchase fish. If the Lord Prior is at the Hermitage or at Fonte Buono, the purchased fish is taken to the Hermitage and divided equally in his presence, reserving a tenth for the guests and for those on mission at the communities or at neighboring monasteries. But if the Prior is absent, the division is made the same way at the Hermitage. Edible gifts offered by devoted faithful or by brethren of the Congregation are also divided the same way. At Christmas and Easter, a bowl and spoon are brought to the Hermitage for each brother. On these feasts, it is customary to distribute two pounds of pepper—one for each feast. In summer, the sacristan of the Hermitage should receive from the chamberlain [*camerarius*] sixty pounds of wax, incense as needed, and oil that is usually needed each month, namely a small barrel. Each year they should be given three portions of lard for oiling their footwear, and as much leather as they need. During summer, they also receive thirty measures [*sextaria*] of broad beans. The stewards placed on our farms should be solicitous enough about the Hermitage to bring the usual offering at Christmas, Easter, and on other occasions. And they should bring the customary provisions of wood at opportune times.

28. *The Provision of Wood*

Wood should be furnished for each cell during the summer, according to ancient custom, so the brethren do not have to interrupt the savor of contemplation because of such needs. The ministers should not delay or be negligent in furnishing the other utensils for the cells: the bag of straw, the pillow, the iron tools, the towel, the lamps, the tallow, the cloth for drying the brethren's feet on Holy Thursday, etc.

29. Clothing

Clothes are prepared before the feast of St. Martin, so as not to disturb the necessary quiet of Lent. They are made so that they appear neither too shabby nor too beautiful, since excessive or affected filthiness is as displeasing as exquisite elegance. The former is hypocritical while the latter is vain. Those who wear delicate clothing live in kings' palaces, not in monasteries, while those who wear dirty clothes live in hypocrites' dwellings, not hermitages. We should be content with poverty and penury, but not appear horrid or squalid. So, we must buy the goatskins, leather footwear, mantles, tunics, and other clothing that can be gotten easily in this area. Regarding the quantity of clothing, the norms prescribed for cenobites are observed. Hair shirts are given to all those who request them, so that their usage is not imposed, but left to the capacity of each one. For there are many things that are not suited to all in the same way, since not everyone has the same capacity. It is not improper, in many cases, to treat with greater indulgence those who have come from a more delicate lifestyle, because sometimes those who do less in body produce more by their intention. It often happens that an offering that seems of little material value can have greater value because of the sentiment with which it is given. As the Savior testifies, the widow's gift of two small coins is preferable to all the other offerings given by the wealthy.

30. *Care of the Sick*

The care of the sick and the weak should be the greatest concern of the Prior, as well as those ministers delegated to this charge. When someone becomes sick at the Hermitage, the administrator [*provisor*] of the Hermitage who takes the place of the Prior, the sacristan, or the cellarer should quickly visit him, offering him the necessities for feeding the body and the spirit for eight days. If he has not healed within that time, he should be taken to Fonte Buono, where a good quantity of suitable food for the sick can be given him, as well as the other factors that can avail for his healing, until he might fully recover. Once he has recovered his physical strength, he should return at once to his customary way of life. But if he should die in that place, he should be brought up to the Hermitage for burial. For it is right that his tomb should be where he lived his holy solitude. If it is necessary to make some concession regarding food or clothing for the more delicate or weaker brethren, it should be done with wisdom and caution, so that merciful discretion shown the needy does not result in harmful laxity among the stronger ones. For the fragility of human nature tends easily to imitate laxity rather than follow the example of proper austerity. A particular or individual concession must not extend to a general rule for the others, so that indulgence toward one or a few does not engender the irregularity of many. Discretion is the nurse of virtues, not the mother of vices.

31. *Avoiding Greed and Wealth*

The Prior and his delegates provide necessities for the healthy and the sick so that no one becomes culpable for murmuring, detraction, or begging. For it was established in the past and is confirmed today by the Prior that none of the inhabitants of this Hermitage presume to ask anything from the guests or possess anything personally that is against the custom of the place and the Prior's permission. For if Ananias and Sapphira were condemned because they wanted to hold on to their goods, how much more damnable are those who seek others' things, accumulating through covetousness goods not their own, as if they were stacking up a pile of mud on their head? We read that the avarice of Gehazi was so accursed that he even transmitted leprosy to his descendants. And we ourselves have seen some hermits, who in every other way seemed praiseworthy, cast out for this fault. So it is customary in this place that the Prior inspects the cells, one by one, through loyal brethren, looking for personal property. Whatever is illicit or superfluous is taken away and an account rendered before all in chapter, shaming the guilty and severely punishing him, so that impunity in one does not incite others to sin. Indeed, a fault that remains unpunished invites new faults to be committed.

32. The Need for Occupation and Stability

Every brother should beware of staying in the cell without doing anything, because idleness is dangerous for the soul and provides an entrance for the enemy's temptations. "Always do something," says an authoritative voice, "so the devil will always find you busy," and discover no way to tempt you. Therefore, each one must apply himself diligently to prayer, reading, discipline, prostrations, or flagellation, so that the entire day and night seem brief and insufficient. Flee the vice of wandering and instability not only by avoiding wandering outside the cell like Dinah, Jacob's daughter, but also by remaining stable and fixed in the cell itself. For it is possible to run the risk of walking around all day in the very cell by some impulse of Vertumnus, the spirit of wandering.

33. *How Manual Labor Is Done*

On days of abstinence, stability should be observed continually, without disturbing the eremitical peace in any way with manual work. On Tuesday and Thursday during Lent, the brethren may perform activity outside the cell after Sext. Outside Lent, on those two days and on Saturday dispensed from abstinence, some manual work can also be done during set hours and in established places—after Sext during the winter, and after the midday rest period during the summer, from None until Vespers, except on feast days, when they should chiefly take time for prayer and quiet, according to the cenobitical custom.

34. *How and When They Go Out for External Work*

In this Hermitage, it is also established that no one presume to go out alone to collect wood or do other manual labor, but that three or more go together, with the Prior's permission or that of one who takes his place. Those who can and are assigned to cultivate the garden or gather hay should do so together—going, working, and returning while singing Psalms—doing all in common and modestly in the Lord's name. By doing so, they can silence the ignorance of the insolent, not giving them reason to find fault with God's servants.

35. *Psalmody*

During the Lents, each brother recites two Psalters with their relative additions every day. At other times during the year, he must recite a Psalter for the living and at least a third, if not a half or entire Psalter, for the deceased. At the passing of any brother of the Hermitage or Fonte Buono, each must recite thirty Psalters or offer thirty Masses. For the deceased brethren in other places of the Congregation, each recites three Psalters or offers three Masses. As far as prostrations, flagellations, blows with switches, and other similar practices are concerned, each must act according as his own capability allows, or utility suggests, or divine grace inspires. For in these matters a spontaneous offering is advised, not imposed as an obligation. In this area, each one must take the measure of his own strength, count the cost, and moderate his feelings, so as not to overreach himself through indiscretion or fall short through laziness. The breasts of our abilities and knowledge are squeezed in four ways: with strength and gentleness by the good; with violence and carelessness by the wicked—with strength, surely, through the rigor of justice, with gentleness through the tenderness of mercy, violently through indiscreet austerity, and carelessly through lazy laxity. Strength squeezes out the butter of holiness and gentleness, the milk of devotion, but violence produces the blood of intemperance and carelessness, the vice of lust.

36. *Perseverance in Remaining in the Cell*

The solitary strives to remain in the cell, always and continually, so that God's grace and assiduous abiding there can render the dwelling sweet to him. As the cell is a prison for the restless and unstable monk, discomforting him with the punishment of a life sentence, so the cell offers the quiet and persevering monk sweet refreshment and blissful silence, like a slice of Paradise. We know many who have so experienced the sweetness of the cell as to despise not only the riches of Croesus or the pleasures of Sardanapallus in comparison, but even power over the whole world. For amidst the aforementioned, they would feel suffocated as though among thorns and briars, brambles and buckthorns. But here, as if in the midst of exquisite delights, they taste how sweet the Lord is, saying: "How great is your goodness, Lord, which you reserve for those who fear you, which you prepare for those who hope in you; there you will protect them in your tabernacle from contentious tongues."[6] Leaving it for a brief time, one seeks out the cell with greater longing; but abandoning the cell for a long time, one often forgets it. And as the sea quickly casts up a corpse, so the hermitage quickly rejects, like a dead man, the monk estranged from the eremitical life.

37. *Avoiding Excessive Presence of People*

The cellarer and every solitary should be careful not to attract the presence of too many outsiders under the pretext of hospitality, almsgiving, or any other motive, disturbing the solitary quiet. This is not prescribed out of a lack of humanity, but to avoid disturbances. Indeed, the duty of hospitality must be observed in every way at Fonte Buono, where the leftovers collected at the Hermitage for the entire week are sent for the maintenance of the poor. For that place was especially built to

---

6   Cf. Ps. 31:19-20.

fulfill the duty of hospitality and, though it was later adapted to the cenobitical norm with the Congregation's growth, in no way should it neglect hospitality. Nothing is more pleasing to the brethren of the Hermitage and nothing more welcome among all the services rendered by the Hermitage than the reception of all guests, especially the poor and pilgrims, with all due honor, as the Apostle says: "Show hospitality, and do not forget to share your things with others and to do good. In this way, some have received angels into their homes and pleased them."[7] For Christ Himself is received in the poor, as He Himself maintained: "Whatever you have done to the least of mine, you have done to me."[8] So, the ministers with this charge should often gather to take stock of things and even seek out the Prior with modest suggestions, so that hospitality is not neglected. If it is sometimes neglected, it will be understandable that the brethren's anger will begin to become a bit enkindled and, despite their interior moderation, burst out exteriorly with a certain zealous indignation. As the prophet says: "Zeal for your house devours me,"[9] and, "Zeal for you consumes me."[10] Let the ministers there, like Martha, devote themselves to every service connected with good hospitality; let the brethren here, like Mary, sit at the Lord's feet by applying themselves to holy contemplation. There, let Leah bear the practical fruits of her fertility by the care of administration; here, let Rachel preserve her beautiful and luminous countenance by purity of intention.[11]

---

[7] Cf. Heb. 13:2.
[8] Mt. 25:40.
[9] Ps. 69:9.
[10] Cf. Ps. 119:139.
[11] Cf. Gen. 29:16f.

38. *The Mandrakes of Leah*

Rachel sometimes desires the mandrakes of Leah's son Ruben; that is, she yearns for the occupations of external services and devout fertility, interrupting a bit the application to contemplation. But she ought immediately to return to her commitment to contemplation. For a momentary intermission usually restores her for this principal service, but too long a pause makes for a cooling or forgetting of the pristine purity. We know that some desire with great ardor the mandrakes of temporal administration and would like to be involved with them always. Others abhor them, so that they will not even look at them. Both attitudes are reprehensible and blameworthy. The sweetness of contemplation must always be found in the will, while the occupations of administration—if ordered by the superior—will be undertaken when necessary. Mandrakes, that cure sterility, have human semblance, and produce fragrant fruits, symbolize rightly-ordered human services. Religious and contemplatives at times yearn for them blamelessly, as a means for their virtue and holiness to shine forth, or to bear fragrant fruits of integrity, and to receive good testimony from those outside.

39. *Virtues of Hermits: First of All, Humility*

Having said these things, we should add something about the virtues necessary for God's servants, especially solitaries. First comes humility, the root and guardian of all virtues. For as all vices sprout from the root of pride, so also the young shoots of all virtues spring from the origin of humility. Humility signifies the baseness of earth, and so the humble person is said to be like earth. Indeed, as earth is an element inferior to the others, but is the foundation and support of everything, so the humble person will consider himself inferior to all, even to those to whom he furnishes the means to subsist. The more often the earth is trod upon, the more fit it is found for walking; the more it is worked over with iron tools, the more abundantly fecund with fruits it becomes. Humility is also more fertile in tribulations, more glorious in disdain, more fruitful among reproaches and insults. It is the ladder of salvation for everyone, the gate of life, the beginning of holiness, and, above all, necessary for hermits because where the life is stricter, self-awareness must be all the humbler. The devil, king over the sons of pride, plots more against those whom he sees resisting him more, because his traps are choice and he believes that the Jordan—that is, the multitude of the saints—will flow into his mouth. He does not persecute his own soldiers, but concentrates on attacking those who have distanced themselves from him. Since he cannot knock down the solitaries with open vices, he tries to wound them insidiously with the arrows of pride. Indeed, pride, highborn and of heavenly origin, tempts more severely the exalted and the great. Is it any wonder that what cast down the angels in Heaven and man in Paradise is out to knock down the monks in a Hermitage? The ancient enemy is chiefly conquered on earth by that virtue that he disdained to observe in Heaven. Blessed Benedict distinguished twelve degrees of humility that we can summarize into six virtues. These can be summed up in the following verse, so as to impress them more steadfastly upon our memory: "The mind that meditates—silent, patient, devout—obeys with sobriety." [*Mens meditans tacite, patiens, pia, sobria obedit.*]

40. Obedience

To begin from what we just mentioned, obedience is the first and principal companion of humility, like the most salutary fruit or young shoot from the best root. Through it, we truly unite ourselves most closely to Him who humbled Himself, becoming obedient unto death. Since humility is an inclination of the soul and body to rightly bow before God and man, obedience is its first offspring, the humble observance of God's commands, or of those who rule in His stead. This virtue is necessary above all for solitaries because, as they live a harder life, so they must more fully observe obedience. For some refuse the yoke of obedience, with the excuse of leading a holier life. They consider themselves released from the law of obedience, because they see themselves as bound to the stricter practice of the eremitical life. But the observance of obedience must be even greater where the lifestyle is more fervent and austere. Obedience represses self-will, submits to the order of another for God's sake, conquers the enemy, opens Paradise, imitates the angels, and always joins one to God by an indivisible bond. This virtue is divided into three kinds: the necessary, the voluntary, and the delightful—the necessary in divine matters, the voluntary in adversities, and the delightful in prosperity. Indeed, it is necessary to obey when God commands something, because one must obey God rather than men. Whenever things hard or humiliating are prescribed for us in God's name, even if they seem impossible, we must submit to them willingly and not obstinately refuse them. However, if you quickly and voluntarily accept to obey something pleasurable and honorable, you are obeying your fancy rather than the authority of another. But if you obey against your will and as though constrained to do so, your obedience proves to be not delightful, but almost necessary.

41. Sobriety

Sobriety follows this virtue because, as you repress your own will with the latter, you strive to slay the flesh and all its vices with the former. And so sobriety is the moderation of the soul that represses, with just discretion, the desires of the flesh and the other vices. The Apostle's words—"not to be more wise than is fitting, but to be soberly wise"[12]—should refer to every activity: eating, fasting, waking, sleeping, standing still, walking, talking, being silent, and other similar actions that must be performed with moderation and sobriety. We must treat our flesh soberly in such a way as to nourish a helper, giving it its due, and not destroying a servant by withholding what is necessary, or fostering an enemy by conceding what is superfluous. We must extinguish the concupiscence of the flesh, not nature. When Abraham was ready to immolate his son, he was commanded by the Lord to let the child live, and he killed as a substitute a ram that had entangled its horns among briars. So also you must learn to immolate in your heart and body not your natural feelings, but thorny and bestial obstinacy, destroying the desires of the flesh that militate against the soul, not the sensible members that serve the soul. You must live in this age soberly, justly, and piously, so as to know how to provide for yourself in sobriety, to come to the help of your neighbor in justice, and to serve God in piety.

---

[12] Cf. Rm. 12:3.

42. *Piety*

Piety is also extremely necessary for solitaries, so that they may learn to be more human, kind, merciful, and meek. Piety is the kind disposition of heart toward the infirmity of others, to whom one bends with humanity and mercy. For solitaries, under the pretext of eremitical severity, have the habit of appearing too austere and harsh toward others, as if they were not like other people, despising their various brothers with a Pharisaic eye, considering them publicans. This does not derive from the virtue of piety or the spirit of meekness, but from the puffing up of pride. So you who want to be numbered among the holy and devout hermits, seek not to despise proudly those found in sin, but to correct them with a spirit of gentleness, considering yourself lest you be tempted. Do not smash the ships of Tarshish with a furious wind, or rashly crush the pregnant women of Gilead beneath iron wagons. Instead, you must strike dill or cumin with the rod, not with a stick or wagon; that is, you must restrain the little ones and sinners with meek and kind correction, not with immoderate rebukes.

43. *Patience*

One can prove how useful patience is to hermits from the fact that every virtue is a widow if it is not reinforced by patience. But surely, not all patience is commendable, for there is patience of worldly favor, and of a resentful grudge, and of devout intention. The Apostle says of the patience seeking favor: "You who are wise suffer fools gladly."[13] From what follows, we understand he is speaking ironically. One

---

[13] 2 Cor. 11:19.

uses this kind of patience who sees his own brother overtaken by some sin and accompanies him with flattery rather than correction, as if trying to push further into him the arrow wounding him. Of resentful patience, it is said: "To tolerate with hatred is not the virtue of meekness, but a veil for rage." For the malicious tolerate offenses for a little while, but watch all the while for the day of revenge. About the third type of patience, the Savior Himself says: "By your patience you will gain possession of your souls."[14] For true patience is a humble frame of mind that bears offenses and annoyances with equanimity. We read of it in the book of Maccabees: "The sun shone on the golden shields, and from them the mountains gleamed."[15] As the shield is held on the left side to defend the entire body, patience is necessary in adversity. The golden shield, then, symbolizes splendid and sincere patience maintained for love of the heavenly reward that Christ, the sun of justice, illumines in truth. The other types of patience are not golden shields, but iron and wood, and cannot be illuminated by the light of truth, but are darkened by the gloomy cloud of error.

44. Silence and Meditation

Finally, there follows silent meditation, in which the rule of silence and the vigilant practice of meditation are inseparably united. Neither alone is enough for salvation. Silence without meditation is dead, as though a man were buried alive. Meditation without silence is ineffectual, like the unearthing of a man enclosed in a tomb. United together spiritually, they make for great quiet of soul and perfect

---

[14] Lk. 21:19.
[15] Cf. 1 Macc. 6:39.

contemplation. There are three kinds of silence or quiet: of action, of the mouth, and of the heart. Isaiah says of the first kind: "Cease doing evil."[16] David says of the second kind: "Repent on your beds of what you say in your hearts,"[17] so as to correct evil thoughts by silent compunction. The same prophet says of the third kind: "I have placed a guard on my mouth and a door on my lips, so not to sin with my tongue."[18] It is not enough to abstain from sinful words in the mouth, if you do not keep silent from evil deeds in the body and wicked thoughts in the mind. What good is it to keep quiet with the tongue, if one's life or conscience is in a tempest? What good is there in keeping silence with the mouth and having a tumult of vices in actions or in the mind? The house of God rises in sacred silence, and the temple that will not collapse is built up by keeping silent. They heard neither hammer nor axe in Solomon's temple, for in the temple of a quiet and peaceful soul, the hammer of demonic temptation or the axe of worldly persecution cannot prevail. "Misfortune will not strike you, nor will any scourge come near your tents; you will walk upon the asp and the basilisk, and you will crush the lion and the dragon,"[19] for you will overcome all the ruses of the evil tempter, remaining quiet and humble, and not fearing the power of the flesh. For the waylayer does not gain mastery where the heavenly dweller rests. "Upon whom will my spirit rest, if not on the one who is humble, and quiet, and who trembles at my words?"[20] "The ocean says, 'He is not within

---

[16] Cf. Is. 1:16.
[17] Cf. Ps. 4:4.
[18] Cf. Ps. 39:1.
[19] Ps. 91:10,13.
[20] Cf. Is. 66:2.

me'; the abyss answers, 'Nor is he with me.' "[21] God does not dwell in the land of luxurious living, because He does not abide in the tumult of the heart, duplicity of the mind, or the pleasures of the flesh, but He has made His dwelling in peace, and His habitation in Zion. Wisdom resides in the silent soul, dedicated to quiet and meditation.

45. *The Entreaty of the Quiet*

"I adjure you, by the gazelles and deer of the fields, do not wake my beloved until she wishes."[22] This entreaty is as glorious in its spiritual meaning as it is absurd in its literal sense. It is a fruit with a coarse peel, but the sweetest pulp. The gazelles are naturally gifted in their agile running, have sharp eyesight, and prefer the food on the heights. Deer are just as fleet and have extraordinary gifts: killing serpents, bearing one another's burdens, and neutralizing deadly poison by a draught of water. The two orders of blessed spirits—angelic and human—are represented in these two kinds of animals. For they are so swift that, without difficulty or delay, they get past obstacles; they are so keen that they see God; and they are so set on eating heavenly food that they taste and see that God is sweet. They scatter the hellish serpents, help others in need, and expel the poison of vices with the saving water of wisdom. Any wonder, then, if the holy and quiet soul of a contemplative does not want to be deprived of their sight and enjoys their companionship? It is right that he entreats us with the authority of those whose company he loves, whose nature he imitates, whose grace he contemplates, and whose

---

[21] Job 28:14.
[22] Cant. 2:7.

sweetness he tastes—wanting to rest in their meditation rather than to dwell in the tents of sinners. There are three kinds of meditation: one may search into the lamentations, the canticle, and the woes. The laments of penance come through the recollection of sins, the canticle of the heavenly fatherland through the contemplation of its felicity, and the woes of Gehenna through the consideration of its torments. And so, while pondering both good and evil matters, things both pleasant and harsh, one aspires to flee the crooked and the bitter and to cling always to the pleasant and the sweet.

46. *The Meaning of the Seven Trees*

The list of the seven virtues includes humility, their root, and is symbolized by the seven trees planted by God in the desert. "I will plant in the desert," he says, "the cedar, the acacia, the myrtle, the olive, the fir, the elm, and the box tree."[23] So, if you wish these trees in abundance, or to be numbered among them, whoever you are, you must live quietly in solitude. For there, you can possess the cedar of Lebanon or become a cedar yourself: a tree of noble fruit, incorruptible wood, and pleasant perfume, fertile in works, eminent in chastity, most fragrant in opinion and fame, and flourishing with wonderful gladness like a cedar exalted in Lebanon. You could also become a useful thorn, that is, healthy and pungent, suitable for making hedges. You could be called builder of hedges, turning away the paths of iniquity, knowing how to puncture and correct your vices and those of others, not caressing or flattering them. For the words of the wise are like thorns or, better still, like spurs and deeply fixed nails. They enclose the Lord's vineyard: "Your ways are

---

[23] Is. 41:9.

surrounded by thorny hedges lest those passing by harvest your vine, or the wild boar from the woods destroy it, or a wild beast lay it waste."[24] You could also become a myrtle tree, a plant with sedative and sobering properties, doing everything with moderation and discretion, appearing neither too just nor too remiss. For there is more grace in the just mean, and between excess [*pleonexia*] and defect [*mionexia*], that is, in the decorous middle of things where, as Severinus says, every good is located. You could also deserve to be an olive tree, symbolic of piety and peace, joy and consolation, anointing your face and those of others with your oil—consoling the mourners of Zion with your works of piety. Like a fruitful olive tree in the house of the Lord, you will produce sweet perfume, like olive shoots around God's table. You could also be a fir tree, lofty in height, densely shady and luxuriantly green, striving to meditate on sublime truths, contemplate heavenly realities, and knock at the doors of the highest dwelling of the divine majesty—understanding things above rather than earthly things. And do not disdain being an elm tree, not distinguished because it is tall or rich with fruit, but always useful as a support. It does not bear fruit, but sustains the vine laden with fruit. This plant can be compared with our Gabaonites, the rustic woodcutters who carry water and perform various useful manual labors, so fulfilling what is written: "Carry one another's burdens, and so fulfill Christ's law."[25] Though they do not come from Israel's stock, they share in their reward by obeying and serving the Israelites. Finally, do not hesitate to be a box tree, a plant that does not

---

[24] Cf. Ps. 80:12-13.
[25] Gal. 6:2.

grow very high, but easily maintains its greenness. Thus you will learn not to want to taste high things, but to remain bound to the earth by fear and humility and, by remaining on earth, to stay forever green. The prophet says: "Do not lift your horns on high,"[26] and "Whoever exalts himself will be humbled."[27] These two shrubs—the elm and the box trees—are without fruit, but are not useless. Indeed, goatskin cloth and red-tinted hides appear humble and ugly, but with their ugliness they watch over and protect precious things within. No one should disdain or despise the simplicity of those who give themselves to external activities and works of the ministry, because often things that appear homely on the outside are more beautiful within. Be, therefore, a cedar through nobility of sincerity and holiness, a thorn through the piercing of correction and penance, a myrtle through the discretion of sobriety and temperance, an olive through the good cheer of peace and mercy, a fir through the loftiness of meditation and wisdom, an elm through the work of support and patience, and a box tree through the model of humility and perseverance.

47. The Perfection of Charity

When you come to possess these trees of the solitary life—these virtues of this withdrawn way of life—you will arrive at the perfection of charity that, by casting out fear of punishment, sweetens all things and makes everything shine. What had previously seemed strict and stifling, hard and unpleasant, you will now experience as spacious and ample,

---

[26] Ps. 75:5.
[27] Lk. 14:11.

pleasant and mild, as the prophet says: "You have placed my feet in a spacious place,"[28] and, "You have leveled my steps and they did not falter,"[29] and, "I have run the way of your commands, when you enlarged my heart."[30] The yoke of this virtue is sweet; its burden is light. O happy joy, O glorious sweetness, that only charity can perceive and only the perfect can experience, tasting and seeing how sweet the Lord is! Woe to me, unfortunate man as I am, and to all those like me who still have not arrived at these virtues. I am not talking about the perfection of love, but just the beginning of fear. O that someone would give me the wings of a dove, so I could fly and be at rest in holy solitude and be worthy to grasp a twig of the aforementioned trees, the virtues! There is only one thing in which I have confidence and have presumed to hope: that my soul has felt the desire to attain these justifying deeds, so that what I lack effectively I do not lack affectively. I presume this and dare to hope, not through my own merits, that are nothing, but through the mercy of God, who exceeds the merits and prayers of the supplicant and bestows His gifts on the lover rather than on the worker. Be careful, whoever you are, be careful, because the good you seem to do may be in vain. But it cannot be that I would love your actions in vain.

48. Life, Teaching, and Virtues of the Hermitage's Prior

Now is the time to describe the one with whose governance and doctrine all the aforementioned can be observed efficaciously. We speak about these matters toward the end, that they may remain more deeply impressed on your

---

[28] Ps. 31:8.
[29] Ps. 18:36.
[30] Ps. 119:32.

memory. It is right that you find his model after instruction in the rule—he who must first learn to observe the rule, and then teach it while observing it. The master of the order cannot be one who has not first been a disciple of the regular life. The Prior must be elected by the brethren of the Hermitage, some representatives of Fonte Buono, and numerous other members of the Congregation gathered into council. He should be one of the brethren of the Hermitage, if a suitable one can be found there, or chosen from among the other members of the Congregation—one who has learned the eremitical life with study and experience, who is commendable both for his knowledge and his manner of life.

49. How the Prior Should Preside

Once elected, he must remember he has been called to service, not dominance, to labor, not pleasure, because he will be among the hermits as one of them. To the good and the modest, he should show himself an equal, and to the unruly, the proud, and the rebellious, he must know that he is a prelate. God did not create man to rule over men, but over the birds of the sky, the beasts of the earth and the fish in the sea, that is, over the proud, the greedy, and the curious, who are governed by the concupiscence of the flesh and of the eyes, as well as by the pomp of life. Nature begot us all as equals; sin has set some over others. Where he sees vice, let the Prior exercise his role as prelate, reproving and rebuking with all patience and doctrine. Where he recognizes virtue, he should fulfill his role of minister, entreating and cooperating in all humility and knowledge. To the former he shows severity and rigor, so that an excessive humility does not damage the authority of rule; to the latter he acts with meekness and cheerfulness, striving to make himself their example in the Lord, so that they can see in his conduct and actions what to do and what to relinquish. The doctrine and life of prelates is like a kind of inscription and bas-relief before the eyes of their subjects, where they can read or attentively consider a model for their behavior. Thus, they say of the chief priest that in the cassock he wore, the whole world was represented, and in the four rows of precious stones were sculpted the great deeds of the ancestors.

50. The Cassock

The cassock represents consummate justice and the perfection of holiness, as the prophet says: "Your priests clothe themselves in justice."[31] And the Church bears witness: "He has clothed me with a garment of salvation and surrounded me with a mantle of justice."[32] The garment is called "*poderis*" because it reaches to the feet, that is, it lasts a lifetime. "Be," he says, "faithful until death, and I will give you the crown of life,"[33] and, "Whoever perseveres to the end will be saved."[34] The circle of the world is represented in this garment, so as to indicate there the perfect circle of the virtues. For the world fulfills an entire revolution, returning to its point of departure. No order is stable where the beginning does not rejoin the end, rendering stable its turning. Therefore, the earth's circle is rightly achieved when the end of our life is recalled to its beginning, namely Christ, so that our every virtue and action always begins from Him and ends in Him.

---

[31] Ps. 132:9.
[32] Is. 61:10.
[33] Rev. 2:10.
[34] Mt. 24:13.

51. The Great Deeds of the Ancestors

The great deeds of the ancestors sculpted into this garment are the virtues and works of the ancient fathers, namely: Abel's innocence, Enoch's holiness, Noah's longanimity, Melchisedech's sacrifice, Abraham's faith, Isaac's piety, Jacob's prudence, Joseph's modesty, Moses' meekness, David's penitence, Phineas' zeal, Joshua's constancy, Elijah's abstinence, and Eliseus' sobriety. Coming to more recent exemplars, we also find sculpted: John's austerity, Peter's charity, Paul's severity, Andrew's fortitude, John's virginity, Benedict's sincerity, and the glorious justice and temperance of Antony, Macarius, Arsenius, Eulalius, and the other saints whose virtues are worthy of imitation by all, but especially by hermits. The Prior of the Hermitage must demonstrate to his disciples these marvels of the saints and great deeds of the ancestors not only as written through his assiduous good works, but also as sculpted through the expression of his holiness, intimating them with his discipline and molding them with his conduct.

52. The Variety of Precious Stones

These virtues are sculpted in four rows of precious stones—each row containing three stones. In the first row we find the green of jasper for the vigor of faith, the heavenly hue of sapphire for the loftiness of hope, and the brilliance of chalcedony for the light of charity—shining pallid because today's charity is pallid and far from perfect. But in the future it will no longer appear like a pale lamp, but like the sun shining in all its splendor. In the second row we find the brightness of the greenest emerald for the beauty of contemplation, the whiteness of sardonyx for the glory of virginity, and the red of sard for the fruit of fervent humility. In the third row are placed the golden beauty of chrysolite for the treasure of wisdom, the opaqueness of beryl for the pallor of abstinence, and the many colors of topaz for the generic form of justice. In the fourth row shine the golden-haired chrysoprase for the teaching of prudence, the watery reflections of hyacinth for the cleansing of mercy, and the blood red of amethyst for the imitation of the Lord's passion and most ardent patience. Therefore, into these four rows of twelve precious stones, through which the full array of the virtues is signified, are sculpted the models of holiness, the lives of the saints, and the doctrine of piety.

53. *The Severity and Discretion of the Prior*

Whoever leads the devotees of the solitary life must show these sculpted virtues and similar ones to those entrusted to him by the example of his deeds, painting them by his zeal for authenticity and conveying them by the intent of his mind. Examples are more efficacious than words, and it is much better to teach by deeds than by sermons. He should gather often in chapter with the brethren and, prostrating himself, confess his faults and make amends for his sins as an example of amendment to the others. He should do nothing offensive to others' eyes regarding walking, standing, dressing, talking, or acting, but always act in a manner befitting eremitical holiness. He should be severe with himself and discreet with others, so as not to become a castaway after preaching to others. For some require and impose on whomever is entrusted to them hard and stringent tasks, while themselves remaining unwilling to lift a finger to help. Diverse weights and inconsistent measures are an abomination in the Lord's sight. This proverb brands those who impose lighter tasks upon themselves and heavier ones on those placed in their charge, tiring out their flock during their journey by forcing them to do more than they themselves do.

54. Reverence for the Hermitage

With the greatest care, he should take further steps to provide that the Hermitage be venerated as head of those who dwell at Fonte Buono or in other places and dependencies of the Congregation. All should honor the brethren who dwell there, for greater respect is due where the life is stricter. For their part, the brethren should receive these honors with a humble attitude, not a haughty heart—not demanding them, but recalling that respect is due them commensurate with their fervent charity, not as lords and masters. The acceptance of monks, the governance of monasteries, and all other principal affairs should involve the presence or counsel of the hermits. Abbots and priors of this Congregation are exhorted to fulfill their annual visits to the Hermitage, as is customary. Should they refuse or neglect to do so, they should be seriously punished for neglect, and more so for a refusal, because the rigor of discipline should not be relaxed by an evil patience. For this reason, the general chapter of the Congregation will be celebrated annually with the counsel of the brethren of the Hermitage and in the presence of some of them, at an opportune time and place. It will serve to reform any observances that have broken down and to confirm reformed observances, by the decision of those who are qualified, and with common consent, in the name of the Lord.